THE
BAGHDAD
LAWYER

THE BAGHDAD LAWYER

FIGHTING FOR JUSTICE IN SADDAM'S IRAQ

DR. SABAH ARIS

Cover and interior design by Monica Alejo/Ankerwycke.

In 1215, the Magna Carta was sealed underneath the ancient Ankerwycke Yew tree, starting the process that led to rule by constitutional law—in effect, giving rights and the law to the people. Today, the ABA's Ankerwycke line of books continues to bring the law to the people. With legal fiction, true crime books, popular legal histories, public policy handbooks, and prescriptive guides to current legal and business issues, Ankerwycke is a contemporary and innovative line of books for everyone from a trusted and vested authority.

Printed in the United States of America.

19 18 17 16 15   5 4 3 2 1

Library of Congress Cataloging-in-Publication Data

Aris, Sabah, 1935- author.
  Baghdad lawyer : fighting for justice in Saddam's Iraq / Dr. Sabah Aris.
    pages cm
  Includes bibliographical references and index.
  ISBN 978-1-62722-968-5 (alk. paper)
  1. Aris, Sabah, 1935- 2. Criminal defense lawyers--Iraq--Biography.
I. Title.
  KMJ110.A75A3 2015
  340.092--dc23
  [B]
                        2015004197

Discounts are available for books ordered in bulk. Special consideration is given to state bars, CLE programs, and other bar-related organizations. Inquire at Book Publishing, ABA Publishing, American Bar Association, 321 N. Clark Street, Chicago, Illinois 60654-7598.

www.ShopABA.org

For my family:
Aida, Tariq, and Edward

CONTENTS

When law can do no right,
Let it be lawful that law bar no wrong,
Law cannot give my child his kingdom here,
For he that holds his kingdom holds the law.
—William Shakespeare

PROLOGUE

"There is a higher court than courts of justice and that is the court of conscience. It supersedes all other courts."

—Mahatma Ghandi

THEY'RE GOING TO KILL HIM, doctor. My father says that you can help. Will you return to Baghdad to save him?"

It was the early hours of June 15, 2006. I had just returned home from the casino and was on the verge of going to bed, but the man who spoke to me on the telephone in an urgent tone now had my attention.

"How did you find out about me?" I whispered, quietly shutting my office door, not wanting to wake my wife who was asleep upstairs.

"My father said that you were once one of the best lawyers in Iraq," the man quickly answered, with a hint of desperation in his voice. "He has asked for you personally. Without your help, he has no hope."

I was flattered. My criminal law office in Baghdad had once been very successful, but I had been semi-retired now for over fifteen years. It had been a long time since I had been before a criminal court. Was I really ready to work on a case that had the eyes of the world upon it, the so called "trial of the century," the trial of Saddam Hussein? I wasn't sure.

"I will consider your request very carefully," I said, hearing the man sigh with relief. "Please call me tomorrow. There are a few things I need to think over first."

As the man thanked me profusely, I hung up the phone, my head spinning. It was hard to take in what had just happened. Sitting behind my oak desk, I put my fingers to my temples and tried to digest it all.

Having left Iraq just before the Gulf War, I had lived a peaceful life in the United Kingdom. Despite being semi-retired, I had continued to work on a few legal matters, but in comparison to my Baghdad days, they were relatively minor. I had come to accept that my days as a swashbuckling trial lawyer were at an end. I was now in my seventies. My time had come and gone. Yet this was an opportunity to get back to what I did best, a chance to act on the biggest stage of all. It was hard not to be tempted.

Perhaps the most compelling reason to return, however, was that I truly believed that my potential client, Saddam's co-defendant, Awad Hamed al-Bandar, was innocent.

When I had worked as a criminal lawyer in Baghdad, al-Bandar had been at the top of the legal tree—the president of Iraq's Revolutionary Court. Many times I had argued cases before him and had found him a just, fair, and virtuous judge. Even though he answered directly to Saddam himself, al-Bandar seemed very much his own man. He was certainly someone I respected.

The more I thought about the trial, the more I got worked up. By the morning, I was ready to pack my bags to make my way to Baghdad, but my wife, Aida, made me think again. "What do you think you are going to do, Sabah?" she shouted, trying to get me to see reason. "You could put on the best courtroom performance of your life, and it wouldn't make any difference."

I had to admit, she had a point. I had once been one of the most feared criminal lawyers in Baghdad. It was a profession that had led me to work on some of the most horrendous and complex legal cases, usually under intense pressure. I had certainly earned my dues. Nevertheless, I had to acknowledge that this was in a different league altogether.

As I pondered this point, Aida continued to ram home the folly of the idea. "Two of the lawyers in this case have already been murdered," she warned, her anger bringing her close to tears. "Do you want to be next?" Again, she was right. Two defense lawyers had mysteriously been killed just days into the trial.

Lowering her voice, Aida took my hand, looked me in the eyes, and pleaded with me to come to my senses. "We have a good life here, Sabah. You have a nice home. You are surrounded by friends and family. Why do you want to put all of that at risk?"

As she spoke, I looked at a picture of my late father, Edward, that I had lovingly hung on the wall above my desk. Looking at him peering out at me with his broad, kind face, I wondered what he would want me to do.

In the early years of my career, my father had been my greatest supporter. For hours he would sit in the courtrooms of Baghdad watching me plead for the lives of my clients, who were often accused of the most horrific offenses. No matter what they were said to have done, my father always preached to me the virtue of a fair trial. "If a man is given a fair trial," he would say, "then justice will inevitably follow." It was a nice concept, one with which I agreed in principle, but I had learned the hard way that fair trial or not, justice was not always the end result.

I was torn. In my heart I desperately wanted to go, but in my head I knew that it would be a huge risk. My career had led me to some dark places, but this had the potential to be the darkest of all. Baghdad was now a war zone. Nearly every day stories emerged of yet more atrocities. Even if acting on the case itself didn't put my life in danger, just merely being in the city was a hazard in itself.

Despite my concerns, I realized that this certainly wouldn't be the first time that I had put my life on the line in the name of justice. During my time in Baghdad I had worked on some horrendous cases involving murderers, pedophiles, and honor crimes. Indeed, such was the danger involved that I had been forced to carry a gun in order to ensure my safety. This was just a way of life for a lawyer in a country where trouble was never far away. As I reflected on this, I realized that almost right from the start, I had learned that a lawyer's life was cheap on the streets of Baghdad . . .

1.

THE FIRST STEPS

"The first requisite of civilization is that of justice."
—Sigmund Freud

ON THE FIRST DAY OF MY "legal training," I was shot in the head. As I lay poleaxed on the dry, cracked mud, I put my hand to my dust-covered face and felt warm blood trickle through my fingertips. Running my bloodied hand along my scalp, I feared that half my head had been blown off.

"The boss has been shot!" I heard one of my workers cry out as he put his hand under my arms and tried to drag me away. "Quickly! Quickly! Help me lift him."

Rushing to my side, my workers tried to shelter me from any further attacks as bullets and stones continued to rain down on our camp. I knew that I might face a difficult reception, but this was crazy. Sheltering from the bombardment with my head split open, I began to think that perhaps I had bitten off more than I could chew. Less than twenty-four hours after I had arrived, I was already seriously considering returning to the relative safety of Baghdad, if I even managed to survive that long.

Not long before this event I had dreamt of going to university and training to become a lawyer. This had been my father's wish for as long as I could remember. But fate had intervened. Now fate had left me lying in a pool of my own blood with any plans I had of becoming a lawyer seemingly in tatters. So how did I get myself into this situation?

Before I was born my father had lived in Syria, where as a young man he had worked in the accounts department for one of the country's most prominent lawyers, Fathallah Saqqal. Inspired by Saqqal's legendary exploits, my father desperately wanted to follow in his footsteps, but unfortunately events conspired against him. First, after the First World War, Syria suffered a bitter recession, which meant that he could not afford to devote his time to legal studies; and second, he fell in love with my Egyptian-born mother and needed to support them both.

By the time I was born in 1935, my mother and father had left Syria in search of a more prosperous future. Baghdad, the capital city of Iraq, was their destination. Upon their arrival they would have found a city undergoing enormous change. Having been under Turkish Ottoman rule for centuries, Iraq had been liberated by the British at the end of the First World War. This, coupled with the discovery of oil in 1927, helped the country quickly catch up with the rest of the modernized world as electricity, a postal service, telephone, radio, and television were all suddenly introduced, while horse drawn carriages were replaced by buses, taxis, and private cars.

When Britain pulled out of Iraq in 1932 and supposedly gave the country its independence, the sky looked to be the limit. For the first time in hundreds of years, Iraq seemed to be truly free from outside rule. Finally, the Iraqi people felt that they were on the verge of a bright new dawn. However, all was not quite as it seemed.

Before leaving, the Brits had installed a new monarch, King Faisal, to rule Iraq. This was meant to give the impression that the country was independent, but it soon became clear that the monarchy was still very much under British control. Slowly but surely a well of resentment started to build as Iraqis felt they had been cheated.

At the start of the 1930s Iraqis had looked forward to a glorious new era, but by the end of the decade, things were going downhill. The peaceful and prosperous country that my parents had immigrated to was now in real danger of imploding.

Perhaps the first sign that all was not well occurred in 1939 when King Ghazi (King Faisal's successor), who had stood up to the British, was mysteriously killed in a car crash. As his infant son, Faisal, was too young to take the throne, Prince Abd al-Llah became the ruling monarch. While this did not initially cause many problems, it would, in time, lead to a revolution that would have a dramatic impact not only on Iraq but also on my own life.

With political tensions rising, Baghdad also became embroiled in the horrors of the Second World War. Although I was too young to have many memories from this time, I do recall one awful incident that is rarely mentioned, the so-called Farhud, or as some call it "The Iraqi Holocaust."

In the 1930s the population of Baghdad was estimated to have been 200,000, of which there were approximately 100,000 Muslims (including Shias, Shi'ites, and Kurds), 80,000 Jews, and 12,000 Christians, with the small remainder made up of a mixture of other religions. By and large the religious communities mixed well and respected one another. Indeed, it was almost impossible not to have a friend from a different religious faction. Growing up I was friendly with both Muslims and Jews. Most families thought nothing of it. We learned to respect and tolerate beliefs different from our own, even going so far as to celebrate Ramadan and Christmas together. I especially enjoyed the month of Ramadan, as Baghdad would be transformed. The Muslims would fast all day, and then the streets would come alive at night as they feasted on the sweets, pastries, and fruits that had been made especially for the occasion. It was wonderful.

Yet over the course of the war, religious bigotry began to creep into the consciousness of some Iraqis. One of the main reasons for this was that some members of the Iraqi press repeatedly regurgitated the Nazis' anti-Semitic propaganda. When the government of Rashid Ali collapsed, feelings between Muslims and Jews had reached a breaking point. With no government in control, many Muslims embarked on a reign of terror, which resulted in hundreds of Jewish-owned shops being destroyed and synagogues burned to the ground.

As the troubles intensified, hundreds of Jews were dragged from their homes and murdered in cold blood. Thousands more were seriously injured as gangs set upon them, beating them to within an inch of their lives. Some Jews were even attacked by the police after they had called for their help.

Such was my own family's fear that my father and uncle gathered all of our valuables into a bag and placed it by the front door. They reasoned that if someone should attack, that person was less likely to do us harm if we were able to hand over our money and jewels instantly. We were, of course, Christian, but the attacks had become increasingly indiscriminate, and we didn't want to take any chances.

During the nights my father and his brother, Antwan, armed themselves with shotguns and took turns keeping watch by the locked front door. Hiding in my bedroom, I remember feeling a real sense of terror as I heard the sound of screams and gunshots reverberate outside. Mercifully, the nights passed without our house becoming embroiled in the troubles, but many others were not so fortunate.

When British troops eventually arrived, two days after the troubles began, they imposed a curfew and tried to bring things under control by shooting rioters on sight. However, by this stage, the damage had already been done. Fearing for their lives, most of the Jews in Iraq had fled the country and never returned.

Once the horror of the Farhud was over and Iraq tried to stabilize itself, my father enrolled me in one of the finest schools in the country in the hope that his legal ambitions for me would prosper.

Having been established in 1931 when Pope Pius XI arranged for American Jesuit fathers to establish a secondary school for boys in Iraq, the school had been an instant success. Right from the start it was flooded with children from some of Iraq's most prominent families; even Muslim children enrolled, such was the school's sterling reputation for academic achievement.

Located near the banks of the glistening Tigris River, the white school buildings were surrounded by palm trees, and the fathers—with Irish-American names such as Sullivan, MacDonnell, Kelly, Sheehan, and Mahan—endeavoured to deliver a rich education to their pupils.

Patient, understanding, and encouraging, the fathers really brought subjects to life, and as they were American, we also learned a lot about their culture. While we played foreign sports, such as baseball and basketball, we were also thrilled to hear their stories of mystical-seeming places such as New York and Hollywood. The school was a magical place, and it seems amazing now to look back and think just how well-respected those American fathers were in Baghdad. Sadly, times have changed since those halcyon days.

Under the fathers' tutelage, I soon learned that I had a talent for public speaking and quickly became the star of the school's elocution contests. When I reached my fourth year, I was even appointed president of the Debating Society, where I eventually won a gold medal for my oratory skills. Law school, followed by a legal career, seemed to be the natural progression. But it was not to be.

Sadly, all of the university entrance exams were in Arabic, and while I spoke the language fluently, my studies at Baghdad College had been in English. As a result, my written Arabic wasn't up to scratch. Unsurprisingly, I failed the governmental secondary exam, and it seemed that my dream of a legal career was at an end. What was I going to do with myself?

To make ends meet, I initially bought a few second-hand cars, fixed them up, and then, armed with a salesman's flourish, managed to sell them for a profit. Seeing that I was doing well, an engineer I knew called Joseph made me aware of an enticing business opportunity. Having worked in the construction industry for a number of years, Joseph saw that Iraq was about to experience a construction boom and that there was a chronic shortage of suitable equipment. He suggested that if I bought a Caterpillar tractor, he would be able to rent it out on my behalf for thirty dinars a day. At this time a good wage was ninety dinars a month, so obviously I was intrigued. Following his advice, I quickly bought the machine.

Before long, the tractor was rented out every day, which led me to expand, buying more equipment, taking on staff, and even branching out to take on projects myself. Soon money was pouring in and I had more jobs than I could manage.

Although I was extremely busy, a director from the German contractor Strabach made me a very tempting but dangerous proposition.

"Mr. Aris," the director started, before outlining the details of the job. "We have a contract to build a major road just outside Karbala. It needs to be built through heavy palm tree plantations, which the government has issued compulsory purchase orders for."

This sounded simple enough, but there was a catch. "Regretfully," the man continued, "we have encountered some problems with the locals."

"What sort of problems?" I asked.

"I must be frank," he replied. "Our last contractor walked off the job after being attacked. Some of the farmers don't believe that they have received a fair price for their land and refuse to move. In some cases, we have had to start work on land where the owners haven't yet received any compensation. We know it is a dangerous situation, but we have a tight deadline that we must meet. If you agree to work on this project for us, and deliver, we will reward you handsomely."

"How handsomely?" I inquired, almost certain that I would turn down such a hazardous job in any event.

"One dinar for every four cubic meters you remove."

This was a massive sum. I was staggered. Despite the high risk involved, I just couldn't turn it down. It was an amount that could really set me up and put me at the forefront of earth-moving contractors in Iraq. So, without hesitation, I made my way to Karbala, a staunchly Muslim city, as a Christian, not quite sure what I would find. Within twenty-four hours of my arrival, I had my answer.

Throwing bricks, bottles, and shooting guns, the locals did their best to scare us away as my workers and I tried to set up camp on the banks of the Tigris River. To a large extent, these tactics worked. Some of my men walked off the job and refused to come back. It was during these scuffles that I was shot in the head, giving me more reason to turn my back on the job than anyone. But thankfully, I enjoyed a lucky escape. While there was an unbelievable amount of blood, my injury turned out to be just a flesh wound that required a few stitches. The bullet had missed lodging itself in my skull by a matter of millimeters. I was alive, although badly shaken.

Recovering in my tent, I gave serious thought to packing my bags. Yes, the money was fantastic, but what use would it be if I ended up dead? My mother would have been horrified if she knew the situation I had gotten myself into. Despite this I knew what my father would say: "Stay." No matter how dangerous or difficult something appeared, my father always had faith that I would prevail. Having his confidence in me made me feel as if I could achieve anything. Thinking of him, I

THE

BAGHDAD

LAWYER

decided that I had never walked away from a fight, and I wasn't going to start now.

The next day I hatched a plan. If we were attacked again, this time I would be ready. Arming my men with an array of weapons, we spent the night in the darkness waiting for our foes to return. It was a very dangerous situation. There was no doubt that people could get hurt or killed, but the men who stood by my side refused to be scared away. Holding a shotgun in my hand, I hardly slept as I waited for action to commence. Without warning, at around 4:00 a.m., the first shots were fired.

Running out of my tent, I shouted to my men, "Quickly, turn on the lights!" Following my orders my men turned the camp floodlights toward where our attackers had gathered. Suddenly, we could see them, but they could no longer see us. Panicking, they tried to flee as my men and I charged at them. Filled with anger and adrenaline, I pumped my shotgun furiously, shooting into the air to warn them away. I had no desire to kill anyone, but I certainly wanted to do everything possible to scare them.

To my great relief, my gamble paid off. From that moment onward they left us in peace, knowing full well that we would fight fire with fire. However, while I had scared off the most hostile of the locals, I was still greeted with a degree of skepticism by the inhabitants of Karbala. It was a sacred city, where millions of Shi'ite Muslims visited the Imam Husayn Shrine on pilgrimage every year. A young Christian like myself—dressed in European-style suits, with a moustache instead of a beard, and with my slick black hair not covered by a headscarf—stood out like a sore thumb.

If I was to be accepted in the city, I now knew that I would have to respect the Shi'ite culture, and hence I made every effort to fit in. To a large degree this worked in my favor, so much so that I was soon invited to luncheons with some of the highest-ranking officials in the city, where they affectionately called me "Abu Tariq."

Having been left to get on with the job, I soon had the road built. It was one of my finest accomplishments and perfect legal training. I learned how to negotiate in hostile conditions, to stand my ground when being bullied and provoked, and to also adapt when necessary.

You can read about all of these things in textbooks but to experience them all, in such extraordinary conditions, was something else.

However, although I made a small fortune upon completion of the job, I started to consider just where my life was heading. Did I want to continue to make money where my life was at risk? Surely my luck would run out sooner or later. Most importantly, despite my success, I felt empty. Something seemed to be missing.

But while I considered my future, my mind was made up for me on July 14, 1958, a date that is forever ingrained in my memory, as it is for most Iraqis, for that day changed not only the course of my destiny but also that of Iraq.

2.

REVOLUTION AND CIGARETTES

"In the absence of justice, what is sovereignty but organized robbery?"

—Saint Augustine

MY FAMILY HAS ALWAYS JOKED that I could sleep through a riot, and on the night of July 14, 1958, I pretty much did just that.

Following a party at my Uncle Antwan's house, I had retired to bed completely oblivious to the storm that was about to engulf us all. As I slept, soldiers who were loyal to the anti-British nationalist movement had stormed the al-Rahab Palace and had proceeded to murder King Faisal II and Prince Abd al-llah, as well as other members of the royal family. Slain without mercy, Prince Abd al-llah's remains were then hung outside the Ministry of Defense as a warning to those who opposed the coup.

Having tried to flee the melee, the prime minister, Norrie al-Said, who was particularly loathed by the nationalists for his pro-British stance, was spotted in a Baghdad market disguised as a woman. With unimaginable ferocity he was lynched before his mutilated remains were dragged through the streets.

For several days mob violence ruled as those who were perceived to be traitors to the nationalists' cause were beaten and murdered in the cold light of day. It was a terrifying time for everyone. To avoid becoming embroiled in the troubles, my family and I once again locked ourselves in our house, as we had done during the Farhud, until the worst of it was over.

Finally, when the dust had settled, the leader of the nationalists, Abd al-Karim Qasim, was made prime minister. Under his rule Iraq immediately severed its ties with the West and began aligning itself with communist countries such as the Soviet Union. Just like that, times had changed.

It became immediately clear that if my work as a contractor had been difficult before, it was now going to be almost impossible. I felt that not only would it be too dangerous to proceed but the boom years in construction had now passed. Weighing these factors, I decided to sell my machinery and liquidate my contracting business.

With this done I started to consider the next step I should take. Thankfully, it didn't take me too long before I stumbled upon the perfect idea.

During this time my father had been having some success importing a brand of Egyptian cigarette paper booklets called Bafra. Sadly, the Iraqi government soon put a stop to this in an attempt to encourage local production, a law was passed that made it illegal to import foreign cigarettes and papers. However, this made me wonder if I could produce the cigarette booklets in Iraq itself.

Realizing that this could be very lucrative, I set off to Bafra's headquarters in Alexandria, Egypt, to try to broker a deal. For over three months I pulled out all of the stops, harassing, pleading, and charming the Egyptian owners to give me, a guy in his mid-twenties with no experience in the cigarette industry, a chance. As you can imagine, this was not easy, and many times I came close to giving up.

Yet just as I was on the verge of returning home, an incident occurred that made me think again. On the eve of departing Alexandria, I was invited to a dinner where at the end of the meal we drank Turkish coffee in traditional small cups. It is a custom in the East that when you finish the coffee, you are supposed to turn the cup upside down on a small plate, where the stains that are left behind will supposedly reveal your fortune.

Normally I would not have engaged in such a superstitious practice, but on this night there was a young lady present who not only was said to be very good at reading the coffee stain but also was very beautiful. So when she offered to read my fortune, I didn't hesitate.

As the young lady started the reading, her mood swiftly changed from light-hearted to very serious. "You have been in Alexandria for some time trying to achieve a special goal that has seemed impossible," she began. "And right now you are close to giving up, but I can see that what you came for will be fulfilled before the next full moon."

I smiled and quickly counted. It would be ten days before the next full moon. And while I had planned to leave the next day, I reasoned that as I had already been in Alexandria for three months, staying ten more days wasn't going to do me any harm. Thank God I did. Incredibly, the young woman's prediction came true!

Two days later, almost out of nowhere, I received a call from one of the directors of Bafra. The company had decided to grant me a royalty contract to manufacture its cigarette booklets in Baghdad. It was one of my greatest achievements, and it completely changed my life.

Following this phone call, I swiftly returned to Baghdad where my factory was soon up and running, producing Bafra cigarette paper booklets, which became enormously popular throughout Iraq. The success I achieved was beyond my wildest expectations; before I knew it I was earning more money than I had ever dared to dream. But for some reason I still felt unfulfilled. Why?

One day it hit me. After a night out in Baghdad I overheard a group of men talking about me. Listening to what they were saying, I heard a well-respected doctor say dismissively, "Yes, Sabah Aris may have a lot of money, but he has no university education." The remark upset me. Yet on reflection I had to admit that there was some truth in what was said.

It had, of course, been my intention to go to university, but I had failed the Governmental Secondary exam. I now realized that in spite of my success in business, I had an inferiority complex at not having a university degree. Whenever I was at a social event in Baghdad, I always had a feeling that some people held this against me. I could have been the richest man in the room, yet in some of their eyes I was still inferior. And looking deep within myself, I had to admit that I felt inferior.

Perhaps another significant reason behind me feeling so empty was my father. Of course, this was never intended on his part, because he was very proud of everything I had achieved, but I knew that deep down he would be the happiest man on earth if I were to become a lawyer. No one in our family had ever achieved such a thing. While we had all been relatively successful in business, we had not as yet made our mark in the academic world.

Reflecting on what the doctor had said and looking within myself, I knew that there was only one thing for it: I had to become a lawyer. And not just any lawyer, but the best lawyer in Baghdad.

3.

A DELIBERATE ACCIDENT

"Fairness is what justice really is."

—Potter Stewart

I **T IS QUITE REMARKABLE, SABAH,**" my law school professor said, shaking my hand on graduation day, "that despite running a cigarette paper factory and attending law school, you still have the best attendance record in your year." I smiled in return. This was true. Yet all was not quite as it seemed.

When I first entered the doors to law school, I had great intentions. Truly I did. Not only did I want to attend every single lecture, all of which were held in the evenings because most students also had full-time jobs, but I also wanted to immerse myself in all aspects of university life. Regretfully, I hadn't considered that continuing to run my cigarette paper factory while also attending law school would be quite so testing.

Many times I would have my bags packed and ready to travel the ten-minute journey from my factory to law school only to be called back inside to deal with a work matter. Other times I was so immersed in my work that I forgot the time completely and missed a class. And there was also the occasional time where I have to admit that I succumbed to the temptation to merely give the lectures a miss just because I wanted to spend some time with my friends.

13

Unsurprisingly, with such a terrible attendance record, I was soon told that if I didn't improve, then I could face expulsion. This was just months into the four-year course, so I knew I faced an uphill battle. And while I desperately wanted to attend lectures, as I genuinely loved learning about the law, it was virtually impossible to attend them all due to running the factory.

While I considered how I could somehow balance the two, I had a moment of inspiration. I had noted in the lectures that I did manage to attend that each student had a designated number on the back of his or her chair. If that chair was subsequently empty, a clerk would instantly know that the student was not in attendance. It was a simple but effective system, but I soon got around it with a simple but effective solution of my own.

Whenever I could not make a lecture, I sent my driver to sit in my designated chair for me. Looking back this was quite funny as he was totally illiterate. He once told me that a fellow student had approached him during a break and asked a question regarding a point of law. My driver turned to him and said, "Don't ask me; I am just a donkey!" Thank God a lecturer never asked him a question in all his time there!

However, this ruse paid off. Suddenly I had one of the best attendance records in law school. Amazingly, in all my time at the university, nobody ever realized what I was doing. Yet while I did not attend all of the lectures, this did not mean that I didn't do the required work.

In law school I had struck up a friendship with a fellow student named Khalid. We were probably the two youngest students on the evening course, which was mostly attended by the likes of majors from the army or older businessmen, so we had sought each other out. And while we were the same age and were both Christians, we also shared a great love for Iraqi poetry. In fact, Khalid had far more than a love for it; he was an exceptional poet in his own right. After law school he even went on to publish two books of poetry that in my opinion include some of the finest poems ever written.

In any event, thanks to Khalid, who always dutifully attended lectures, I was able to keep up with the course in my own time, as he always supplied me with his notes. And while I worked very hard to pass the written exams, I found that when it came to the verbal tests, I always excelled, even with little time to prepare.

But while I tried my best to learn the law, an incident occurred that made me realize that if I truly wanted to become a great lawyer, then the rules alone would not suffice.

During my second year at law school my father and Uncle Antwan worked from the third floor of my factory as agents for an Egyptian insurance company called Le Shark. I used to take great pleasure in having us all work under the same roof together and would regularly pop up to chat.

One such day, I entered the office in a jubilant mood only to be met by a somber atmosphere. It was as if someone had died. "What is it, Abu Sabah?" I asked, noticing the pained look on my father's face.

"We have just had bad news from the court," he replied. "Now we have to pay a murderer 10,000 dinars!"

This was a huge amount of money. At the time this was the equivalent to something like $33,000, while today it would run into the millions. While the sum itself was substantial, what really caught my attention was that my father had used the word *murderer*.

"What has this man done, Abu Sabah?" I asked.

"He has killed his wife, that is what he has done," my uncle angrily interjected, unable to keep his cool any longer.

"So why do you have to pay him?"

"He came to us a while ago," my father said, pacing the room. "He wanted to insure his wife for a large sum against accidental death, so we gave him a policy. A few months afterward he claimed that while he was cleaning his shotgun it accidentally discharged and shot his wife in the face, killing her instantly. The criminal court initially sentenced him to twenty-five years for murder, but today an appeals court ruled it was an accidental death. Now he has come looking for us, demanding we pay the policy."

I was astounded. The whole thing stunk. "So what are you going to do?" I asked.

"We will fight it," my father suddenly shouted, turning to face me. "I have spoken to the owners of Le Shark in Egypt, and they have authorized me to hire the best insurance lawyer in Iraq to defend the claim."

Indeed, my father had already done exactly that. He had hired a man by the name of Nasart Al Farasi, who not only was regarded as a top lawyer but also was Iraq's former minister for justice. In addition, he had also hired two junior lawyers who had good reputations to assist him.

With Al Farasi working on the case, I was confident that my father's troubles would soon be over. However, despite Al Farasi preparing a defense, the court still ruled that the claimant's wife's death, under the terms of the insurance policy, had indeed been accidental. As such, Le Shark was now liable to pay him the insured sum of 10,000 dinars.

My father was stunned at the verdict. That night he vowed never to pay the "murderer" a single penny. It wasn't even his money, but he was disgusted that a man would seek to be rewarded for such a blatant and reprehensible act. Seeing my father's deep distress, I asked him if I could have a look at the policy in question.

With the policy in my hand I bounded down the stairs to see my great friend Anwar, who worked as a lawyer from an office in my factory. Anwar was a very intelligent man and a great lawyer, and therefore I hoped he would somehow be able to spot a weakness in the man's claim.

After I had outlined the case to Anwar, he immediately began to dissect the fine print of the policy. Suddenly he stopped. A smile slowly formed on his lips as he began reading the following clause out loud: "If the beneficiary deliberately causes the accident insured against in the policy, he will be deprived of the benefits of the policy."

"So what does that mean?" I asked, not quite following. "The man has claimed the incident was an accident, and the court has agreed with him."

"You are correct," Anwar replied, thrusting the policy into my hand and jabbing his finger at the relevant clause. "But this clause uses the wording 'deliberately causes the accident.' This is a big difference than just a mere accident."

Anwar was right. While a court had ruled that the incident was an accident, no one had yet made the case that the man had deliberately caused it. It was a very delicate point, one not recognized in Iraqi law, or most other legal jurisdictions, but under the terms of the policy, it was absolutely crucial.

Rushing back up the stairs with the policy in my hand, I outlined the clause to my father and uncle. They were both intrigued yet still skeptical that a court would accept the argument that someone could deliberately cause an accident. Nonetheless, they asked me to meet with Al Farasi that night to discuss it.

At the meeting Al Farasi was blunt and to the point. "The case ends here," he said before anyone could speak. "I do not advise an appeal. A criminal court and a civil court have now ruled the incident to be an accident, and we have nothing else to plead." At this point my father gave me the signal to talk.

As a law student I was well aware that Al Farasi was one of the finest lawyers in Iraq, with decades of experience, yet I was still confident that what I was about to say would strike a chord with him. "Your Excellency," I began, pointing out the vital clause in the policy. "This says that if the beneficiary has deliberately caused the accident, then he shall be deprived of the benefits of the insurance."

To my surprise Al Farasi didn't even read the clause. Instead, he looked me up and down dismissively and said, "You're a student aren't you? What year are you in?" I knew he was being sarcastic, but I still took the blow with grace and merely responded that I was in my second year. "So what did they teach you about accidental incidents?" he sneered.

At this remark I again picked up the policy and underlined the clause with my finger. "What they taught me at law school has nothing to do with this," I said, raising my voice. "This is different. A precedent that may not be in Iraqi law but should be."

Al Farasi didn't respond. It was clear that he had washed his hands of the case and his arrogance wouldn't allow him to listen to a law student, even if I had raised a perfectly valid point. Turning to my father, Al Farasi shook him by the hand and said, "I like you, Edward, but my work here is done. I advise you not to go any further."

However, as he then went toward the door he suddenly stopped, turned around, and said to me, "By the time you graduate, things will look clearer to you."

Having had enough of him trying to belittle me, I merely replied, "It doesn't make any difference what I learn in law school. Anyone can see that justice has not been done in this case, yet the answer is right in front of our faces." At that Al Farasi stormed out, his work on this case at an end.

With Al Farasi out of the room my father turned to the two junior lawyers who were still waiting. "Do we have a case?" he asked.

For a moment there was silence as they pondered this. Then one of them suddenly said, "Yes. You have a case, but I don't know if you will win."

My father put his hand on my shoulder. "With Sabah in court, we will definitely win," he replied, full of confidence.

It was a huge sign of his faith in me. After all, I was just a law student, and a top lawyer had already advised us not to appeal, as our case involved pleading a point that was not recognized in Iraqi law. And there was another problem. I was not officially a lawyer and also did not work for Le Shark, so I wouldn't even be able to speak in court.

However, when I discussed this issue with Anwar, he came up with the perfect solution: "Have Le Shark employ you as a manager of the agency." I wasn't sure that Le Shark would be happy to do this, but when my father explained how vital it was to have me in court, they agreed. Now we were all set. I just hoped I could repay my father's faith.

Before our day in court Anwar and I helped the junior lawyers draft our appeal. To really ram home the claimant's offense, I ensured that we called him "the killer" at every opportunity. Unsurprisingly, this was the very first thing the claimant's lawyers objected to when we started the case. Standing to address the court I bellowed, "Your Honor, the claimant is a killer. They say he killed by accident. We say he killed deliberately. Either way, the man is a killer."

The president of the court smiled. "The remark will stand," he said. From that moment I knew the president would be open to our defense.

While the wording in the policy offered us some hope, I knew that if we were going to be successful in court we still had to show that the claimant had deliberately caused the accident. This would be difficult. After all, the facts surrounding the incident had already been discussed at length in the criminal trial as well as at the appeal. In both instances the court had heard that when the claimant had been cleaning his shotgun, opening and shutting it as he did so, a bullet had discharged that subsequently struck his wife in her face. Considering all of the facts that had already been disclosed I suddenly realized something that had not yet been raised but was absolutely crucial.

At the time I was a keen shooter and therefore had a reasonable knowledge of how certain cartridges would discharge from shotguns. In this case the cartridge in question was a no. 5 Elay cartridge, which had 150 to 200 pellets in it. Once the gun had been fired and the cartridge was subsequently 20 centimeters from the barrel, the pellets would then disperse to hit as wide a target as possible. However, in this case the pellets had not dispersed into the wife's face. Instead, the fully intact cartridge had penetrated her eye. This could mean only one thing: the gun must have been fired within 20 centimeters of her face, which is not a distance at which you would expect any sane human being to clean a gun, unless of course he or she wanted to kill someone.

Despite this new piece of evidence I was still hamstrung by the previous ruling in the criminal case, which the claimant's lawyer kept interjecting and referring to. This meant that I could not say that the man had pulled the trigger, as it had already been ruled that he had not. Therefore I had to say that when cleaning the gun, the man must have kept closing and shutting it just 20 centimeters from his wife's face before a bullet discharged. He may not have killed his wife in the traditional sense, but he certainly deliberately manufactured an accident that resulted in her death.

Unsurprisingly, the claimant's lawyer tried to rubbish our case as having no principle in Iraqi law. Indeed, he raised another point, "How can someone deliberately cause an accident?"

On the stand I outlined how this was actually pretty simple. I provided an example where if someone were to deliberately drive his or her car very fast on a road where people were walking, that person could be said to have deliberately caused the accident by intended negligence. I then referred to the article of the law that stated that negligence can be so serious that it borders on intent, which was clearly the case here.

Again, the lawyer turned to the judge and reiterated how preposterous this was. But I could see that the judge was clearly taken by this concept, perhaps because it offered him a path to justice.

The claimant certainly did not do himself any favors in the eyes of the judge when he took the stand. Under questioning from the junior lawyers he either refused to answer, stating that this matter had already been dealt with in the criminal trial, or said that he could not remember. Despite the fact that I was not a lawyer, I stepped up to question him about the firing of the gun, trying my best to elaborate on the discharge of the cartridge.

Setting upon him furiously, I asked why a man would choose to clean a gun with a cartridge still loaded in it. And worse yet, why would a man choose to clean it just 20 centimeters from his wife's face? The man tried to bat away my questions, but then suddenly something else crossed my mind, something that was absolutely crucial.

"When you open a gun," I began, untangling my thoughts, "the cartridge automatically falls out doesn't it? The man suddenly shrunk backward, knowing full well where I was going with my line of questioning.

"I . . . I . . .," he stammered, desperately trying to scramble away from trouble.

Coming to the rescue the claimant's lawyer suddenly leapt up. "Your Honor, please stop this man from questioning my client. He is not a lawyer and is therefore not permitted to discuss such legal issues."

I snapped my head towards him. "This is not a legal issue," I answered. "I am just discussing how your client accidentally fired a gun into his wife's face from 20 centimeters away. No one needs to be an expert on the law to discuss this."

The president of the court glared at the lawyer. "Mr. Aris is permitted to question your client under these parameters," he said to my relief. The lawyer was stunned as the president then turned to the claimant and said, "Now answer the question. Does a cartridge fall out when you open a gun?"

The man looked to his lawyer for help, but none was forthcoming. He was on his own. "Sometimes," he finally murmured.

To this reply I shouted, "No, it happens every time you open a gun! Therefore, while you have previously told this court you were opening and shutting the gun when it went off, the gun must have been shut all along, as only then could the cartridge have still been loaded. Isn't this the truth now?"

"I can't remember how it went off," the man replied, desperately trying to cling on to something. "All I know is that I was cleaning it, and I suddenly shot my wife by accident."

"Yes," I said, raising my voice. "A deliberate accident. One that is not covered in the insurance policy you took out for your wife, and that you are trying to claim under now."

Nothing more needed to be said. I had proven two very crucial things: the man's story did not add up, and it was indeed possible to cause a deliberate accident, something that was higher than gross negligence but just less than criminal intent.

With the case at an end my father felt that we could have done no more. I agreed. "I don't know if we will win," I said to him, "but we have given it everything." My father replied, "The judge will see that justice will be done, of that I am sure."

On the day of the judgment I was not able to attend court as I was unwell. However, as I lay in bed one of the junior lawyers called me with the verdict. As I tentatively answered the phone, he merely said, "When you graduate from law school I might come and work for you." I knew then that we had won the case! And not only had we won the case but we had also established a new principle in Iraqi law, that of "deliberate causation of an accident," a principle that is still in force to this day.

As you can imagine, my father was delighted, not only at not having to pay a murderer a large sum of money but also because I had proven myself in the courtroom. Indeed, the directors of Le Shark were so pleased with the outcome that they wanted to pay me for my services. Regretfully, as I was not a lawyer, I was not entitled to receive a fee. However, while I could not receive a monetary reward, I suggested that if they did want to reward me in some way, then I would very much like a law library with which I could start my own law firm. And they duly delivered, providing me with a comprehensive library of over 700 books.

But despite this success, nothing could match my father's pride on the day of my graduation. In the audience, he stood, beaming, alongside my mother as I shook my law professor's hand, and accepted his compliments for my excellent attendance record with a straight face.

I had learned a lot in law school, even if my attendance was not the best. But perhaps my most important lesson was that despite what the law might state, a good judge and/or lawyer is always looking for ways to procure justice, even if that might conflict with the written law. This was a lesson that would prove crucial for the rest of my career, especially in cases where the law itself was against me.

With a law degree, and a big case already behind me, my father and I dreamt that I could now embark on a high-flying legal career and realize both of our dreams. Unfortunately, I soon learned that best laid plans do not always immediately come to fruition.

4.

THE WARNING

"If we do not maintain justice, justice will not maintain us."
—Francis Bacon

I'M WARNING YOU, MR. ARIS.** If you do not stand down from this case, then you are putting yourself in grave danger."

My first major case as a qualified lawyer, and already my life was under threat. With the trial just days away, I had been approached in my office by four men. Far from looking like your typical Baghdad thugs, they were well dressed in smart navy blue suits, had well-groomed moustaches, and initially spoke in a polite manner. In fact, they could have quite easily passed for fellow lawyers.

The leader of the group, an older man with graying hair, had started our conversation by offering to pay me an enormous amount of money to step down, an offer I refused point blank. It was only after this that the tone of our meeting changed. Now I was being told that if I didn't step down, things could get nasty.

Standing just inches from my face, so that I could smell the stale odor of his breath, one of the younger men, who was built like a refrigerator, tried his best to intimidate me. In return I did what came naturally: I took a step closer so that he could see I was unmoved.

"If you do not leave my office now," I said defiantly, "I will not hesitate to call the police."

The man smirked. "Watch your step, Mr. Aris," he warned. "You don't know who you are dealing with. You should be very afraid."

"If I allow fear to dominate my work, I would not be the criminal lawyer that you're afraid of," I replied, staring intensely at him. "Tell the person who sent you that not only will I see him in court but I will also go after him with every resource I have at my disposal."

For a moment there was silence. It was clear that the man was not used to being spoken to in such a manner.

Sneering in my direction, he suddenly backed away. "Very well, Mr. Aris," he said. "You will be seeing us again shortly."

"So be it," I confidently replied.

With that the men stormed out of my office, making it very clear that they were unhappy with the outcome of our meeting.

Peering out of my second floor window I watched the men as they walked up the busy street and out of sight. At least I knew they would not be lying in wait for me outside. Not now anyway. Taking a seat behind my desk, I tried to get on with some work, but my head was all over the place.

I already knew that being a lawyer could be a hazardous occupation in Baghdad. That is why so many of us carried guns, although if you had grown up in Baghdad, it was already expected that you knew how to look after yourself. But up until now I had not had the misfortune to experience this bare-knuckle brand of law. I expected it to cross my path one day, but why did it have to happen during my first major case?

Unable to settle, I packed my papers into my suitcase, bade farewell to my young assistant, Fahker, and left the office for the day. Walking tentatively out of the entrance, I took my time to look up and down the bustling Rashid Street, which was full of juice bars, shisha cafes, and men playing backgammon. I knew that it was very unlikely anything would happen here, on a street that was one of Baghdad's main shopping areas, but I had learned the hard way not to underestimate anyone or anything.

Watching my step, I walked briskly to the parking lot at the back of my office and got into my brand new convertible Ford Falcon, an American car that was the envy of many. Convinced that I was not being followed, I finally set off, meandering through the dusty streets of

Baghdad in the early evening sunshine, weaving through animals, beggars, and market places until I finally reached the middle-class Sadoun district on the outskirts of the city. There was someone I needed to speak to, the one man whose advice I valued more than any other: my father.

Before I had a chance to ring the bell, my younger sister, Kawther, excitedly opened the door.

"Mummy," she cried, looking toward the dining area where my mother was preparing food. "Sabah is here!"

Walking into the house I kissed my mother on the cheek and sat at the table alongside my father and my other sister, May.

"You should have called, habibi," my father said with a smile on his broad face. "We were not expecting you."

"I'm sorry," I replied earnestly. "I need to speak to you about something."

"OK, but let us eat first. Your mother has been hard at work all day."

My father was besotted with my mother. Ever since they had met in Syria in the early 1920s, they had been inseparable. When it was time to eat he liked to forget about the stresses of the day and devote as much of his attention to her as possible. In all of my life I do not think I have ever seen two people as in love.

As we ate a dish of chicken and rice, I was very quiet. This was unusual for me. Usually I was loud and talkative, but tonight I could not concentrate on small talk. The case and my fledgling career were bothering me.

After graduating from law school, I had spent my first few months in the legal world rapidly learning that life as a criminal lawyer was not as glamorous as it had once seemed. While my father looked after my factory, I established my own firm, which I ran from a second floor office in the hub of the city, initially spending my time dealing with relatively small matters while tirelessly waiting to find a big case where I could prove my worth. However, now that one had finally come my way, my life was under threat. Nothing came easy.

The defendant in this case was a very wealthy and powerful businessman who stood to lose everything if he was convicted. Not only could he afford to hire a hit man to take me out but also he was the type of individual who would try to bribe everyone who stood in his way. And to think, I didn't stand to make a penny from this case; I was doing it pro bono.

I played around with the food on my plate for over half an hour, pondering all of this in my head, until my father finally ushered me into the living room. "What is troubling you, habibi?" he asked, inviting me to take a seat. "You're not yourself."

"I may be in some sort of trouble, Abu Sabah," I replied.

"Tell me about it," he urged, as always filling me with confidence that he had the answer to every issue.

Taking a seat next to me, he listened intently as I told him everything I knew at this stage.

The case in question had come to me completely out of the blue. One afternoon I had been chatting to some colleagues in the private lawyers' quarters at the old courthouse in central Baghdad when a clearly distressed woman staggered into the room, tore her dress in half, and screamed, "I am a woman, and I need your help. Will someone please help me?"

The dramatic tearing of her clothes was an Iraqi custom that women did to appeal for a man's assistance. On this occasion, however, most in the room chose to ignore her plea, having become accustomed to such dramatic acts in their long legal careers. Yet I was intrigued.

Having finally managed to calm her down, the woman told me, in between heaving sobs, "My daughter has been killed by her father. He is a very rich man, and he is doing everything in his power to cover it up. I need a lawyer to help me."

The woman went on to explain that while a public prosecutor had already been appointed, she now needed to appoint a lawyer to claim damages under a procedure known as prosecution by the victims of crime. Unlike in Western legal systems, the families of victims of crimes in Iraq are able to claim personal damages against the defendant during the course of the criminal trial itself instead of in a separate civil hearing.

Not only was I moved by the woman's deep distress, but as she briefly explained the details I also saw that this was the opportunity I had been waiting for. It was a high-profile case where a rich and powerful defendant thought he was above the law. If I could win, then I would really make my mark in the courtrooms of Baghdad as well as to ensure the most important thing of all: justice.

"I am a poor woman. I have no money to pay you," the woman confessed.

"Do not worry about money," I reassured her, holding her hand in mine as the other lawyers in the room looked on. "It is not my concern here. Justice is. I will help you." At this she broke down. Crying on my shoulder, she thanked me over and over for my assistance. Confidently I told her to leave it with me; everything would be fine. At least I hoped it would.

As the details were still sketchy, I contacted the public prosecutor and asked for the case file, something he was happy to provide. Sitting with my feet up on my desk, I pored over the papers, working until the early hours of the morning trying to piece it all together.

The first document in the file was the woman's witness statement, which gave me some good background information:

> I was married to the defendant for fifteen years, during which time I gave birth to our daughter, Yasamin. Regretfully our marriage ended after my husband had an affair, and he swiftly remarried. While I was forced to raise Yasamin alone, my husband's new wife gave birth to two little boys.
>
> When Yasamin reached her sixteenth birthday, her father demanded that she live with him so that she could act as a maid, with one of her chief duties being to look after his sons. Yasamin was terrified of her father. He had beaten her in the past, and she really did not want to go, but she felt she had no choice.
>
> During her time working in her father's house, Yasamin told me she was treated as a slave and had to do every duty you can imagine—such as cooking, cleaning, bathing the children, and shopping—all without pay. Many times she told me that she complained to her father about her treatment, but when she did so he beat her with a stick. On one

occasion she even told me that she had tried to escape the house, but he found her and then chained her to her bed as punishment. I tried to talk to my ex-husband about this situation, particularly about him repeatedly beating her with a stick, but when I did so he told me to mind my own business. I also told the police what he was doing to Yasamin, but nothing happened.

When I heard that Yasamin had died, I knew that it would have been at the hands of her father. He is a violent man who had beaten me severely when we were married, and I have no doubt that he is responsible for Yasamin's death.

Digesting the mother's statement, I flinched in horror thinking about the ordeal this poor girl must have endured. But how did the father come to be arrested for the crime? Flicking through the file I came across a statement that caught my eye. It was on behalf of a doctor whose name I recognized, Dr. Marlyn. I knew that Dr. Marlyn worked in Baghdad General Hospital, and she was actually a friend of my sister, May, who was training to be a doctor herself. Quickly scouring through the statement I realized that it was due to Dr. Marlyn that the defendant had been arrested:

I was working the night shift in Baghdad General Hospital when the defendant and his wife entered the emergency room in an agitated state carrying the body of their daughter. It was immediately clear that she was dead and had been for a few hours. The defendant claimed that she had fallen down the stairs and after feeling unwell had gone to bed. He said that when he had checked on her a few hours later, she was dead.

However, I have treated many people who have fallen down stairs, and the deceased's body showed none of the usual injuries. Usually you can expect there to be a head injury, cuts, bruises, and maybe even broken bones in different areas. Yet in this case the deceased just had a large bruise on her lower back. There was no other injury present.

When I told the defendant that I wanted to examine the body further, he suddenly became very angry. He warned me that if I did not issue a death certificate immediately then I would be in trouble. The longer the process took, the angrier the defendant became. Suspecting that there was more to this than met the eye, I called the police, and the defendant was subsequently arrested.

Things were now starting to get interesting. Quickly rummaging through the file I found what I was looking for: the coroner's report. Surely his opinion on the fate of the deceased would be crucial.

Having examined the body of the deceased, I found there to be just the one injury present, namely a large bruise on the base of her spine. Further examination revealed that the deceased had in fact fractured her fifth vertebrae and that this injury would have caused her death. An injury such as this is usually consistent with receiving a heavy blow from an object.

And surely that was it, the smoking gun that would put the defendant away. The evidence all painted a picture of a violent man with a prior history of beating his wife and daughter. On top of that his suspicious behavior at the hospital and the coroner's report both proved that his story did not add up. There was very little chance that the daughter had fallen down the stairs. The obvious conclusion was that the defendant had once again beaten her with his stick.

On the facts of the case I was confident that I could get a conviction. However, when I looked at the court docket and realized who my opponents would be, I began to wonder if this really would be straightforward after all. One of the defense lawyers was a well-known politician who had built an outstanding reputation in the courtroom while the other was someone I knew personally, one of my old law school professors. I've never been afraid of a challenge, but I knew that this case would really test me to my limits.

After outlining the facts of the case to my father and informing him of my theory—that the defendant had beaten his daughter—I then proceeded to tell him about the unsavory events that had occurred in my office that afternoon. Before he even opened his mouth, I knew what he was going to say.

"Continue with the case," he urged. "You are a man, and they cannot intimidate you." My father already knew that if things got out of hand, I could handle myself, especially after my experience as a contractor in Karbala.

However, in this case I was determined to see that justice would be done in the courtroom. I would not be sidelined by vendettas or violence. That was the domain of thugs. I wanted to prove that I could prevail with the law. Yet I was also not naïve enough to think that I did not require a backup plan. I felt that I needed to send a message to the defendant that I was not a man to be messed with. But what? Then it struck me.

When I walked toward the courthouse on the first day of the trial, I was stopped in my tracks by the four men who had confronted me at my office.

"If you go into that courtroom, you will pay with your blood," one of the men threatened.

I smiled. Behind me were over fifty of my workers from my factory. These men were hardened, working-class Iraqis to whom I was very close. They did not take kindly to my life being threatened.

"If anything should happen to me, then you will have to answer to all of these men," I cautioned. "They know who you are and who your boss is."

The man suddenly backed away, clearly intimidated.

Marching into court I felt that I had won a small victory. Entering the oak-panelled courtroom with a slight spring in my step, I saw that my father was already sitting in the first row behind the lawyer's bench, alongside May and her friend, Dr. Marlyn. My father had dreamed that one day I would argue at a big trial such as this, and he wasn't going to miss it for the world.

"May God be with you, habibi," he said, grinning, as I made my way to the bench. I smiled back at him. I knew there was still a long way to go, but the day had certainly started well.

Once the judge had got the trial underway, one of my first tasks was to question Dr. Marlyn, who had first examined the body. As expected, she confirmed that the body had an unusual bruise on the base of the spine and that, in her experience, this was not consistent with an injury sustained when falling down the stairs. Dr. Marlyn also discussed the defendant's agitated demeanor at the hospital, where instead of acting like a grieving father, he had been more interested in making threats toward her. So far so good. Yet things then took a turn for the worse.

I had expected the coroner's testimony to be a formality, as he had already stated in his report that the fatal injury could only have been incurred by a heavy blow. However, after swearing on the Bible, the coroner stunned the court by changing his position.

Under questioning by the public prosecutor, the coroner now claimed that the injury was probably caused by a fall down the stairs and that he could see no evidence to support the theory that Yasamin had been struck. His testimony was greeted by a torrent of abuse, which led the judge to call for order. I was seething. Glancing at the defendant, I could see him smiling smugly. I had little doubt that he had bought off the coroner.

I was itching for my turn to question him. There was no way I would let this blatant mistruth be allowed to stand. When my time finally came, I set upon him in a furious manner.

"Have you seen the stairs the victim fell down in this instance?" I asked.

The coroner hesitated before saying, "Yes, I inspected the house."

"I assume you would have measured the width of the stairs. How wide were they?"

Again, another pause, as the coroner took a long sip of his water. "One hundred centimeters," he finally answered, sounding less than convincing.

"Very well," I said, now moving in for the kill. "Then can you please explain how a person can fall down the stairs and only receive this one specific injury?"

"I cannot answer this. A body can fall down a flight of stairs in any manner of ways."

Sensing that the coroner was now beginning to flounder, I increased the ferocity of my questions.

"Sir, do you seriously expect this court to believe that someone can fall down a flight of stairs and receive only this one injury in this unusual place? Surely there would be some other cuts, bruises, or perhaps broken bones?"

"I do not know how she fell down."

"Well surely you must have some idea, doctor? After all, you are an expert on stair injuries."

"It is impossible for me to say."

"Don't you find it incredible, doctor, that a body, which is 150 centimeters tall, can roll vertically down stairs that are 100 centimeters wide and sustain nothing but a severe injury to one spot on her lower back?"

"No. It is possible."

"Have you ever come across a case such as this?"

"Yes."

"Well, can you provide us with the file?"

Finally, he snapped. "What are you trying to say? Are you insinuating that I'm lying?"

Before I could answer, his lawyer, who was my old law school professor, jumped in.

"Your Honor, the lawyer of the personal prosecution is clearly harassing a very valued and well-respected expert witness. He should be referred to the disciplinary committee at the Bar of Lawyers for such improper conduct."

Burning with rage, I turned to face my old professor, who I actually liked very much, and said, "I am sorry."

"I am glad to hear it," my professor replied.

But then I continued, "I am sorry that you were my professor."

He looked at me in shock as everyone in the room looked toward the president of the court. Thankfully, the president dismissed my professor's request and instead excused the coroner from giving any further evidence. It was obvious that he was far from impressed with the coroner's testimony, as he took the unusual step of calling for a three-week adjournment so that the autopsy report could be re-examined.

As we were leaving the courtroom, my old professor approached me. "Are you really sorry that I was your teacher?" he asked, making it clear he had been stung by my words.

"How can I be sorry when you have taught me so well that I can stand up to you in the courtroom?" I answered.

He smiled, pleased with my answer. Shaking my hand he said warmly, "I'm proud of you."

Three weeks passed without any further incident. It seemed that the presence of my men had made the defendant think twice about removing me from the equation. I was still worried, however, that he would attempt to bribe anyone he could to get the verdict he craved. Although I had got off to a good start, I recognized that there could yet be many more twists and turns. And this proved to be the case.

When the case finally resumed, I was delighted to find that Dr. Wasfi Muhamad Ali, the head of the coroner's office, had been called to give evidence. This clearly showed that the court had been less than impressed by his colleague's testimony at the last hearing. I had made my point that day, but now I had to hope that Dr. Ali, a highly respected man, had not also been paid off.

"After reviewing the records and pictures of this incident," he began, upon taking the stand, "I am of the opinion that the deceased could only have received this injury by being hit with an object."

As he spoke, you could hear a pin drop. This was a huge moment for my case. I knew that the defendant was now pushed into a corner. It seemed that even he could not bribe Dr. Ali.

Continuing his testimony Dr. Ali said, "I cannot accept the assertion that the deceased fell down the stairs, as such a blow to the back would mean that the girl would have fallen head first. This would definitely have injured her skull, an injury that was not present here. Furthermore, in almost all stair-falling cases, there are an array of different injuries. It would be very unusual for there to be just the one."

Scrambling for something to cling to, my old professor asked, "But what about the opinion given by your colleague?"

Smiling, Dr. Ali replied, "You have answered your own question. It is an opinion he is entitled to, but on the evidence it is not one that I agree with."

For a few more minutes, the defendant's lawyers tried to cast doubt on Dr. Ali's evidence, but it was clear that he was too well prepared to slip up. Finally, they realized they were fighting a losing battle and left me to question him.

I knew that the court would now be satisfied that Yasamin had died as a result of receiving a blow. This was crucial to my case. Now I needed to highlight the brutal element of the crime.

Standing up, adjusting my black robe as I did so, I looked at Dr. Ali and asked, "Would the deceased have died instantly as a result of this injury?"

"It is very unlikely," he responded. "Usually it would take a few hours to die from such an injury."

"If the deceased had been brought to the hospital immediately, is there a chance that she could have been saved?"

"With spine injuries, it is hard to say, but I have certainly heard of cases where people have received similar injuries and prompt treatment saved their lives."

"Are such injuries painful, doctor?"

"Yes. The pain would have been indescribable. Like someone putting a red hot poker into your back."

"For how long do you think she would have endured this pain before she died?"

After considering my question, he finally said, "Anything up to six hours."

For a moment I didn't say anything. I let the courtroom digest this answer.

"Six hours, doctor?" I finally said, wanting to labor on this point.

"Yes. Six hours," he replied.

"Would she have been conscious during this time?"

"It is possible."

After asking the judge for permission to approach Dr. Ali, I proceeded to hand him a stick.

"Doctor," I said, as he examined the stick, "is this the kind of object that could be the cause of the deceased's injuries?"

Dr. Ali looked at the stick, and then at me before he finally answered, "Yes. This type of stick could have caused the injuries that I inspected."

"Your Honor," I said, now turning to face the judge, "I would like to admit this stick into evidence. It was found at the home of the defendant by the police, and it is the object that the deceased girl's mother has testified her ex-husband had previously used to beat her and the deceased."

This caused a few mumblings in the courtroom. The doctor's testimony, and now this vital piece of evidence, had cast severe doubt on the defendant's story.

With the stick admitted into evidence, and the judge apparently content with Dr. Ali's testimony, I then faced my hardest task: cross-examining the defendant. He had already claimed that Yasamin had died due to falling down the stairs. It was my job to now paint the real picture for the court—that he had beaten her to death. However, I knew there was no way he would simply admit this, so I had formulated a plan.

Looking at the defendant as he made his way to the stand made my flesh crawl. He was a small man with jet black, greasy hair who had a habit of smirking at every question he was asked. He struck me as very arrogant. Whenever he was asked a question that didn't meet his approval, he squinted his eyes into narrow slits, his crow's feet spreading across his face. I had no doubt that this was a stare his daughter had been subjected to on many occasions.

Deciding to deal with his violent past first, I set the scene that the defendant had habitually beaten his ex-wife, something he of course denied. I also asked him to answer the allegations that he had chained his daughter to her bed and had beaten her with a stick.

Narrowing his eyes, he said with steel in his voice, "These are just lies created by my ex-wife. She has never forgiven me for leaving her, and now she wants to punish me by blaming me for this accident."

"Sir," I began, walking toward the stand, "I put it to you that on the night in question, your daughter confronted you over your treatment of her. Enraged by her complaints, you did what came naturally to you; you grabbed the stick with which you had beaten her in the past and struck her across her back."

"These are just lies," he laughed. "What are you, a storyteller?"

"After beating Yasamin," I continued, "you then dragged her upstairs to her room where you chained her to her bed. As we have heard from the coroner, she would have been conscious and in intense pain for anything up to six hours. Despite hearing her cries for help, you sat downstairs with your wife and did nothing. Effectively, you left her to die."

"What is this bullshit?" he replied, looking at the judge, who rebuked him for using foul language in the court.

"When your daughter had been silent for a few hours, you went to check on her only to find that she was dead. You waited until the early hours of the morning before taking her to the hospital. You knew that it would be quieter then, and it would be less likely that questions would be asked. You needed to get a death certificate quickly, and that is why you were so agitated with the doctor. That was the case, wasn't it?"

"You don't know what you're talking about."

"We've heard that you used to beat your ex-wife and daughter with a stick, the same stick that was found at your house, and that stick is consistent with your daughter's injuries. We've also heard from a respected doctor that your attitude and demeanor when bringing your daughter to the hospital were not those of a distraught father. Far from shedding any tears, you were more interested in getting a death certificate, so much so that you even threatened the doctor for not giving it to you. You killed your daughter, sir, as your ex-wife always feared you would. Isn't that true?"

"*No!*" he shouted aggressively, banging his fist on the wooden stand in front of him. "You are full of shit. You're a liar."

For a moment I let the defendant continue with his tirade against me. I knew that it was extremely unlikely that he would ever admit to killing his daughter, but this display of anger was showing the court something very important. Here was a man who struggled to contain his temper and was quite capable of lashing out in frustration.

As he continued to yell and stood up to gesticulate at me, I then delivered my final blow—I winked at him. Unable to contain himself, he suddenly, leapt forward and tried to grab me. I quickly swerved out of the way as two policemen rushed forward and restrained him.

"Your Honor," I said, as the defendant continued to rage behind me, "the current charge against the defendant is assault leading to death. I believe that this charge is wrong. While it was initially an assault, it later became murder when this man did not help his daughter when it was clear she was distressed. I now ask that the court consider giving the death penalty to the defendant for such a crime. I am sure the public executioner will be more merciful to him than he was toward his own daughter."

This last sentence provoked uproar in the courtroom. As the defendant's lawyers leapt from their chairs to try to shout me down, a number of supporters from both sides broke into scuffle. Several police officers struggled to bring the melee under control as I too became embroiled in the fracas as someone from the gallery took a swing at me. Wrestling the man to the ground, I held him by his throat until security managed to drag him away. Even in the courtroom, under the eyes of the judge, the police, and over fifty of my men, I still was not safe. It took over ten minutes for security to bring the courtroom under control. It was like a tinderbox. I knew it wouldn't take much to set it all off again.

"Order, order!" the judge bellowed at the top of his voice. "The lawyers will give their closing statements before I will retire to reach my verdict."

As I gave my closing statement, I was very conscious of the number of enraged eyes boring into the back of my head. It was clear that if given half a chance, these people would take great pleasure in doing me harm. Still, I was undeterred. Over the cries of Yasamin's mother, who sat behind me, I set out the facts of this horrific crime and how the court had seen firsthand just what a violent man the defendant was. Even though the defense team tried its best to paper over these cracks, I was confident that I had done enough.

However, as I waited outside the courtroom for the verdict surrounded by my workers, I noticed that many of the defendant's supporters were drinking sharbat, a drink that is usually only drunk in instances of celebration. Having personally witnessed the lengths the defendant was willing to go to in order to ensure a not guilty verdict, I suddenly felt sick to my stomach. While I had focused all my energy on the facts, had the defendant gone right to the top and bought the judge? If he had, then all of my best efforts would have been in vain. While this thought swirled around my head, the court officer suddenly asked everyone to return to the courtroom. A verdict had been reached.

After entering the courtroom, the judge directed everyone to take a seat while the crowd waited with bated breath for him to speak.

"The court has deliberated for a long time on this matter and has come to the following decision," he said, before taking a sharp intake of breath. This was it. Was my faith in the justice system about to be shattered? "The court finds that the defendant has committed a grave assault on his daughter, and this directly led to her death. He is thus ordered to spend fifteen years of hard labor in prison and is also ordered to pay the deceased's mother 5,000 dinars in moral compensation."

My heart soared as the defendant angrily cried, "Bullshit. Bullshit!" Suddenly his supporters joined in. There was chaos as the police tried to take him away. Leaping onto the officers, the defendant's supporters tried to pry him free, but they were viciously beaten back by truncheons. The next five minutes were some of the most outrageous scenes I have ever witnessed in a courtroom. It was sheer pandemonium.

Yet amid the chaos, almost unmoved, remained Yasamin's mother, who held a picture of her dead daughter in her hand. I sat down beside her, and while at first she seemed to be in a daze, she suddenly hugged me with all of her might. Digging her fingernails into my flesh, I could feel her tears stream down her cheeks as she thanked me over and over for helping her. I have to admit that I also became very emotional. As I held her frail, sobbing body in my arms, I felt tears well up in my eyes. No one said that justice would always bring happiness.

I had dreamt of a moment like this, of delivering justice in the face of adversity. But now that I had achieved my goal, I felt sad. A young girl had needlessly lost her life. Nothing could make up for that.

While I hugged the mother, I saw the cheerful figure of my father walk toward me with a broad smile on his face. Enveloping me in a hug, he whispered in my ear, "I'm proud of you, habibi." That meant more to me than anything in the world, far more than money and success. I was on my way. My legal career had truly begun and what a way to start. In my first major trial I had encountered threats, bribery, and fighting in the courtroom, but if I had thought it would get any easier, I was wrong. This was merely the calm before the storm.

5.

THE CONFESSION

"There is no such thing as justice, in or out of court."
—Clarence Darrow

AFTER MY FIRST MAJOR LEGAL victory, I became inundated with requests for my legal services, and as I usually ended up on the winning side, I rapidly developed a successful reputation. No matter the circumstances, I always felt confident that I could win, especially with my father supporting me from the front row of the courtroom. But when I stood up to give my closing statement in one of Iraq's most notorious cases, I knew my winning streak could be about to come to an abrupt end.

The case in question had captured the imagination of the public, and as such, the courtroom was packed with friends, relatives, lawyers, and even the media. Everyone wanted to know how I was going to defend the indefensible, a murder charge where my client had a motive to kill, had been the last person seen alive with the victim, and to top it all, had already confessed to committing the crime. For all intents and purposes, it looked like an open-and-shut case.

Preparing to give my final argument, I took a sip of water and felt sweat drip down my forehead as I struggled to work out what I could say in the face of such damning evidence. If I couldn't come up with anything, then my client would hang.

Other than his initial confession, my client had refused to say anything else on the matter, not even to me, his lawyer. I had repeatedly
begged him to tell me the truth, but all he would say was, "I have nothing to tell you. Save me if you can."

"Save you with what?" I would cry. "I am not a magician. We have
nothing, and you're facing the death penalty." But even this prospect
wasn't enough to persuade him to talk.

All I knew at this stage was that the defendant's sister had lived with
her husband and their two young children in a small village in the
north of Iraq. One day the alleged victim, who worked as a medical
assistant, came to live in the village, and he immediately struck up a
friendship with the sister before they suddenly disappeared.

At this time the defendant was in prison serving twelve years for
manslaughter. When he was finally released, he set off for his village so
that he could be reunited with his sister only to find that she was no longer there and hadn't been seen in three years. Her husband explained,
to the defendant's disgust, that she had run off with the medical assistant without even leaving so much as a note. Unhappy at hearing of
such a betrayal, and fearing the effect his sister's actions would have on
his family's honor, the defendant vowed to find her.

Hearing whispers that his sister had settled in Baghdad, the defendant immediately set off for the city, aiming to scour every nook and
cranny until he found her. After a few days he had a stroke of luck when
he spotted her shopping in a prominent marketplace. Although he was
furious when he first confronted her, he soon calmed down when his
sister tearfully told him the true story of what had happened.

It transpired that the medical assistant had taken her against her will
to Baghdad, where he had raped her repeatedly, which subsequently
left her pregnant. Her choices were stark. She could either stay with the
rapist medical assistant and raise a family with him, or she could try to
escape and return to her village, heavily pregnant, and face the wrath
of her husband, who would no doubt kill her for bringing such shame
upon his honor. Neither choice was desirable. Yet if she stayed with the
medical assistant, she felt she had a better chance of staying alive.

Giving his sister the benefit of the doubt, the defendant demanded
that she take him to her home to meet the medical assistant. While

she protested, the defendant told her that he came in peace. He merely wanted to help arrange it so that she could marry the man and stop living in sin. Believing this to be true, she took the defendant home and introduced him to the medical assistant, where after an awkward start, the two men apparently got on so well that the defendant decided to stay for a few days.

On the third day of his stay, the defendant asked the medical assistant to show him around Baghdad. Together they set off, but in the evening the defendant returned to the house alone, where he told his sister that he had asked the medical assistant to allow her to return to her family. The medical assistant had apparently agreed to this, so the defendant and his sister soon returned to their village, where upon their arrival the defendant told her husband the true story. Despite being very upset, the defendant managed to persuade him to forgive his sister, and to welcome her back to their home.

Over three years went by with no one reporting the medical assistant missing. Not even his family suspected anything untoward. As far as they were concerned, he had enlisted in the army, as he had always promised he would, and had not returned from the war with the Kurds. This was certainly not unusual, as thousands of men had met their fate on the battlefield in that conflict.

Indeed, no one suspected that the defendant may have been linked to the medical assistant's disappearance until the night he got into an argument with a friend in a bar. After a scuffle, the friend said to the defendant, "Don't act like a man now. If you were any sort of man, you would have killed your sister after she disgraced your family's honor."

To this the defendant was said to have replied, "I avenged my honor. I killed the man who kidnapped her."

Following this very public admission, the defendant was arrested. While he did not deny that he had made this confession, he told the police that he had nothing more to say on the matter. And that was that. The case looked all but closed.

However, despite searching hospital records, army records, and death certificates for any trace of the medical assistant, the police found nothing. The only thing they had to go on was the defendant's motive and subsequent confession, both big chunks of evidence, but without a body, there was no definitive smoking gun.

Did I believe the defendant was innocent? I wouldn't have taken the case if I had thought otherwise. Although there seemed to be overwhelming evidence against him, I felt in my gut that he hadn't committed this crime. I had nothing concrete to go on, but I was usually a good judge of character. When I looked into his eyes, I thought I saw a man who had been caught up in events beyond his control.

However, by this stage in the trial I had already cross-examined the arresting police officer, the medical assistant's mother, and one of the sister's neighbors. Nothing in their testimonies had shed any further light on what had actually happened. They merely confirmed that the medical assistant had been missing for a few years and that the defendant had admitted to killing him.

Now, with all eyes on me, it was time for my closing statement. My heart was beating so fast I thought it would explode through my chest. Behind me all I could hear was the furious scribbling of pen to paper from a journalist by the name of Yahia who was covering the case for *The Baghdad Times*. His opinion in his column that morning did not look good; as far as he was concerned, my client was going to the gallows.

Starting slowly I addressed the president of the court, who was peering down at me from his seat. "My client was confronted with the greatest challenge faced by men in the Middle East," I began. "Someone insulted his honor. And when faced with such a slur, a man is expected to do his utmost to defend it, or he is not recognized as a man." Thankfully this met with approving murmurs from the courtroom.

I don't think people in the West realize just what a big deal honor is in the Middle East. Any insult, no matter how slight, on someone's honor can lead to dire consequences. Retaliation is almost seen as being compulsory. If you don't strike back, then you can almost certainly expect to be shunned and mocked in your community. Because of this, people take matters of honor very seriously. The Iraqi legal system even allows defendants to use harm to their honor as a mitigating circumstance in murder cases.

Continuing on this theme, I went on. "When my client was confronted in a busy bar by a man claiming that he had no honor, what could he do? He could not say that he had killed his sister—an act that would have been understandable in his community, given the circumstances—as they knew she was alive. Therefore, the only thing he could say to save face was that he had killed the medical assistant, someone who hadn't been seen in some time."

Turning away from the judge, I looked toward the gallery, who were now hanging on my every word. There in the front row, as always, was my father. A judge had once said that I presented all of my cases to him, rather than to the court, and I suppose that was true. When I spoke under such intense pressure, I was always comforted to see my father nod along to my every word.

Looking at my father, rather than the judge, I said, "When my client was subsequently arrested for making such a claim, his honor would have been hurt further if he admitted that he had been lying. Faced with this predicament, he neither retracted his statement nor said anything further in regard to the disappearance of the medical assistant."

My father nodded and smiled, urging me to continue.

"Throughout this case the prosecution has revealed no evidence other than the supposed confession of my client. They have acted under the assertion that this confession was truthful, but I would ask that the court please consider the following when coming to its verdict."

Gradually raising my voice, I then went on to deliver my final words, in the hope that they would be enough to save the life of my client, who was now peering at me desperately.

"After the disappearance of the medical assistant, neither his friends nor family reported him as missing. Doesn't this strike you as strange? Surely if one of your family members had been missing for so long, and you suspected something had happened to him, you would contact the authorities?

"We have seen evidence that at the time of the medical assistant's disappearance, he was a reserve soldier with the army. As we well know, this was during the time of the conflict with the Kurds, where many reserve soldiers went to fight and never returned. To this day thousands of men are thought to have died on the battlefield without ever being identified. Is it not possible that the man simply went to fight the Kurds, after the defendant told him to stay away from his sister, and was then killed in battle?

"Indeed, as no body has ever been found, it is certainly possible that the medical assistant may even still be alive. If I were to tell the court that the man was in this courtroom right now and pointed him out, I'm sure that you would all look to where I was pointing, as no one can be 100 percent certain that he is in fact dead."

Having set out my defense, I sensed that the mood in the courtroom had changed. For the first time since the trial had begun, it seemed that some were beginning to question whether the defendant was in fact guilty, as everyone had originally assumed. Stopping to have a sip of water, I knew that I now needed to strike an emotional chord with the president of the court, as well as his two co-judges

"Your Honor, may I please approach the witness stand?" I asked. Bemused by my request, the president of the court nevertheless indicated that I was allowed to do so. Striding up to the stand, I grabbed hold of the Qur'an, which had been left for witnesses to swear upon.

Holding the Qur'an in my hand, I walked back toward the prosecutor and said, "This is the Holy Qur'an. Could you, before God, put your hand on it and swear that you are 100 percent fully convinced that the man you're representing has been killed by the defendant?"

The prosecutor was taken aback. The eyes of the courtroom were upon him. Everyone waited to see what he would do. Even I wasn't too sure. Eventually he stuttered, "I am just a lawyer. I am not required to swear on evidence at a trial."

His reaction was enough. It showed to the court that he was not confident enough in his own case to swear on it. After waiting a few moments to let this register, I returned to the witness stand and picked up the Bible.

"I am a Christian," I said, turning to speak to the gallery with the Bible in my hands. "I swear on this Bible that I am personally not sure if my client is innocent, but at the same time I cannot swear that he is guilty. I have no more information about this case than does anyone else in the courtroom. Everyone here must have a semblance of doubt as to what has taken place. No one can say for certain whether my client has in fact committed the crime he is accused of. For that reason, can we afford to have blood on our hands when such uncertainty is present?

"If my client is found guilty, he faces the death penalty. What would happen, as is quite possible, if you discover that one day you were wrong and you had sentenced an innocent man to death? This is a very real possibility. I leave in Your Honor's hands the fate of a man who could very well be a killer but who at the same time could merely be an innocent man who is just trying to save his honor. May God almighty guide you to reach your decision."

The atmosphere in the courtroom was electric. I sensed that many now felt that this case was too close to call. With the hearing at an end, we were ordered to leave the courtroom while the judges tried to reach a verdict.

Waiting outside, the journalist, Yahia, came to greet me. "You couldn't have done anymore," he told me, "but I'm not sure if it will be enough to save your client."

I had to admit, deep down I agreed with him, but my father thought differently.

"Habibi," he said, his face glowing with pride. "After that performance, no court on earth would convict that man." As always, no matter the odds, my father backed me.

Three hours passed slowly, the tension becoming unbearable. Pacing up and down the corridor, I tried to remain calm, but I really didn't have a clue what the court would decide. My client's life was on the line. I prayed that I had done enough, but still I felt that the odds were stacked against him. As these thoughts raced through my mind, the usher suddenly announced that the court had reached its verdict. This was it.

Everyone rushed inside the courtroom, packing the room until not another soul could fit. It seemed that everyone in the building was desperate to see how the court would rule.

Finally, after the three judges had taken their seats, the president of the court began reading his verdict. His summing up of the case only served to increase the tension as we all waited for the only words that mattered: guilty or not guilty.

As the president finally reached his conclusion, I closed my eyes and prayed.

"According to Iraqi law," he began, "when defendants are charged with a crime that carries the death penalty, then the court is under an obligation to find a defense for them, even if they fail to present one.

"When considering this, in conjunction with the fact that the body of the deceased was not found, that his family did not report him missing, and that the defendant may have made the admission to save his honor, based on the evidence presented, the court is unable to determine whether the defendant is in fact guilty of murder. In light of this, the court has no option but to rule in favor of the defendant."

I was stunned. I had won in the most improbable of circumstances. As I tried to take it all in, a huge commotion broke out in the courtroom. No one could quite believe what had just been said. Everyone swarmed toward me to offer congratulations, but as always, my father was the first to shake my hand. Not for one moment had he doubted that I would win.

Forcing his way through the melee, the journalist, Yahia, grabbed my arm. "Can I meet with the defendant in your office?" he asked excitedly. "Now is the time for his side of the story."

I said I would do what I could and that he should meet us there in an hour.

After almost half an hour of these extraordinary scenes, I finally managed to bundle my father and the defendant into my waiting car so that we could make our way back to my office. Under the circumstances, I had expected my client to be ecstatic, but he was like a robot. On the journey he hardly said a word, hardly made a sound, hardly batted an eyelid. This made me very uneasy. What was he thinking?

When we finally arrived at my office, I ushered him in and closed the door behind us. I was desperate to see if he would at last reveal the truth. Taking a seat beside him, I softly said, "The case is over. You're free. Would you now tell me what actually took place?"

Still my client looked nervous. "Is everything really over?" he asked. "Yes," I replied.

Wringing his hands together, he slowly began to tell me his story, reaching the point where he had gone off to explore Baghdad with the medical assistant.

"The man took me to a place on the outskirts of Baghdad called Hamorabi Park," he confided. "Feeling hungry, we went to a restaurant

that was surrounded by gardens. For days I had tried to bury my feelings against the man, but as we ate I found myself becoming consumed
by anger. When we had finished our meal, I knew what I had to do."

"And what was that?" I probed, my palms sweating with anxiety.

"Walking in the park together, I waited until we were out of sight
before pulling a dagger from my pocket."

I flinched. I knew what was coming next. I just didn't want to hear it.

"When he turned his back to me, I lunged forward and stabbed him
repeatedly until he was dead."

As he said those words, my stomach dropped. I felt sick. Noticing the
stunned look on my face the man suddenly became angry.

"You are a man!" he shouted. "You know my community's tradition!
You know I had no choice!"

For once I was at a loss for words. Slowly nodding my head I tried
to process this shocking information. I always knew that this could be
possible, but when the reality hit me, I didn't know if I could face the
truth.

Wanting to get the whole story off his chest, he continued. "I hid his
body in the bushes while I returned to my car to collect a big suitcase
and a hunting knife. When I returned to the body, I cut it up into little
pieces and then dumped the remains into the bag. I then took the suitcase to my car and put it in the trunk.

"Returning to my sister's house, I told her that I had arranged for
her to go back to her husband, as she had wished, and that everything
would now be fine. She didn't ask me what had happened. She was just
overjoyed that she could go home.

"On our journey to her village in the north of Iraq, we passed
through some mountains where there had been some vicious battles
between the Iraqi army and the Kurds. I knew this would be a good
place to dump the body. Stopping the car, I took the bag containing the
man's remains out of the trunk and threw it off the side of the moun-
tain. I reasoned that even if people found the remains, they would think
he was a victim of the war.

"Once I had disposed of the remains, I continued driving to the village, where my sister and her husband were reunited. I stayed with
them for a few days, as I was expecting that a police investigation would
have commenced and that I would need to hide, but nothing happened.

Feeling safe, I returned to Baghdad and made some discreet inquiries regarding the whereabouts of the man. Most people believed that he had gone to live with my sister in a village outside Baghdad, while others felt that he had joined the army. No one thought there was anything strange in his disappearance, and after his own family failed to report him missing, I started to relax.

"Obviously, three years later I was involved in the incident in the bar where I confessed to the killing. As a matter of honor, I did not want to say that I was lying, but I also did not want to give the police any more information, as I knew I would then definitely face the death penalty. However, until you took on my case, I never thought I would get off. That is why I could not tell you any more. I needed you to fight for me with the conviction that I was truly innocent."

I didn't know what to say. I was sickened by the whole affair, but at the same time I knew that in this man's world, he truly believed that he had no choice but to kill his sister's kidnapper. It was a matter of honor.

Standing to leave, while also thanking me for my work, the man suddenly stopped and turned to face me. "I had no choice," he said. "Believe me. I had no choice."

He took my hand and tried to kiss it, but I pulled it away. Despite this, he tried to take me in his arms while uttering, "Thank you. Thank you."

I remained still, having nothing more to say.

When the defendant finally left my office, I sat alone for a few minutes, trying to digest what I had heard. I was very troubled by the whole experience. A man is always entitled to a defense, but I felt that I had been duped. I almost felt as though I couldn't face my father and Yahia, who were waiting for me outside. What could I tell them?

After running this over in my head for a good ten minutes, I finally decided to leave my office. Unsurprisingly, Yahia immediately pestered me with questions. He was desperate to know what my client and I had discussed.

"Nothing really," I told him. "He just wanted to thank me for defending him."

Yahia was clearly unconvinced. "I have always believed every word you have said," he replied, "and I will try my best to believe what you are telling me now."

I shook his hand and thanked him for his support, but he could tell that something was amiss.

In a daze I walked back into my office and sat behind my desk. For a couple of minutes he left me alone with my thoughts. but then suddenly he asked, "Was he guilty?"

"Yes," I replied, looking up at my father. "He killed the man."

My father was shocked. "Listen," he began, as he tried to process his thoughts. "Whatever he has said to you now you could not have known when you were in court. You presented your defense believing truthfully in every word that you said. You can do no more. Don't be too hard on yourself. I am proud of you."

I smiled at these words. My father was right. When I was in court I had truly believed every word I had said. All defendants should be represented by their lawyers to the best of their ability. Based on what I knew, I could not have done anymore. I realized that I was in an impossible situation. If the same thing happened again tomorrow, then there wouldn't be much that I could do about it.

The legal system is flawed at times. Justice does not always prevail. But I had acted truthfully before the court and had represented my client to the best of my ability. Ultimately, the verdict was down to the judges, who had to make a decision based on the facts that were set before them. Justice may not have prevailed, but I believe I did my duty.

6.

THE WRESTLING BEAR

"Justice and truth are two such subtle points that our tools
are too blunt to touch them accurately."

—Blaise Pascal

AS THE 1960S CAME TO A CLOSE, I looked back on the decade with
enormous satisfaction. Bafra cigarette papers were now acknowledged as one of the top brands in Iraq, and my success as a lawyer had
surprised even me. Things were going better than I could have ever
imagined.

With my legal work becoming my main focus, I moved my office
from the old part of Baghdad to the up-and-coming Karrada area,
which had the Tigres River running along both sides and was rapidly
becoming one of the most affluent areas in the city. Once settled I soon
put together one of the finest criminal law firms in the country. Using
all of my charms, as well as offering huge financial inducements, I managed to persuade some of the best lawyers in Iraq to work for me.

The legal expertise I assembled at this time was second to none. I
hired not only vastly experienced lawyers but also respected judges,
such as Sadiq al-Khudiary, who had once worked as the vice president
of the Court of Appeals, and Said Jawad al-Mousawie, who had been
president of one of its chambers.

My brief to my team at our weekly meetings was never to accept a
case just for money. My cigarette factory was making money; my law

firm was there to make a difference. I wanted us to only take cases where we could fight injustice and help people who usually couldn't afford a lawyer. Of course, in some cases we were rewarded handsomely for our efforts, but there were many other cases where we worked for free.

Often I took a case just for the challenge or for an unusual reward. I remember once leaving court and a small, bearded man asked me, "Are you a lawyer?"

"I am," I replied. "How can I help you?"

Coming closer, almost whispering, he said, "I have a case, but I can't afford to pay you. However, if you will take this case, I will give you a good meal in a restaurant I know."

"Work for food?" I questioned, finding the concept very amusing, to which he nodded his head. Thinking the offer over, I eventually decided that it would be a lot of fun. But I told the man that I would only represent him on one condition, that my friends would also be able to join me at the restaurant for the meal, something he was happy to agree to.

The court case was a very trivial matter. I forget the facts now, but in any event, I successfully defended the man. Soon afterwards, with my ravenous friends in tow, I set off for the restaurant. Arriving at two o'clock we took our seats and proceeded to order virtually one of everything on the menu: steaks, kebabs, chicken, rice, salad, and more. The man was stunned. I laugh now when I think of his face. It was clear that we were in a hungry mood, and he was obviously frightened I was going to get more than my money's worth.

As four o'clock came and went, the afternoon developed into a gluttonous feast. Just to see the look on the man's horrified face, I continued to order more and more, knowing full well we would struggle to eat it all. Every time I ordered, I had to stop myself from laughing, as it was becoming so ridiculous.

At one point the man even whispered in my ear, "Please. I can't afford all of this."

In a deadpan voice I replied, "A deal is a deal. Keep the food coming."

To the man's credit, he kept ordering the food, but I could see he was really panicking. Of course, my extravagant orders were just in jest. I am not that cruel. When he disappeared for a few moments, I settled the bill in full, having thoroughly enjoyed my meal.

As I started to leave the restaurant, the man came running after me, shouting, "You have saved me on two occasions. The first when you represented me in court, and the second when you paid that bill!"

These truly were great days, and feeling happy with the way things were progressing, I decided to treat myself. The finest house in Baghdad had come on the market, and without thinking twice, I snapped it up. At that time I was still a bachelor and had no need for a house with over twenty rooms, but I have to say that it was quite magnificent. Situated in the luxurious al-Hindia district, which is Baghdad's equivalent to Beverly Hills, the house stood on the banks of the Tigres River, with all the city spread before it. I used to enjoy sitting on my veranda and taking in the splendor of it all while waving to the captains of the boats, who sounded their horns in acknowledgment as they sailed past.

The house was also ideal for parties, as the garden was enormous at 3,500 square meters and boasted two pools. Many a Sunday afternoon I would invite my close friends over for an impromptu celebration. For a time, my house was the place to be seen in Baghdad.

Yet as always, when things appear to be going well, disaster is never far away. My father, who was my closest friend in the world, suddenly became very sick, and after a short illness he passed away. I will never forget his last words. For days my father had been bedridden and was so ill he was unable to speak, yet as he neared the end, he held my mother's hand, and summoning up his last speck of energy, he whispered to her, "I am sorry for leaving you." His death broke my mother's heart. They truly were soul mates.

For a number of weeks I could not face going to court, as I knew that my father would no longer be in the front row to give me helpful advice or just offer an encouraging smile when I needed it most. It was a very rough time, and even to this day I still feel enormous pain when I think of him. He was so much more than my father; he was my best friend. I knew that no matter how long I lived, I would never get over his loss.

However, even in death, my father inspired me to save the life of a client. Before he had passed away, I had acted in a case where a man named Hamed was very unfortunate to have been given the death sentence for murder. I was stunned at the verdict and took it very hard, but even in ill health my father told me to stop blaming myself.

When my father passed away, Hamed wrote to me from death row to express his sympathy. He said, "I wish I could have given my cheap life for the dear life of your father. Yet if I am executed, and I meet him in the next life, I will tell him how you mourned his death and how dear he was to you."

My father had liked Hamed, and I knew he would want me to do all that I could to save him, so I immediately launched an appeal.

After distributing my pleadings to the twenty-seven judges who would read the case, I was comforted when shortly afterward one of them said to me, "Your dear father will not be disturbed by any message taken to him from earth." I knew then that Hamed was saved.

A few days later I had it in writing. Instead of receiving the death penalty, he would now serve just seven years in jail because the court felt that he had acted in "excess self defense." Again, even in death, my father still inspired me to strive for something that everyone else thought was impossible.

Although this was tremendous news, I still felt very down and struggled to motivate myself. To help me get over my pain and so that I had some company in my huge house, I started to visit a market in central Baghdad, which was held every Friday, to buy animals. At this market you could buy virtually any animal you could think of. Soon my back garden resembled a mini zoo. I had monkeys, a gorilla, fighting cocks, dogs, lizards, scorpions, and even two parrots who would incessantly chant my name: "Sabah. Sabah. Sabah."

One Friday while visiting the market again, I was keeping my eyes out for something really special, an animal that not even a zoo would have.

Due to the fact that I always made a purchase, I was a very well-known face in the marketplace, so as soon as I arrived, I was besieged by traders trying to sell me things.

"Mr. Aris," one man cried, "come look at my monkeys. I will give you a good price."

Waving him away, I continued browsing, hoping for something to catch my eye.

Just as I was giving up hope, a man approached me. "Do you want to buy a wrestling bear?" he asked.

I couldn't believe my luck. "Why not?" I excitedly replied.

Taking me to a nearby warehouse, the man told me that this bear had once been one of the best wrestling bears in Iraq and had travelled all over the country with the circus. I was thrilled; I couldn't imagine a better addition for my zoo.

Apprehensively I entered the room containing the bear, prepared to be confronted by a fearsome beast. Yet as I entered the creature did little more than raise his eyes forlornly toward me. Looking at him lying flat on his belly, barely moving an inch, I would have sworn he was dead if his eyes had not followed me. As I slowly approached him, I could tell that he was very sick and tired. It was clear that the man had hardly fed the bear in an attempt to keep his energy and strength levels low. It broke my heart to see such a beautiful animal so malnourished and close to death.

Without wanting to waste any more time, I told the man that I would buy him. Happy with the sale, the man immediately loaded the bear onto the back of his pickup truck and brought him to my house.

However, when he arrived I realized that I had a problem. I had been so caught up with the idea of owning a wrestling bear that I actually hadn't considered that I didn't have anywhere to keep him. But while I had no building or cage that was suitable, I didn't want to let this poor creature return with the man, as I was sure the bear would almost certainly die. As such, I hammered a stake into the ground and then tied one end of a rope around the bear's front leg and the other end to the stake. It would have to do while I had a special cage built.

For days the bear did nothing but lie flat on his stomach, barely moving or making a sound. There was no doubt that he had suffered greatly. Animals had always been one of my greatest passions, and I therefore made it my mission to nurse him back to full health.

A vet advised me to feed the bear one hundred baguettes a day as well as an array of vegetables, but I was never, under any circumstances, to feed him meat. He said that the reason for this was if people ever had an open wound around the bear, he would smell the blood and possibly attack them, thinking they were food. Such an attack could most certainly lead to serious injury or death.

While the bear slowly regained his strength, I had a spacious caged area finished that allowed him to walk around unchained. In the caged area I also built a small pond for him to play in, which he loved so much that he would even fall asleep in it at night.

In Iraq bears have always been regarded as primitive creatures, and as a result the circus had christened the bear "Abu Fahmi," which means "low intelligence" in Arabic. Yet it was abundantly clear to me that Abu Fahmi was very bright, and we soon developed an incredible bond.

At first he would just delicately put his enormous paw on top of my hand, but as he gradually grew stronger, he managed to stand up and would embrace me in a bear hug. I did not panic, as it was very clear that he meant me no harm. There was no doubt that he could have squeezed me to death if he had chosen to, but he applied minimum pressure around my body so as not to hurt me.

Soon, however, it became apparent that what Abu Fahmi really loved to do was wrestle. I learned that if I were to tap him on the top of his head and then go into a wrestling stance, he would stand up and fight. This may seem crazy, but not once, in all of our wrestling fights, did he hurt me. Putting all of my strength up against him, I would try to push him backward, and while he would push back furiously, he was always careful not to overcome or hurt me with his claws. I was amazed that such a big animal could be so tender and understanding. It got to the point where I could even put my arm into his mouth. However, although Abu Fahmi was gentle with me, he wasn't quite so tame with everyone he met.

Greek wrestling was a very popular spectator sport in Iraq at this time, and all the participants were treated as major stars. One day the best participants the sport had to offer came to Baghdad to engage in a series of high-profile contests. Being a huge fan, I invited all of the wrestlers to a party at my house. As could be expected, Abu Fahmi was the main attraction. When I wrestled with him, everyone gathered in a circle around us and cheered. Abu Fahmi certainly enjoyed the attention and was excited to see so many people take an interest in him.

However, one wrestler could not see that this was all just a bit of fun. After a few drinks he became very determined to fight Abu Fahmi and started to shoot off his mouth. I tried my best to deter him, and explained that Abu Fahmi did not hurt me because he trusted me but that I had no idea what he would do to someone he didn't know. Still, this didn't stop the wrestler. He was so arrogant that he actually thought he could win. To the amusement of my guests, he began boasting about how he was going to knock out the bear with one of his famous "munch" elbow moves. As you would expect, the wrestler was a huge man who was very famous for his wrestling conquests, but I really didn't give him much of a chance.

Everyone at the party begged me to let them fight, and despite my warnings and reservations, over sixty people soon gathered on the lawn to watch the contest. With Abu Fahmi towering in front of him, the man lunged toward him and landed an elbow to his rib cage, which made him roar in pain. It was clear that he was hurt. But just as I was about to stop the fight, Abu Fahmi delivered a knock-out blow. Swiping violently with his paw, he caught the wrestler across the temple and sent him crashing to the ground. Knocked unconscious, the man lay limp as Abu Fahmi tried to tear him limb from limb. People started screaming, as there was a real fear not only that the man was dead but also that Abu Fahmi would go on a rampage.

Approaching him quickly, I put my hand on Abu Fahmi to try to get him to stop. Amazingly, as soon as he saw me, he stepped away from the wrestler and was calm. While the panic subsided, there was real concern for the health of the fighter, as he was not moving and had blood coming from his mouth. Two doctors who were at the party came to his aid and immediately called an ambulance. Thankfully, the wrestler survived, and after a few days in the hospital he was released with just a few stitches and broken ribs. Perhaps the greatest injury was to his pride, as he did not wrestle again for some time, and I'm pretty sure he never took on a bear again.

This incident was the only time I ever saw Abu Fahmi hurt anyone. He was a very timid, peaceful animal who had only lashed out after being provoked. I remember that at nighttime I could let him out of his cage, and he would sit with me on the veranda. It seems incredible to think about it now, but at the time it almost seemed second nature. I treated Abu Fahmi just like you would treat a beloved family pet, and none of my staff were scared of him, as they knew he had such a friendly nature.

However, his presence in my house and my famous wrestling parties soon became very well known, and I was inundated with requests from people who wanted to come see him. One such request almost certainly could have changed my life in the most drastic way imaginable.

At this time I had all of my suits handmade in Baghdad by a tailor named Harooq. He was very popular and was renowned for being the best in the business. With such a reputation this meant that he came into contact with all manner of important and famous people. From time to time he would even bring some of them to my house for dinner. I was always glad to have company and welcomed them with open arms.

One Sunday afternoon Harooq called me and said, "Sabah, is it ok if I come to visit you with a friend today?"

"Of course," I replied. "But out of interest, who is he?"

"You don't know him yet Sabah," he answered excitedly. "But soon you and all of Iraq will know his name!"

Harooq was prone to exaggeration, so I was not overly impressed.

"What is this man's name?" I asked.

"Saddam Hussein," he proudly announced.

It's true, at this time I didn't have a clue who Saddam Hussein was. Unless a policy or an individual was directly affecting my life then, I paid very little attention to politics. However, looking back now it is clear that Saddam was already making quite a name for himself in political circles.

Saddam had first come to prominence in 1959, when he was allegedly backed by the CIA and had unsuccessfully tried to assassinate Prime Minister Abd al-Karim Qasim, whose left-leaning politics had enraged the West. After his failure, Saddam escaped to Egypt, where he spent the next few years in hiding. Following the 1963 coup, where Qasim's government was overthrown by members of the Ba'ath and Arab Nationalist Party, Saddam returned to Iraq, but his freedom was short-lived.

When the new president of Iraq, Abd al-Salam Arif, cracked down on prominent Ba'ath Party members, who he saw as a threat, Saddam was one of the first people he imprisoned. However, in 1967 Saddam escaped jail and soon started plotting a coup, along with Ahmed al-Bakr, that saw them seize control of Iraq in 1968. At that time Saddam became al-Bakr's deputy, which was his start on the road to eventually becoming president in 1979.

When Harooq first mentioned Saddam's name to me, it was before the 1968 coup, and therefore most people in Iraq would not have known who he was. Despite this, I still invited Harooq and his friend to join me for a drink, as I did not want to appear rude. Yet Harooq wanted more than this.

"Sabah," he said. "Saddam does not wish to have a drink. He wants to see you fight the bear."

Normally this would not have been an issue, as on many occasions I had fought with Abu Fahmi for my guests' entertainment. But for some reason, on this day, I was tired and in no mood for such activity. I was also annoyed that Harooq and his friend weren't coming to spend time with me but were more interested in seeing me perform some circus show. In no mood for such a spectacle, I told Harooq, "If all you and your friend are interested in is seeing me wrestle, then I would prefer it if you didn't come over." And that was that.

At the time I had no way of realizing what an important decision I had made. Throughout my career I never wanted to be seen as having any sort of political connections, as I always thought that could have the potential to interfere with my job of procuring justice. Iraq was also not a country where you could freely discuss political ideas. If you nailed your support to the mast for one party and another party subsequently seized power, then you could expect to be killed. To those in Western countries, it seems incredible to think that this is the case, but I can promise you that it is a fate that has fallen on hundreds of thousands, if not millions, of people in Iraq over the years. If I had met Saddam in a social setting that day, then judging by what came later, any possible friendship between us could have made my job, and life, very difficult. Thankfully, such a situation never came to pass.

While Saddam would in time have a major effect on my life, unfortunately my tales of Abu Fahmi the bear end here. A few years later I moved and rented my mansion to the Japanese Embassy. Understandably, the embassy was concerned about having a bear in the garden, and as my new house could not cater to him, I was advised to donate Abu Fahmi to the zoo. Although I did not want to do it, as I knew that Abu Fahmi was happy in my mansion, I was persuaded that as he was very old, it would be in his best interests.

When representatives from the zoo came to take him away, I could tell that Abu Fahmi was very unhappy. Although it broke my heart, I reasoned that the zoo would be able to look after him far better than I could. However, the zookeepers did not want to transport him while he was conscious and were adamant that they had to give him a tranquilizer. Despite my protests, they injected Abu Fahmi and reassured me that everything would be fine. Before they took him away, I kissed his head and promised to see him soon.

But for some reason after they left, I was very worried about Abu Fahmi. Something just didn't feel right. Fearing the worst, I called the zoo later that day to ensure that everything had gone as planned, but my question was greeted with an awkward silence. Finally, the zookeeper told me the worst possible news: Abu Fahmi had died. At hearing this I dropped the phone and wept.

We may not have been able to talk to each other, but I believe that both Abu Fahmi and I always understood what the other was feeling. We had an incredible bond that went beyond words. Even to this day my house is covered with pictures of the happy times that Abu Fahmi and I shared together and I continue to miss him greatly.

7.

DEATH PENALTY X

"Spare me through your mercy, do not punish me through your justice."

—Anselm of Canterbury

MR. ARIS, THERE IS A MAN outside with a machine gun who is demanding to see you."

I raised my head from a stack of papers to look at my secretary, whose voice quivered as she spoke.

"What do you mean?" I replied, glancing toward the door.

"I told the man we were closed for the day, but he stormed in and said he had to see you tonight. I can see that he has a machine gun under his coat. What shall I do?"

"Send him in," I said, opening my drawer and searching for the one thing I hoped could save me.

"Don't you want me to call the police?"

"No," I replied, pulling out my gun. "It is too late for that."

With that my terrified secretary left my office as I prepared to be confronted by someone who obviously wanted to do me harm. Maybe it was a former client, or someone I had helped send to jail? Maybe it was someone mentally unhinged? Regardless, someone was in my office with a machine gun and needed to be dealt with.

As my office door slowly opened, I raised my gun, clicked the safety, and put my finger on the trigger, ready to shoot as soon as the man made a wrong move. My heart was beating fast, yet everything was happening so quickly that I didn't have time to be scared.

With my finger primed, ready to shoot, a small man suddenly marched into my office.

"What do you want?" I shouted, pointing the gun toward him.

"Don't you remember me, Mr. Aris?" he said, continuing to walk toward me.

I looked closer, recognizing the man but not able immediately to put a name to the face. Then it struck me. "My God," I suddenly blurted. "I thought you were still in prison."

"I served seven years, thanks to you," he replied. "I was released last week."

It was true. The man, whose name I now remembered to be Halain, had indeed served seven years thanks to me. And at the end of his trial, he had thanked me profusely, as it certainly beat the charge he had been facing—the death penalty.

Looking at Hailan standing in my office, I thought back to how I had first become involved with him. I remembered that after speaking in court one day a man had approached me and asked if I would represent a relative of his who was charged with killing his sister as well as her daughter. It turned out that the accused's relative was Hailan. Apparently Hailan had killed them both to defend his families' honor after finding that his sister had been pimping out her daughter as a prostitute.

Complicating matters further was that Hailan had only just finished a five-year prison sentence for attempted murder, the result of a bar fight where the victim had shot at Hailan first. The case seemed an impossible challenge. Hailan had already been convicted of an attempted murder and was now being charged with double homicide. Surely there would be no escape from the death penalty.

Despite my misgivings, the man continued to harass me to take the case. He desperately pleaded that Hailan was a good man who had been caught up in very unfortunate circumstances. Without committing myself, I said I would at least meet with him.

And when I did meet Hailan at the police station, I found a fair, short man in his mid-twenties who was completely broken by what had taken place. Indeed, his guards told me that he had already tried to commit suicide, such was his grief.

It transpired that everything Hailan's relative had told me was true. Hailan really was a good man who was very unfortunate to have been imprisoned in the first place on the attempted murder charge. Then, upon his release, he had returned to his village to find that the two people closest to him in the entire world, his sister and niece, were now working as a pimp and a prostitute, respectively. When he tracked them down, he had indeed killed them. There was no defense other than that it was an honor crime, something that the Iraqi court accepted as a mitigating circumstance.

Despite Hailan being in a very difficult situation, I decided I would take the case. It was clear that we would be facing an uphill battle to avoid the death penalty, but I felt that if I could get across to the court the true circumstances, then perhaps Hailan would serve a life sentence instead.

In court, I passionately outlined how Hailan had tried to defend his honor to uphold the laws of Iraq. It was a crime that had completely destroyed his life and had left him alone, yet he did what he thought was best. After commiting the crime, he had also voluntarily handed himself over to the police, knowing full well he would probably be facing the death penalty.

Incredibly, despite his attempted murder conviction and the double homicide charge, Hailan avoided the death penalty and was instead sentenced to ten years of hard labor. It was quite a result and certainly one of the most memorable victories I had earned in the early stages of my career.

Yet now, seven years after his trial, he was back in my office, holding a machine gun.

"Please, Hailan, what is it that you want?" I asked, confused as to why he would turn up like this.

"I need your help," he said softly.

"Anything," I replied, offering him a seat, relieved to see that he didn't intend to use the gun on me.

With that he sat down and the reason for his visit soon became clear. He told me that after being released from jail three years early, he had returned to his home to find that everything was gone. Worse still, he found that his name was no longer on the deeds for the land. Further investigation revealed that his next-door neighbor was responsible. The neighbor had not only stolen everything but had also fraudulently put his name on the deeds.

"Do you want me to start legal proceedings against this man?" I asked.

"No," he replied.

"Then how do you want to deal with it?"

Hailan lifted his machine gun.

"You can't kill this man, Hailan!" I said. "Please, let me deal with it. If you commit a murder now, this time I cannot save you from the death penalty."

Hailan shook his head and stood up. "It has been good to see you again, Mr. Aris," he said before turning away and walking toward the door.

I shouted after him, "Please, Hailan. Don't do it! Don't do it!"

He turned, and nodded, before disappearing.

Four months passed without any further incident. I was relieved that it seemed as though Hailan had listened to me. But then one day, as I visited the court to catch up with some old friends, I heard one of the ushers shout from the criminal court, "Lawyer Sabah Aris! Lawyer Sabah Aris!"

I was confused. I did not think I had a case that day, but nevertheless I went to investigate.

"Have you made a mistake?" I asked the usher. "I am not scheduled to be in court today."

He glanced down at his list. "It says here you represent Hailan Hassan? His case is on now!"

My stomach dropped. I instantly knew Hailan had killed the man and had then told the court that I represented him. Flustered and confused, I merely nodded and entered the courtroom, unsure as to how I would proceed.

As I walked toward the bench, I glanced up to see the president of the court, a man I didn't like very much, glaring down at me.

"We have been waiting for you," he said gruffly. "You should know that when a man is facing the death penalty, you should not keep the court waiting."

I glanced at Hailan, who stared at me with pleading eyes. I couldn't let him down. "I am very sorry, your Honor," I apologized, swallowing my pride. "I got the times confused."

"Have you seen the file?" the president asked, to which I replied that I had not. With that he gave me thirty minutes to consider the facts of the case before I would again plead for a court to spare Hailan's life.

I took the file to a bench outside the court where I quickly scanned through the pages, trying to get an idea of what had taken place. It seemed that Hailan had confronted his neighbor about what had occurred only for the neighbor to turn a gun on him. But before the neighbor could fire, Hailan shot him dead. Again, as in the previous case, there was no denying that he was guilty of murder, but again, there were significant mitigating circumstances.

Nevertheless, I knew that this was a man who had already been convicted of attempted murder as well as murder. And now, less than a week after being released from jail, he had killed someone else. I fully expected the prosecutor to forcefully demand the death penalty, and I was not disappointed.

As soon as the case recommenced, the prosecutor opened by stating, "Your Honor, the defendant's previous convictions and facts of this case speak for themselves. I almost feel as if I need say nothing more. The death penalty was tailor-made for a man such as this."

Instantly I interjected. "The crimes my client has committed have never been accompanied with the malicious criminal intention usually connected to a murderer. In his first case he was involved in a fight that was not of his own making. In the second case he was defending his honor after his sister and niece became a pimp and a prostitute. And now in this current case, he confronted a man who had stolen everything he had in the world, only to be met by a gun! This was nothing but self-defense. My client is not a murderer in the traditional sense. He has merely been extremely unfortunate and has taken actions many others would have in the same positions."

These comments sparked a backlash from the president. "This is ridiculous!" he bellowed. "You are inventing a defense to try to save a clearly guilty man."

With this slur I lost my temper. "This is not a defense I have created," I shouted. "It was put forward by my client before I was involved in this matter. In all of my career I fear that this is the first time I have attended a case where the judge has already made his decision!"

With that the president slammed his gavel against the table. "I will hold you in contempt if you continue," he shouted.

Yet still I carried on. "Your Honor, it is clear that no matter what my client says, or what I say on his behalf, you have already made up your mind. We may as well do away with this hearing and just let you pass what you have already decided."

For a moment no one spoke. I don't think anyone could believe what I had said. And I have to admit, as I started to calm down, I realized that I may have gone too far.

"One more word from you, and I will have you arrested. Is that understood?" the president finally said, glaring at me.

I said nothing in return, having made my point, and knowing that if I did indeed utter another word I would be spending the night behind bars.

The subsequent pleadings in the case were predictable enough. The prosecution demanded the death penalty, owing not only to this crime, but also to the catalogue of similar previous offenses. Meanwhile I begged the court to see beyond the crimes themselves and consider the reality of the situations in which my client had found himself. With both sides going for the jugular, the judge finally called an end to proceedings and retired to consider his verdict.

Over three hours passed before we were called back into the courtroom. I waited with trepidation and wondered if my client's luck had finally run out. After all, three people had met their deaths at his hand. If the judge opted to give Hailan the death penalty, then I could not blame him. Indeed, I had begged Hailan not to go through with this crime. If he were to hang, then he would have no one to blame but himself.

As we reentered the courtroom and took our seats, the president began to talk, shutting up the conflicting voices that were swirling around my head.

"I have considered this case very carefully," he began. "On the face of it the circumstances dictate that the defendant should receive the death penalty." My heart sank, but then he continued. "However, I have taken into consideration that the victim was indeed armed and had carried out a crime on the defendant himself. In light of this I have decided to sentence the defendant to twenty-five years in jail without parole."

I nodded at the president in admiration at his sense of justice. I was glad that we had managed to put personal differences aside to ensure that an unfortunate man did not have to suffer the ultimate punishment.

"Remember this case always," the president said as I passed the bench. And I have, as proof that Iraqi judges can be merciful even in the face of crimes that seemed tailor-made for the death penalty.

Making my way to Hailan before he was taken away, I took him in my arms.

In between tears he said, "You have saved me again. I only hope I can repay you one day."

I replied with a smile on my face, "Hailan, I will always remember you, and I think you are a good man, but truly I hope we never meet again."

And we didn't. I don't know if Hailan died in jail, or if he might be alive to this day, but I am glad that I saved his life not once but twice.

Yet despite being against the death penalty on this occasion, I would soon be back in court holding an opposing point of view, this time demanding a man be put to death in the name of justice.

8.

THE CAGE MAN

"Law and order exist for the purpose of establishing justice, and when they fail in this purpose they become dangerously structured dams that block the flow of social progress."

—Martin Luther King Jr.

THE MOST BRUTAL CASE I ever dealt with occurred in the ancient city of Baquba, ironically the purported cradle of civilization where the Garden of Eden was once said to be situated. There was certainly nothing civilized about the crime that took place there. In fact, to this day, it is the one case that continues to haunt me.

On a searing hot day I was cooling myself under my fan at my desk when my secretary called to say that there was an old man and his family waiting to see me. People wanting to see me without an appointment was not unusual. Indeed, on most days I could expect a handful of unannounced visits. As such, I told my secretary to send the visitors in. However, when they entered I was immediately struck by the old man's appearance. Deep, dark circles surrounded his small eyes, while his face, gaunt and tired, was framed by a long, white, unkempt beard. Accompanied by his wife and other relatives, the man looked as though he was on the verge of a mental breakdown.

I asked the man to take a seat, for fear he could keel over at any time, and sent my secretary to fetch us some tea. For a few moments we exchanged pleasantries, but as soon as the man looked comfortable and had a cup of tea in his trembling hands, I tentatively asked, "What is it that I can do for you today?"

Taking a deep breath, and with his voice shaking, the man started to tell me a deeply unsettling story.

"Six weeks ago my three young sons went shopping in the local market," he began slowly, as if each word was getting stuck in his throat. "While my oldest son inspected a book stall, his two younger brothers stayed to chat with a man who was selling birds on the corner of the street."

The man suddenly looked at his wife, who had tears welling in her tired eyes, and grasped her hand for support before continuing.

"After a few minutes had passed my oldest son looked up from a book he was reading to find that he could no longer see his brothers. Rushing from the shop he quickly scoured the area for them. At first he assumed that they had wandered off to another stall, but after ten minutes of frantic searching he realized they were gone. One of the stall owners in the area told him that he had seen the boys leave with the man selling the birds.

"Quickly my son came home and told me that his brothers were missing. He said that a man he referred to as 'the Cage Man' had taken them. Not wanting to waste any more time, I called the police, and they immediately started searching the area, but it was useless."

Suddenly the man whimpered like a wounded animal. I passed him some tissues while he struggled to compose himself. Choking back tears he tried to get the words out. "It was useless. It was useless . . . my boys. . . my boys . . . they were gone!"

Burying his face into his chest, the man smothered his white shirt in tears. "The police started to interview people," he said, the tears now running off his white beard. "They spoke to those who had been in the vicinity at the time my sons had gone missing, but while some remembered seeing them with this Cage Man, no one knew who he was. He was a ghost.

"For two weeks the police searched for him until one day the man suddenly reappeared at the market selling his birds. Immediately recognizing him, one of the stall owners called the police, and he was arrested, thank God. An identification parade was swiftly set up, but my oldest son could not accurately identify him. He could not remember the Cage Man's face, you see. Although my oldest had clearly seen his brothers looking at the birds, he had only caught a fleeting glimpse of the man selling them. But my son knows that it was the man selling the birds in the cages who took his brothers."

With his voice rising in anger, the man suddenly jumped out of his seat and grabbed my shoulders. "And this is the man! This is the man! The Cage Man!"

"Where is this Cage Man now?" I asked, looking up at the man's desperate face.

"Still with the police," the old man replied, his face red from anger and tears. "But I've just been told they will have to release him in a few days. This can't happen. It mustn't happen. That animal knows where my two boys are. Something must be done. I don't know where else to go, and everyone I have spoken to has said that you are a man who can help."

I couldn't fail but be moved by the man's story. He was clearly at his wits' end. It was obvious that he was not wealthy and would never be able to meet my legal fees, but that didn't concern me. I wanted to help.

"I'll visit this man at the police station," I said reassuringly, "to see if there is anything that can be done."

"Bless you," the man cried. "When you see this man you will know in your heart that he is responsible."

The next day, at the crack of dawn, I set off to Baquba, the village where this incident had taken place, and where in the small police station the Cage Man was now being held. Upon arrival at the station I introduced myself and asked if it would be possible to see the suspect. There was no issue with my request, but I was told by an officer that while I could see the man, I would not be allowed to question him in any way. This was slightly disappointing but not unexpected. Reluctantly I told the officer that it would not be a problem.

When the man was finally brought into the room, a shiver went up my spine. He was greasy, unshaven, and slight, and his stale body odor immediately filled the room and made me retch. When he opened his mouth to sneer in my direction, he revealed that several of his teeth were missing and that he had black, rotting gums, as well as deep purple scars etched across his face.

If all this didn't unsettle me, when he sat down and looked into my eyes, I almost recoiled in horror. During my career I had looked into the eyes of some of the most ungodly creatures to have walked the earth, but nobody had ever looked at me like this. His eyes were like black, bottomless caverns. I swear, when I looked into them, I could see an uncontrollable rage, the likes of which I had never seen before.

As I tried to gather myself, the man spoke in a harsh, arrogant tone to the police officer. "When am I getting released?" he demanded.

The policeman looked a little intimidated, as if he almost expected this man to flip out at any time, but he replied, "Not until you confess to killing those two boys."

The Cage Man's lips curled into a thin smile. "I don't know what you're talking about. If you don't release me now, I'll tell the judge you kept me here with no evidence."

I sat in silence as the Cage Man eyeballed me. "What are you looking at, you cockroach?" he snarled.

I kept quiet and continued staring in his direction. So many questions ran through my mind but, as promised, I kept my thoughts to myself. Besides, no matter how many questions I may have had, I already had my answer to the most important question of them all: this was clearly a dangerous man who looked more than capable of kidnapping and murdering children.

Just a few minutes after he had arrived, the Cage Man was dragged in chains back to his cell.

"Tell me," I said to the police officer when he returned, "how much longer are you able to detain that man?"

"Just a couple of days," he replied. "But unfortunately he is right. At the moment we have no evidence, and we are running out of time to charge him."

The thought that such a clearly dangerous man would soon be set free was a worrying prospect. I knew that I had to act fast.

With no time to lose I made an appointment to see the investigating judge at the courthouse in the village. At that point I wasn't quite sure what I would say to him, but I felt that I somehow had to ensure that the

Cage Man would be kept in custody until evidence was found linking him to the crime. However, the judge investigating the case was notorious for abiding by the rules. I knew that the chances of me persuading him to bend them in this case were very slim.

Sitting in the judge's chambers we chatted briefly about the crime before I confessed that I had already met the suspect at the police station. I expected the judge to be surprised, or even to rebuke me, but he didn't seem fazed. In fact, when I told him that I was certain that this man was guilty of the crime even though there was no concrete evidence present, he seemed in agreement but added, "Mr. Aris, I sympathize with what you're saying, but I have already had this man detained for over a month. We have investigated this matter as thoroughly as possible. The only thing we have on him is selling birds without a licence. I'm afraid that I can't keep him too much longer."

If we were to adhere to the strict letter of the law, he was correct. However, I got the feeling that he was looking for a persuasive argument so that he could keep this man detained for a little longer. Then I spotted something that could help my cause. Staring at a picture of the judge's family on his desk, I asked, "Are these your children?"

"Yes," the judge replied, with a proud smile on his face. "My son is ten, and my daughter is fourteen."

"I can tell by your smile that you love your family very much," I said, now becoming more serious. "And the man who has lost his two boys in this case also loved his boys dearly. Please look at this case as if your own children had mysteriously disappeared and the man who you think kidnapped and murdered them was in custody. Would you be happy to see this man free to walk the streets because of legal technicalities?"

I could tell that the judge was really struggling between his legal duty and his feelings as a father. "What I'm asking, Your Honor," I continued, "is are you going to use legal procedures to set free a man who we have good reason to believe is a child killer, or are you prepared to go deeper?"

After taking what seemed like an age to weigh all of the conflicting thoughts in his head, the judge finally responded, "I will summon this man for a direct investigation in two days' time, where you can also be present to question him. If I am of the opinion then that no evidence is present, then I will have no option but to release him. If, however, I feel that there is something there, then I will transfer him to a special forces police division so that they can investigate him further." It was a brave step for the judge to take. It was certainly not the norm, but it was clear that he was very uncomfortable with setting the Cage Man free.

Two days later I attended the judicial investigation while the boys' father waited outside for the verdict. When the suspect was brought into the room, he launched into a furious tirade against the judge and the police, which certainly didn't do him any favors.

Arrogantly, the Cage Man then refused to answer any questions. To every query he merely responded, "You have no proof of anything. Let me go." After half an hour of this fruitless exercise, the judge ordered the suspect to be returned to his cell.

Exasperated by this ordeal, the judge invited me to his chambers to discuss the matter further. Following this hearing, and having seen the man first hand, I knew that the judge was now in a very difficult position. There was still no concrete evidence present, and according to the law the Cage Man should now be released, yet his demeanor and attitude had only served to emphasize that he was indeed a danger to the public. It was also obvious to everyone he was hiding something.

As I took my seat, I wasn't quite sure what the judge would decide, but he put my mind at rest when he said, "I share your point of view, Mr. Aris. That is a dangerous man. I have no hesitation in referring him to the combat police who will now investigate this matter further."

The combat police! This was a big deal. That division had quite a reputation in Iraq for uncovering the truth in all kinds of unsavory ways. For a moment, I flinched at the thought of the horrific ordeal the Cage Man was about to endure, but before I could really sympathize with him I reminded myself that this was a man who had kidnapped and probably murdered two small boys. We needed the truth. And in my eyes it didn't matter how we found it.

Relieved by the judge's decision I left his office and informed the father, who was waiting for me outside in my car, that the case would be investigated by the combat police. "Thank Allah," he cried. He certainly didn't have any sympathy when I told him that the Cage Man was likely to be tortured.

Days later I was summoned to see the chief officer involved in the interrogation. This man's reputation was notorious throughout Iraq, as he had been involved in a number of major cases where his merciless methods had unearthed key evidence. With the boys' father alongside me the chief officer asked us both to inform him of the details of the case. As we spoke the father broke down several times, his body wracked with emotion. The stress of it all was taking an enormous toll on him. I can rarely recall seeing a human being endure such abject suffering.

After listening to the facts of the case and being moved by the father's obvious distress, the chief officer looked into the father's eyes and said, "Trust me. If this man has kidnapped your sons, I will make him confess."

Jumping from his seat the father knelt down at the feet of the officer and tried to kiss his hand. Pulling away the officer said, "You do not need to thank me. This is my job. I will do whatever is necessary to uncover the truth." There was no doubt in my mind that not only would the officer get the man to confess, but also he would enjoy doing so.

After a few days with no news, I received a phone call. "I need to see you right away," the chief officer ordered. Without any hesitation, the father and I set off to meet him, not knowing what lay in store for us.

On our arrival the officer wasted little time getting down to business. "The suspect has confessed," he said, with a hint of satisfaction that his methods had once again proved fruitful. "He has agreed to take us today to where he buried the bodies. We want you to be present with us."

At this news the father let out a howl of emotion straight from the pit of his stomach. It was news he had long suspected but now knew to be true. His two sons were indeed dead. As I processed this horrific news, I also recognized that my instincts had been correct. The man was guilty. And while over a month of doing things by the book had yielded no results, just a few days of torture had led to a confession. It was a sobering thought.

The father was shaking and crying uncontrollably, so the officer asked him if he would sit outside for a moment. When we were alone, the officer said to me, "As soon as I set eyes on that man I knew he was a hard-core criminal. At first he was quite stubborn, but I made it very clear to him that if he did not confess to the crime, I would see to it that he died here. It was his choice. For days he messed around with us, repeatedly changing his story. One minute he said he did not sell the birds in a cage, the next he admitted there was a cage, and so on until finally we managed to break him."

Hearing the phrase "break him" come from this man's lips left me in no doubt that the suspect had indeed been taken to his very limits. I felt no pity for him. I asked the officer if I could see a copy of the Cage Man's confession. I remember almost vomiting as I read it. This matter happened almost forty years ago, but still the contents of the confession are fresh in my mind. It read as follows:

> When I was young I was raped by an old man, and following this I began to have a sexual tendency toward young children, as I wanted them to suffer the same ordeal I had.
>
> On the day of the incident the two young boys in question approached me to look at the birds I was selling. As I looked at them I suddenly developed an uncontrollable sexual urge. I informed them that I had some very rare birds for them to see, and they decided to follow me.
>
> When we arrived in a field and were out of sight, I tied them up before raping both of them. I was not intending to kill them, but the older boy kept crying and shouting. He said that he would tell his father no matter what I threatened. At that moment I lost control and beat him over the head with a rock. When the younger child also started screaming, I had no option but to beat him with the rock as well. Before I knew it I was covered in blood, and they were both dead.

In my worst nightmares I never expected the death of the children to be so horrific. I started to cry. The suffering those brothers must have endured was too much to take in. How could a human being inflict that much pain on two defenseless children?

Trying to gather myself I asked the officer, who sat in silence, also feeling the gravity of the offense, "Do you really believe that this confession is true?"

Slowly he nodded his head. "I do," he solemnly replied.

Before we could go to the scene of the crime, we needed to convene at the judge's chambers. When the Cage Man was brought in, he looked like a different man from the sneering, arrogant monster I had seen just days before. Two officers, who stood either side of him, virtually had to hold him under his armpits to keep him upright, as days of having his feet beaten by cables had left him unable to stand. All of his bravado had withered away. He was a shell of a man.

Confronting him, the investigating judge demanded, "You will now take us to the place where you committed this crime, and you will show us where you buried the bodies. Is this understood?"

With no strength to resist, the Cage Man slowly nodded his head and grunted.

As we drove to the location of the crime, the father and I were silent. We both knew that what awaited us was not going to be pleasant, and we needed this time to try to steady ourselves for what was no doubt going to be a horrendous experience.

On our arrival at a field on the outskirts of the village, the Cage Man was dragged out of the car as the officer bellowed, "Where are the bodies?"

Terrified and eager to avoid any further punishment, the Cage Man pointed to the far corner of the dried out grass. Two officers raced to the spot and stuck their shovels into the ground. As they did so the Cage Man began to wail, "I'm sorry. I'm sorry. Allah, forgive me. I'm sorry."

After a few moments of shoveling, one of the officers recoiled in horror. He had found what he was looking for. There, just a few inches under the surface, lay the battered, decomposed head of one of the boys. I had braced myself for this moment, but the reality of it was too much for me. Turning away I fell to my knees and retched, while the father had to be restrained from running toward the grave. Screaming and shouting, he lost all control of himself.

"*No. No. No*," he cried. Curling up into a ball, he wailed at the sky and beat the ground with his fists. My heart was with him. What can anyone say at such a terrible moment? I was speechless.

When the two battered bodies had been uncovered, the clearly moved judge said to the Cage Man in a faltering voice, "Where is the rock you used to kill them?"

Limply raising his arm the Cage Man pointed to a large rock near where he had buried his victims. It was still covered in the boys' blood.

We now had all the evidence we needed. The investigation was at an end. But before the court case could get underway, we needed to give the boys a proper burial. Throughout my life I have been to many funerals, for both the young and the old, and while all are incredibly sad, never have I seen such an outpouring of emotion as I did in this case. What could you say to the bereaved? Their two youngest boys had been subjected to a most awful death. I don't mind admitting that I couldn't contain my emotions at the funeral. When I saw those two little coffins and knew that the boys' battered remains lay inside, I swore to myself that there would only be one kind of justice in this case—the death penalty.

Almost three months to the day of the suspect's confession, the trial began. The boys' family filled the courtroom, and there was definitely a very intimidating feeling in the air. Everyone who was present was determined to ensure that the Cage Man would not be in for an easy ride. When he was finally brought into court under heavy police guard, he was subjected to taunts and insults. Yet it all seemed to wash over him. He looked like a zombie.

To most it appeared that this was going to be an open-and-shut case. After all, there had been a confession, which had led to the discovery of the bodies as well as the murder weapon, but I knew that it would not be as easy as it seemed. The defense lawyer was a very capable advocate who would not want to lose to me under any circumstances. We had both had a few run-ins with each other in the past, and it's safe to say that there was no love lost between us. I knew that he would use every trick in the book to try to get one over on me, even if the end result meant setting a clearly deranged lunatic free.

Straight from the opening moments of the trial he went for the jugular. "Your Honor," he said, looking across at me, "the lawyer for the prosecution should be suspended from attending this case since he participated in obtaining the confession from my client through the use of torture."

I suspected that the defense would try to use the torture element in his client's favor, but even I was taken aback when he tried to get me thrown off the case because of it. The president of the court was also clearly caught off guard.

"Is this true?" he asked me.

Knowing that I had to counter this accusation, I stood up and replied, "I have not personally participated in any physical act that forced the confession from the defendant, and therefore such allegations are groundless and slanderous. Indeed, I was not even present on the day that the defendant confessed to these crimes. I was in court, as the record will no doubt reflect."

Jumping from his seat, the defendant's lawyer suddenly interjected, "He's lying!" It was now abundantly clear; this was going to be a dirty fight to the end. The defense was going to sling as much mud as possible in the hope that some of it would stick.

Responding to this slanderous remark, I again addressed the court. "Your Honor, please instruct the defendant's lawyer to behave properly in court. If I have violated any of my professional duties as a lawyer, I can be referred to the disciplinary committee at the Bar, who are indeed authorized to investigate any such charges, but please do not allow such groundless claims to stop or hold up the procedures in a case where the defendant is accused of such an outrageous crime."

The judge stared at me for a moment as he processed all of this information. Then he turned to the defendant's lawyer. "If you have any claims of misbehavior within the legal profession, then this is not the forum for them. As Mr. Aris has said, you should instead address your concerns to the Bar of Lawyers. Under these circumstances, we shall proceed with the case. How does your client plead?"

At this the defendant's lawyer dropped another bombshell. "Not guilty."

Everyone was stunned. Suddenly, the room erupted in a chorus of insults, as the boys' family could not believe what they were hearing.

"Your Honor," the lawyer continued, ignoring the abuse, "my client is pleading insanity as his defense. Therefore, I ask that he be referred to a psychiatric hospital for an examination and that until a report on his condition is provided, all legal procedures be suspended."

This was a tactic I had been expecting. It was the only card the lawyer had to play. Yet it was clear from the discontent in the gallery that they were not happy with any sort of delay.

The president's grim face told the story before he even uttered a word. "In the light of such a defense the court has no option but to suspend procedures while the defendant is referred to hospital for psychiatric examination."

Smiling at the president, the defendant's lawyer knew that this was a small victory. I had to admit, his defense had been textbook. On his way out of the courtroom he looked at me with contempt. This was more than just a court case to him; this was very personal. The man saw beating me as a prize. He had tried, and failed, before, but now he was determined finally to get the better of me in the biggest case of all.

As I collected my files, as well as my thoughts, the boys' father dashed toward me.

"What is happening?" he begged, with a look of sheer desperation. "He's going to get away with the blood of my two sons on his hands, isn't he? How can they let this happen?"

I tried my best to reassure him and told him that this was just a legal technicality, but in the back of my mind I knew that if the doctor's report did rule that the defendant was insane, he would almost certainly avoid the death penalty as well as justice.

That evening the father came to visit me in my office. Although he wasn't crying, he could not stop his hands from shaking. Trying to comfort him, I held his hands in mine, but then his lip started to quiver. I really questioned just how much longer this man could endure this whole ordeal.

"Is he getting away with it?" he desperately muttered. "If he does, I will either kill him or kill myself."

Listening to his voice and observing his whole demeanor, I did not doubt that if the defendant did avoid the death penalty, then this threat would come true.

"Please trust in me and let justice take its course," I begged, but I knew that no matter what I said, if justice failed him, he would take matters into his own hands.

"Mr. Aris, I know this request is unusual," the father said to me with pleading eyes, "but until this case is over, may I spend my days in your office? I promise I will not disturb you or any of your lawyers."

"Why would you want to do that?" I asked.

"When I sit at home, and it gets dark in the evening, everything overwhelms me, and I fear what I will do. When I sit in your office, I feel some kind of peace. Please say it is OK. I cannot stand to spend much time at home while this case continues. I fear I will go crazy."

Seeing this poor man's state, I would have given him anything that he had asked of me.

Knowing just what an effect this case was already having on the father, and what would happen if the defendant was ruled to be insane, I arranged to meet a friend of mine who was a psychiatrist. Over a pot of tea I poured out the facts of the case to him, including what the combat police officer had told me the Cage Man had said when he was being tortured. As I spoke, my friend smiled.

"Do not worry, Sabah," he reassured me. "If the defendant was able to lie and repeatedly cover his tracks by making up stories while under such intense pressure, then that is not the mind of an insane person but of a criminal. Any doctor will be able to see that."

Although I felt somewhat reassured by this valued medical opinion, a meeting with my legal team left me in a quandary. Fawsi, one of my best lawyers and friends, was particularly concerned. "If you inform the doctors dealing with this case," he said, "that the defendant was able to lie under torture, then this could lead to the whole case, being thrown out because you will have to inform the court that he was tortured for the evidence." It was a valid point that needed serious consideration.

Sitting alone in my office, I weighed the options: confess to the torture, which would shed light on the defendant's true mental condition but which could also lead to all the evidence being ruled inadmissible; or keep quiet and run the risk that the defendant may be judged to be insane, which would see him escape the death penalty. It was a catch-22.

That night I barely slept. There was too much to think about. But after tossing and turning, I came to a decision. Upon waking I set off to the psychiatric hospital so that I could speak to the doctor in charge of ascertaining the Cage Man's mental state. By chance I had actually met the doctor a few years before at a mutual friend's party, which meant that on my arrival he greeted me warmly.

After we discussed our mutual friend, I cut to the chase.

"Doctor," I began, "I'm here today in a professional capacity to discuss a man you are currently evaluating. He has been charged with murdering two small boys." Straight away the doctor knew whom I was referring to. Without saying too much, he listened as I informed him of all of the gruesome facts of the case, including the torture aspect. I was taking a huge risk, but I felt that the doctor needed to know that the Cage Man had repeatedly tried to cover his tracks. I didn't want him to be given any chance of fooling anyone. If he was truly found to be insane, then I would have no argument, but I wanted to ensure that those who were conducting the tests had all of the available information at their disposal.

After I had outlined the facts, the doctor put me at ease.

"Do not worry," he said. "I will examine the man myself, and I will subject him to every possible test in order to get to the bottom of his mental capacity. Trust me. It will be virtually impossible for him to deceive me."

Upon leaving, I shook the doctor's hand, looked him in the eye, and said, "The blood of two innocent boys is now in your hands." He nodded his head. He understood what was at stake.

Following this meeting there was an agonizing four-week wait as the doctor subjected the defendant to every imaginable test. As time went by and I considered the Cage Man's actions, I even began to wonder if he may in fact be insane. Why else would a person commit such a horrific crime? And if he was found insane, how would I be able to break such news to the father, who day after day came to my office and sat silently in reception? I couldn't bear thinking about it.

Finally, the day came when I received the medical report. Opening the envelope tentatively, I knew this was a big moment. If the Cage Man was ruled fit for trial, I was sure we would win; if, however, he was said to be insane, then our case was virtually over. Taking a deep breath, I read the report aloud: "After exhaustive tests we can find no mental deficiency of any kind, and therefore we feel that the defendant is able to realize any legal charge made against him." A wave of relief came over me. The finishing line was now in sight.

That evening, when the father came to visit me, I gave him the good news. For the first time since we had met he smiled, albeit briefly.

Looking up to the heavens he cried again and again, "Praise Allah. Praise Allah." It was immediately apparent that a load had been lifted from his mind. I hoped that I could now finish the job with little delay.

When the trial resumed two weeks later, I knew that although we had removed one major obstacle, there still remained the issue of torture. This was the only thing that the defense now had in their arsenal. However, in the time spent since the suspension of the trial my team and I had methodically gone through every single scenario that could occur so I felt prepared for anything that would be thrown my way.

As expected, before I had a chance to sit down, the defense played their trump card. "Your Honor," my opponent said while eyeing me with disdain, "the defense has reason to believe that the alleged confession in this case was brought about as a result of torture. Therefore, we ask that all such evidence procured through this act be judged inadmissible, in accordance with Iraqi law."

The law on such matters was actually a complicated one. While the use of torture itself was strictly prohibited, the law made it clear that if the torture resulted in a confession, that was then supported by other circumstantial evidence, such evidence would be admissible. In this case the confession had of course led to the discovery of the two bodies and the murder weapon.

However, as the use of torture was strictly prohibited, anyone found to have administered such an act was still subject to the full force of the law. In reality most of the people who did administer torture, such as members of the combat police, rarely faced any legal consequences in any event.

Having thoroughly researched the law on torture, I fought back aggressively. In the last hearing the defense had caught me off guard. Now I was more than prepared for them. Addressing the president of the court, I took a gamble. I admitted that torture may have been used, but brought to his attention all of the articles and precedents that supported any such evidence unveiled as a result still being admissible.

"Your Honor," I urged, "please let us finally proceed with this matter. If the defendant and his lawyers want to start criminal cases against the investigating police, then they are free to do so in separate proceedings, but this case should go forward."

I had called the defense's bluff. They had never expected me to admit that torture may have been present in this case. All of the cards were now laid on the table. The judge's decision would prove crucial to how the case would progress. If the evidence was allowed to stand, then the defense had very little to go on. If it was thrown out, then the prosecution's case would be all but destroyed.

Finally, after what had seemed a lifetime, the judge said, "We will proceed with this case, and any complaints you have concerning the investigation can be raised in a separate case at a different court."

A sigh of relief was heard throughout the room. No one had been left in any doubt as to just how crucial this was for the prosecution. But I should have known better than to expect an easy ride, as the Cage Man now played his last throw of the dice. On the day of his admission, when he had cried while revealing where he had buried the bodies, he had been a broken man; now he reverted back to the cocky, swaggering, sneering monster I had first met in the police station.

When the president read the charges and asked how the Cage Man pleaded, he remarked, "I cannot recall what took place." Such a statement saw the gallery erupt in fury. "Murderer" and "scum" were two of the more polite insults that were hurled his way.

Exasperated by the Cage Man's behavior, the president picked up a copy of his signed confession and said, "This is your confession, and there are also many witnesses who were present when you took the police to the area where you buried the bodies. What do you have to say?"

Again the Cage Man played dumb. "I do not remember," he rasped. "I am innocent. This is all a conspiracy against me." Then, as if to prove that he was actually insane, he started to scream and bang his head against the wall. Such behavior earned him short shrift from the judge, who ordered security to subdue him.

In spite of the Cage Man's ridiculous performance, the judge invited the prosecution to make its case. Setting out the facts of the matter, the public prosecutor did an excellent job in highlighting all of the grisly elements that were present. He finished by saying that this was the most violent, brutal, and outrageous case that he had seen in his career.

When it was my turn to speak, I really wanted the judge to see what a needless, violent act had been perpetrated against two innocent boys. Approaching the table where evidence was kept, I picked up the large blood-splattered rock.

Holding the rock before the court I said, "This is the weapon that the accused used to repeatedly beat two innocent boys over their heads until their skulls were cracked wide open. In the Qur'an it is written 'An eye for an eye.' This man is a Muslim; he knows the Muslim traditions. As such he must pay with his life for taking the lives of two young boys in the most horrific crime imaginable."

Putting down the rock I then held up a graphic picture of the decomposed and beaten bodies of the boys. I didn't need to speak. The images said more than a thousand words could have. Many in the gallery were so distressed that they actually ran out of court crying, while the boys' mother fainted and had to be revived.

Handing the pictures over to the president of the court and his two assisting judges, I could see that they were all deeply affected. Tears welled in the president's eyes as he struggled to comprehend just what evil these two boys had encountered.

As the shock at the sight of the pictures continued to reverberate around the court, I then brought the judges' attention to the father, who sat in the front row looking gaunt, crushed, and beyond repair. When I informed them about the horrific ordeal the father had had to endure, with the effects still clearly visible on his creased face, the judges were moved when he started to shake and pray to Allah, muttering between his sobs, "May Allah help me. Please Allah help me." It was a very powerful and sincere moment. By the time I finished, I too had tears in my eyes.

When the defense started speak, I was surprised at their jaded response. I knew that their task was a hard one, yet I had expected more than them just repeatedly raising insanity and torture as a defense, which earned them a rebuke from the president, as these matters had already been dealt with. Having brought nothing new to the table, the defense feebly begged the court to spare their client's life. It was a pathetic effort. After seeing them start the case with such bravado and arrogance, I enjoyed watching them struggle now.

Finally the defense rested and there was nothing more that could be done. The judges retired to deliberate all of the evidence put before them, and I was left to wait. Surely nothing could now prevent justice from being served. However, I had been in the game too long to expect the expected. Sure enough, as I waited, a police officer approached me.

"The defendant has asked to speak with you," he said.

I was taken aback. What could he want? The public prosecutor urged me to ignore him, as no good could come of it, but I was intrigued.

Following the police officer down to the detention area, I saw the Cage Man's wretched figure in his cell. As I approached, he leapt up and aggressively walked toward the bars that separated us.

"You will not get away with this," he spat in my direction. "I've ensured that I will not be sentenced to death. I'm going to serve a prison sentence, and then I will get out. When I'm out, I will kill you and all of your family. You will see. You will see."

The venom in his voice and the madness behind his manic glare unsettled me, but I did not want to give him the pleasure of knowing this. As such, I smiled in his direction, unmoved.

The police officer who was stood behind me said, "Don't worry, Mr. Aris, I heard every word of that and will inform the judge of what he has said."

Pushing his face between the bars, the Cage Man leered at me. "Even if I am executed," he said, "I have arranged for it that you are to be killed. You cannot escape me. I will have your blood."

Tiring of his attempt to intimidate me, I marched toward the Cage Man and shouted, "You do not scare me. You're going to hang for your crimes and will spend eternity in hell!"

"I'll kill you," he screamed. "I'll kill you and all of your family!"

I had heard enough. Marching out of the room, I heard the frenzied cries and threats of the demented Cage Man echo behind me.

When I returned to my colleagues and the boys' father, they were keen to know what the Cage Man had said to me.

"Nothing," I unconvincingly replied. "He just rambled." While I tried my best to play down the incident, I did begin to wonder if somehow the defendant had managed to buy himself justice. I could not see how, as he was poor and did not appear to have any connections, but stranger things have happened.

Another thing on my mind was his threats against me. It was clear that he was a very dangerous man, but did he really know people who would have me killed if he was executed? In the public gallery I had not noticed any of his family or friends present. I therefore doubted it. But still, it was possible.

Half an hour passed with barely a word spoken. We were all going over the case in our heads and playing out every possible scenario.

When we were eventually called into court, I was very nervous. In my eyes this was one of the most open-and-shut cases that I had ever worked on, but I had an uneasy feeling in my stomach. Standing next to me was the boy's father who clung onto my arm for support. If the Cage Man did not get the death penalty, then I was not sure he would be able to withstand the disappointment.

Taking his seat, the president of the court cleared his throat before reading his much-anticipated verdict to a silent gallery. The father grabbed my arm tightly while I closed my eyes and prayed. It was out of my hands now.

The judge's summarization of the case seemed to take an age, but then came the moment we had all been waiting for: "The court finds the defendant guilty as charged, and as such the defendant is sentenced to hang until he is dead."

I clenched my fist. It was done. Justice had been delivered.

Pandemonium broke out as the gallery roared its approval. Looking up to the heavens I thanked God as the father slumped to his chair in disbelief. Kneeling down to embrace him, he held my head in his arms and whispered in a low, trembling voice, "Thank you. Thank you."

Leaving the court after the good wishes and handshakes of the boys' family, I was relieved that justice looked to have been served, but there was still one more hurdle we needed to overcome: the Court of Cassation. In Iraq, whenever a court sentenced someone to death the case was immediately passed on to the Court of Cassation for a second opinion. Although it was rare for the court to overturn the original sentence, it did have the power to substitute the death penalty for twenty-five years in jail.

I had told the boys' father many times that even if the Cage Man did get the death penalty, the Court of Cassation could overturn it. Despite this he was still very upset.

"I told you," he cried. "He's going to get away with it. I know he will."

"Look," I said, trying my best to sound authoritative, "this is just a legal formality. The judges know the facts. Everything will be fine."

Not wanting to take any chances, however, I personally hand-delivered twenty-seven copies of my memorandum of the case to the court. While there would already be one copy of the memorandum for the twenty-seven judges to share, I felt that it was vital that they should all have their own personal copies so that they could fully digest everything. Every one of their verdicts would be crucial. If it was close, then the death penalty would be overturned, which was an unthinkable prospect.

Thankfully, the facts of the case—and my best endeavors—had made it impossible for the judges to quibble with the sentence.

"The decision stands," said the president, confirming the initial verdict. "The defendant will hang for his crimes."

At last I breathed a sigh of relief. Yet the boys' father did not celebrate or show any emotion. He merely appeared to be lost in his own world.

"Rejoice, my friend," I said. "The blood of your two sons has been avenged."

Staggering toward a seat, the father slumped forward and looked bewildered. Then, after I had left him alone with his thoughts for a moment, he suddenly stood up and said, "Thank you for all of your work, but there is one more thing I must ask of you."

"What is that?" I replied, not knowing what he could want now.

"I want to attend the hanging."

I knew this was out of the question. "I'm afraid that there is no way this can be done. Iraqi law does not permit the family of the victims to be present when the defendant is executed."

After thinking about this for a moment, the father answered, "OK. I understand. But will you attend on my behalf?"

I did not want to attend this ugly procedure, but looking into the desperate eyes of this man and hearing his plea, I felt I had no option but to reply, "If that is what you want, then I will go."

Following the father's request, I spoke to the manager of the central Baghdad prison where the Cage Man would be executed. I explained that I recognized this was an unusual situation, but the victim's father had asked that I attend the hanging. The manager thankfully had no problem with this. He informed me that the hanging would take place in a few days' time and that I needed to be at the prison before 5:00 a.m.

Thanking him for this information, I started to feel my stomach knot. It was really not something I was looking forward to. I had witnessed many atrocities during my time in Baghdad but never out of choice.

As I relayed this news to the father, his face twitched nervously. The case had really taken its toll, not just on his physical appearance—he had lost an enormous amount of weight and had not shaved since the day his sons went missing—but also on his mental state. Even after the execution I really did fear that the father would not be able to go on with his life.

So far I had done everything the father had asked of me, so when he asked if he could come with me and wait outside the prison, I saw no reason to refuse him. I told him that I would have to pick him up at around 3.30 a.m., to which he replied, "I will not sleep until that man is dead."

The night before the execution I had to attend a dinner party. I was not really in the mood to go, but it had been in my diary for many months. To cancel at this late stage would have appeared very rude, despite the fact that I had an excellent excuse to do so. Usually, I was the life and soul at such events, but on this night I was preoccupied with the execution and barely said a word.

When I finally made my excuses to leave, the host said to me, "Sabah, where are you going? You never leave a party early."

To the laughter of some of my friends I replied, "I have to attend an execution."

Everyone thought I was joking, for I was renowned for making quips like this. One of my friends even put his arm around my shoulders, winked at me, and said with a grin on his face, "I know you, Sabah. I think you are leaving early to see a lady friend." If only.

Shortly afterward I picked up the father, and we made our way to the prison, which was about a twenty-five minute journey. As we drove through the early morning traffic in the darkness, we said very little. Both of us were completely lost in our thoughts. When we arrived at the prison gates, the father grabbed my hand and looked me in the eyes. No words needed to be said. This was the time for justice to finally be served.

Leaving the father behind I got out of the car and walked up to the prison entrance, where I was swiftly let in. Once inside the old building, I was introduced to a doctor, a judge, and a member of the Muslim clergy, all of whom would also be present at the hanging. Shortly afterward we assembled in the execution room to wait for the Cage Man's entrance. I have to admit, I was very nervous, not only at the prospect of seeing an execution but also because the Cage Man was so unpredictable. Anything could happen when a madman like that was involved.

The steel door suddenly swung open. Expecting to see the arrogant and defiant monster I had seen in court, I was shocked when I set my eyes on the Cage Man. His arrogance and sneer were gone. Now he resembled a frightened child as he shook and begged for mercy.

"Please save me," he wept. "Please, Allah, save me. I'm sorry. I'm sorry."

Despite his horrific crime, even I felt some sympathy for him. I could not comprehend just what a human being must be feeling in the final moments of such a wasted and ruined life.

Hollering and screaming, he was hauled by force toward the noose, but then he suddenly cried, "*Stop!* I want to talk to the lawyer. I must speak to the lawyer."

My stomach sank. What on earth could he want with me now?

The guards were in no mood for histrionics, and despite his pleas they continued to drag him against his will. But for some reason, I wanted to hear what this man had to say.

"Hold it one second," I cried. "Let us grant this condemned man his last request."

Everyone in the room was caught off guard. All eyes turned toward the judge, who was tasked with making the decision.

"Very well, Mr. Aris," he said, "but make it quick."

Taking a few steps forward I looked at the pitiful figure of the Cage Man. When I had first seen him in the police station many months before, I was frightened by the rage and fury behind his eyes. Now, when he looked at me, all I saw was fear, sadness, and regret.

"I am sorry," he said, looking mournfully at me. "I have no grudge against you." I smiled and offered a comforting nod, as he continued. "Do you remember when we were in court, and I told you that I would have you killed if I was executed?"

"Yes, I remember," I replied.

"It is not true," he said, with a hint of shame in his voice. "My family has abandoned me, and I don't have a friend in the world. No one would dream of harming you at my request." Suddenly he began to sob, revealing his blackened gums and scar-lined cheeks. "May God give you the life he denied me," he stuttered in between his tears.

It was clear to me that this was a very damaged human being, one who had been raped and abused as a child. He had never received anything but hardship from life. This didn't excuse his crime, and he deserved his punishment, but it suddenly dawned on me that men are not born of pure evil; circumstances beyond their control often dictate who they become.

"Will Allah forgive me?" the Cage Man asked with pleading eyes. If he had asked me that question any other time in my life, I would have struggled to answer. But at that moment I realized that life had dealt him a very bad hand. Perhaps God would be merciful, and redemption would wait for him on the other side.

"Are you sorry for what you have done?" I asked.

"Yes. I am truly sorry," he spluttered.

"If you are, then I am sure Allah will be forgiving," I said.

At that the guards turned the Cage Man away from me and led him up the steps toward the gallows. As the executioner placed a black bag over his head and a noose around his neck the Cage Man shook violently. I hadn't wished to give such a monster any comfort, but watching him shake and then soil his pants as he stood waiting to meet his fate, I was glad I had.

Almost without warning the floor opened up beneath him and he disappeared below, with the sound of his neck snapping reverberating around the building. Within moments the doctor confirmed the news that we had long been waiting for: "He is dead."

Distressed by the scene I had just witnessed, I made my way back to my car to inform the father that his wish had been granted.

Before I got within twenty yards of him, he ran toward me shouting, "Is he dead? Is he dead?"

"Yes, he is dead," I confirmed.

The father put his hand on my shoulder. "I want to see him," he said. "I want to see the body. I beg this of you. Take me to the body."

By this stage I was very tired and emotional and just wanted this nightmare to end once and for all. However, I sensed that this could finally give him some closure. "Very well," I replied. "His body is being taken to the morgue, but we won't be able to see him for a couple of hours. I'll speak to them and see if we can go later today."

When we returned to my office, I called the officials at the morgue, and thankfully they agreed to my request. At midday they subsequently called to let me know that the body had arrived and that we could see it.

Once again, during our journey, the father and I said very little. I did not know why he was so desperate to see the defendant's body, but I hoped that it could bring him some sort of peace to know that the justice he had craved had actually been delivered.

When we arrived at the morgue, we were told to wait in a room while the body was brought out for us. Fifteen minutes went by very slowly, and I noticed that the father could once again not stop his hands from shaking. What is he thinking? I wondered. But before I could ask, a junior doctor entered and said that they were ready for us.

Following the doctor down a long corridor, we entered a small white room where the Cage Man's body lay on a marble slab. I turned away, repulsed by the sight of his stretched neck and purple face. But the timid, quiet father suddenly went crazy and dived toward the body. Before the doctor or I could react, he had plunged his teeth into the neck. Staring, frozen in horror, we watched as blood spurted out onto the father's white beard as he ravaged the flesh, seemingly intent on devouring as much of the man as possible.

Quickly regaining our senses, the doctor and I rushed toward the father. We desperately tried to drag him away, but he was like a wild dog, his teeth firmly clamped onto the Cage Man's neck. Pulling him with all of our might, we finally managed to dislodge him, but as we did so a large chunk of flesh was ripped from the body.

Panting and wheezing, the father refused to let go of the flesh. I desperately tried to get him to open his mouth by squeezing his face. "What are you doing?" I cried. "Let it go. Let it go." But it was too late. He had swallowed the flesh whole.

Staggering away from the father in shock, I turned my attention to the Cage Man's body. Blood was now pumping out of the gaping hole in his elongated neck. The very sight of it made me so nauseated that I had to hurriedly throw a sheet over the body before I was sick.

Meanwhile, sprawled across the floor, the father had undergone a dramatic change. Seconds before he had been a maniac. Now he shook while muttering quietly under his breath. Blood covered his once-white beard, and he panted heavily as he tried to calm himself. It was a fearful sight. I wondered if he had finally cracked. He had held it together for so long that the moment had come where it had all become too much.

For a few minutes no one spoke. What we had just witnessed had deeply affected us all. Ushering the now timid father out of the room, the doctor tried to get him to drink some water, or at least wash his beard, but he refused. Leaving the morgue, covered in blood, the father still appeared to be in some sort of trance. By now he had stopped shaking, but he would not say a word. Even when I pulled up the car at his home, he got out without acknowledging my presence in any way. I was not sure if he, or even I, would ever be the same again.

I could not bear the thought of spending that night alone in my mansion. I knew that I would not be able to sleep as the horror of the day's events replayed in my head. Once I had dropped the father off I decided to go to my mother's house. As always, she greeted me warmly and insisted that I eat, but she could tell that I was very troubled.

"Tell me what is on your mind, habibi," she said.

But I couldn't. I just sat there with tears streaming down my face. The emotion of the day had completely overwhelmed me.

For days I heard no word from the father, and while I was concerned, I felt that this case may finally be at an end. However, just as I began to think I would never see him again, he suddenly appeared at my office, where his appearance astonished me. Freshly shaven, with neatly combed hair, a bit of weight on his face, and dressed in elegant clothes he looked at least twenty years younger. I was pleased to see him looking so well.

"You may not have been able to bring back my sons," he said, while we sat having tea, "but you did give me justice. You were able to put out the fire that had been burning in my heart day and night. For the first time since my sons' deaths, I have been able to sleep."

I told him that I had just done my job, nothing more, but he interrupted.

"You have done more than your job! Without your help, that man would still be free to rape and murder children."

That thought stopped me in my tracks. Since the Cage Man's tearful apology, his hanging, and then the desecration of his body, I had wondered if the end result was indeed justice. Was this the justice that my father had dreamt that I would one day strive for? A justice that had only come about because of a confession gained through torture? A justice that saw a man sentenced to death? I hadn't been entirely sure.

Torture is barbaric. I do not deny that. But when the might of the law and the intelligence of police, lawyers, and judges cannot provide justice, then I feel that torture must be used as a last resort. I admit that in some cases in Iraq torture was used too liberally, and no doubt many innocent people have been on the receiving end of it. But without it, in this case, the Cage Man would have been free to continue to rape and murder children.

I have never advocated that torture be used as a punishment for a crime, but I feel that if it can unearth vital evidence to prevent future violent crimes, then it is something that should be considered. Some say that torture disregards the rights of the recipient, but what about the rights of those they may harm in the future? For too long now evil men have been able to get away with their crimes while society continues to pay the price. Those who espouse uncivilized standards should not expect to receive a civilized response.

If certain torture methods are allowed in exceptional circumstances under stringent guidelines, then in a world where madmen are still intent on terrorizing the innocent majority, the end justifies the means. In a world blighted by overzealous human rights laws and propaganda, I realize that this is not a popular thing to say. But ask yourself this question: If you knew a man had raped and murdered your two children, and he looked set to walk away, what would you do? Would you shrug your shoulders, say that there is no concrete evidence, and forget about it? I don't think so.

And do such people who flagrantly break society's rules in the most horrific way imaginable deserve to live? As far as I'm concerned, no. If people willingly choose to take someone's life, then they should pay the ultimate price for such an act. Why should they be shown mercy when they could not show it to their victims?

No matter what anyone says, capital punishment also acts as a tremendous deterrent. Of course, murders and crimes still occur in countries that apply it. But when such a strong punishment is in place, it must make some criminals think twice before committing unlawful acts. And if it doesn't, then people who take the lives of others knowing the punishment that awaits them are such a danger to society that they should be permanently removed from it. Society has no place for such animals.

For too long now we have fallen into the trap of fighting for the rights of the accused. It is time we went back to common sense and fought for the rights of the victims. Of course a balance must be struck, but in my eyes victims have had no choice in their fate, whereas the perpetrators of the crime do. If they willingly choose to take such an evil path, then they should face the consequences.

And so I ask: was justice served in the case of the Cage Man? I believe that it was, if not for the two little boys then certainly for the children who were spared suffering a similar fate at the hands of a criminal maniac. Am I proud of the part I played in this case? Yes. I have no regrets. True justice was served, unlike in my next case.

9.

A MATTER OF HONOR

"It is not what a lawyer tells me I may do; but what humanity, reason and justice tell me I ought to do."

—Edmund Burke

HOW CAN I CONTINUE TO ACT for my client when he will not allow me to tell the court the truth?

This was the dilemma I faced as I sat in a police cell cradling a troubled young man in my arms. Sobbing and shaking, he begged for my help. But could I really lie to the court? No doubt the lie would save my client's life, but at the same time those who committed the crime would walk free. Why not just tell the truth?

Grabbing my shoulders, the young man said through gritted teeth, "I beg you. Do not tell anyone of this conversation. If I am to be executed, so be it, but please do not tell anyone what I have just told you."

For once I didn't know what to say.

The case had landed at my door just a few days before. After I had finished in court one afternoon, I had returned to my office to find three men waiting for me in the reception area. After they informed me that they wished to discuss an important case, I invited them into my office.

The old man in the group, who was dressed in Arab robes, began by saying to me, "We were informed by a very powerful friend that you are renowned for dealing with honor crimes. This is why we have come to see you today. Regretfully, my grandson has killed his sister in such a situation, and he is due to appear in court in two weeks. We would like you to defend him."

It was true. I had defended many honor crimes. Muslims did not think twice about asking me to defend them, despite my being a Christian. I knew the traditions and law on the subject like the back of my hand and had built quite a reputation for myself in this area.

However, I told the old man that before I could agree to represent his grandson, I would first need to see the case file. Suddenly, one of the other men arrogantly tossed some papers toward me. "Everything is in there," he said bluntly.

For a moment I stared angrily at him before picking up the bundle.

Flicking through the papers I gathered that the old man's granddaughter had engaged in an extramarital affair that had scandalized their tribe. As a result of this behavior, the woman's brother was so enraged that he stabbed and slashed at her body over forty times. The attached autopsy report contained a graphic picture of the wounds that suggested that some of them had been inflicted long after the woman had died, almost as if to mutilate her body as much as possible. I felt sick.

Closing the file, I shook my head in disgust. Although I dealt with honor crimes on a regular basis, I did not wish to defend a person where such brutality was present. Another factor in my thinking was that while the old man seemed very pleasant, the other members of his family who sat alongside him looked very aggressive. I had no desire to work on a case where they would be involved.

"I am sorry, but I don't think I can help you with this case," I told the old man.

The man who had thrown the file at me suddenly snatched it out of my hands and stormed toward the door.

"Sit down," the old man barked, which made him reluctantly turn back and sit down. It was clear who was in charge.

Turning his attention back to me, the old man said, "What shall I tell the person who advised me to come to you for help? Shall I tell him that you refused the case?"

Nodding my head I replied that unfortunately I was simply too busy to take it on at this time.

"If I tell my friend that, he will say I am lying," the old man smiled. "Please, let me tell you a story that I hope will change your mind."

For some reason I liked the old man. He was warm and sincere, and he was doing everything possible to help his grandson. "Very well," I replied, not wanting to appear rude. "Please continue."

The old man then proceeded to tell me the famous Arabic story of Sheik Hamed. Renowned for his generosity, the Sheik's castle was open to visitors day and night. Everyone was welcome, and on arrival he would treat all of his guests like a king. Subsequently he was regarded in the Arab world as the most gracious of hosts who never turned anyone away.

One day, however, the Sheik was feeling tired, so for the first time he decided to close his doors. But that very night, a man arrived at the castle gates expecting to be received warmly, as all of his friends and family had once been. Despite knocking on all of the doors and shouting for over an hour, no one answered. Faced with no other choice, the man had to spend the night sleeping on the ground outside.

The next morning the sheik asked his guards about the noise he had heard in the night. Upon being told that a man had been refused entry, the sheik set off on his horse to find him.

After hours of searching he eventually came across a man who fit the guards' description. Saddling up alongside him, the Sheik struck up a conversation, but to his surprise the man did not recognize him. When the Sheik asked where the man had spent the previous night the man answered, "At Sheik Hamed's palace."

The Sheik smiled and continued with his questioning, keeping up the charade. "How did he treat you?"

"In the best possible manner," the man proudly replied. "He took me to a big tent where he brought me food, drink, and blankets."

At this Sheik Hamed laughed. "I am afraid, sir, that your story is simply not true. I am Sheik Hamed, and my doors were unfortunately shut last night."

The man appeared to be taken aback. Apologizing profusely, he then told the Sheik why he had created such a tale: "If I told anyone that

Sheik Hamed had turned me away, they would simply not believe me. Your reputation for generosity is so well known that people would ask questions about me or assume that I am lying."

Upon hearing this the Sheik invited the man to be his guest at his castle, where he treated him to every comfort and delight he had at his disposal. By doing so he kept his reputation intact as the most kind and generous Sheik.

After the old man finished his story, I felt I knew what he was saying. His friend had spoken so highly of me that it would be very embarrassing for the old man to say that I had turned him away. I was flattered that someone had thought so much of me, and although I was still very reluctant to take the case, I knew that I could cause him great embarrassment if I did not do so.

"I'm still not sure if I will be able to act," I said, with the pictures of the victim still very much in my mind. "But I will meet your grandson and see if there is anything I can do."

The old man stood up and shook my hand. "Thank you. My friend said I could rely on you."

When I arrived at the police station later that day, I was expecting to meet a very dangerous individual with the same rude manner as some of his relatives. But when he was brought into an interview room, I was shocked. Rather than the aggressive, remorseless man I had expected, my prospective client was a slight young man who was polite and very calm.

Sitting down he thanked me for agreeing to take his case, and while we talked he told me that he had an interest in poetry. Poetry was also a passion of mine, and we soon found that we both enjoyed the poems of Mohammed al-Jawahri, whose writing always gave a very romanticized view of Iraq. When I told him that I had actually successfully represented al-Jawahri in a defamation case, his face lit up. At that moment I asked myself, how can such a pleasant young man be responsible for such a brutal crime?

Turning my attention to his alleged crime, I proceeded to go over the facts of the case with him. While he virtually recited verbatim what was written in my file, I noticed that there was no anger in his voice as he spoke of how his sister had dishonored his family. Usually when I spoke to perpetrators of honor crimes, they seethed with venom when recalling what had occurred. This feeling was clearly not present here. To the contrary, whenever he spoke of his sister, he did it with great fondness, and he said that they had been very close.

Tears suddenly started to roll down his cheeks. This was not an emotion I had expected to see from a dangerous man who was capable of such a brutal crime. Something seemed to be amiss.

After checking outside to ensure that no one was listening, I whispered to him, "Enough with the lies! Tell me now what really happened, or I will walk out of here."

"What do you mean?" the young man stammered.

"Do not waste my time. It is clear that you are not capable of such a crime, so tell me the truth now."

"It is true," he cried. "I killed her! I killed her!"

Still, I was not convinced. "How many times did you stab her?" I probed.

"Many times," came the reply.

Holding up the picture of his sister from the file, which showed her mutilated body, I said to him, "So you did this to your own sister who you say you loved? How did you feel when she cried for mercy? How did you feel as her blood covered you?"

Backing away from my verbal assault, the young man's body shook violently as he sobbed, still saying nothing.

"Did you kill her?" I asked.

"Yes," he spluttered, his voice barely audible.

"*Did you kill her*?" I shouted, my face touching his.

"Yes. God help me. Yes." He continued to snivel.

"Don't mess me around, you fool," I bellowed, grabbing both of his arms. "Tell me the truth now, or I will leave you here!"

For a moment there was silence before he finally whispered, "I . . . I . . . I didn't kill her."

Finally, the truth. But now I needed to get the whole story from him while he was in this vulnerable state.

Lowering my voice, I said, "Well, if you didn't kill her, who did?"

Silence greeted my question. Grabbing him by the shoulder, I knelt down and shook him violently. "Tell me the truth otherwise you are going to be hanged! Is this what you want?"

No answer.

"*Is this what you want*?" I bellowed again.

He tried his best to speak, but no words would come out of his mouth. Finally he mouthed, "No . . . No."

"Then tell me who killed your sister," I demanded.

Gulping down the mixture of snot and tears that engulfed his face, he muttered, "My father and my uncle."

I should have known. The men who I had taken such an instant dislike to in my office were responsible for this brutal crime.

Everything suddenly made sense, apart from one thing. "If they committed this crime, then why are they letting you take the blame?"

Taking deep breaths to calm himself, the young man then finally told me what had really happened.

"When my family found out about my sister's affair, they decided that she had to be killed," he started. "For some reason they wanted me to do it, but I refused. My sister was my best friend. I could not imagine killing her. The very thought of her being dead made me sick."

"So what happened?" I urged.

"When my father and uncle realized that I could not go through with it, they decided they must kill her. But they told me that I had to take the blame. They said that not only had I failed in my duty, and should therefore be responsible, but also I would stand a better chance in court than they would. I am scared of my father. I felt that I had no option. If I didn't take the blame, then not only would he punish me but also so would my community. I'd probably be killed. At least I know that I did not kill my sister and can die with a clear conscience."

Sitting down, I tried to gather my thoughts. What was I to do? It was at this moment that the young man begged me not to tell anyone what had really happened. My head was pounding. I felt that I had to spend some time alone to grapple with my thoughts.

As I walked away from the cell and down the dark corridor, the young man screamed incessantly, "Please don't tell anyone. Promise me you won't tell anyone. Please!"

I was not sure I could keep such a promise.

With the day of the court case rapidly approaching, I didn't have too much time to think. However, I realized that at this time my priority had to be to ensure that the young man did not receive the death penalty. But would I do that by telling the truth or through the family's lies?

On the day of the trial I made the decision that, for now, I would have to stick with the family's story. It was a very tough decision, but at least in court I had some degree of control over the young man's fate. If he were to be freed and his father and uncle prosecuted, then I could not help defend him from his community's retaliation. A young man's life was at stake. The true perpetrators of the crime would have to wait to receive justice at another time.

The only way that I would be able to save this young man's life was to plead that this was an honor crime. I had to hope that the court would accept this as a mitigating circumstance. It would not be easy, especially as I knew that there could be gaping holes in the young man's story. If he made any slip of the tongue during the trial, or if his story didn't add up, then he would be facing the gallows.

During the trial we methodically went over the evidence, and under questioning the young man said sorrowfully, "I was forced to commit the crime. My sister had harmed my family's honor, and our tradition dictates that she must be killed for doing so. If she was not killed, it would have brought great shame upon my family, and we would have had to leave our village in disgrace."

The prosecution and the court seemed to buy his story. It seemed that they just wanted someone to take the blame. In reality they didn't really want to question if in fact this polite young man could actually be responsible for such a horrific act.

Everyone's attention now turned away from the facts of the case to focus on the punishment the young man should receive. This was where my legal skills would come into play. Bracing myself for the prosecutor to ask for the death penalty, as was usual in such a case, I was stunned when he addressed the court.

"Your Honor," he began, "we are all well versed in the nature of honor crimes. We are aware of the defendant's duty in such a case, and it is clear that he has suffered. While the death penalty is an option, we believe that the more suitable sentence in this matter would be twelve years imprisonment."

Usually, I would have been elated at such a lenient sentence, but as the prosecutor had played such a weak hand, I sensed that I may be able to do even better. Watching my words carefully, as the real killers sat in the gallery, I stood up and proceeded to address the court.

"The freedom of our will, in reality, is nothing but the freedom of a bird in a cage," I said. "We are all the slaves of our traditions and culture, and at times we are obliged to act in the manner that is dictated to us by them."

Sensing that the judge was sympathetic to what I was saying, I continued. "Honor crimes are not willful acts but are acts that are strongly dictated by the traditions and behavior of society. This young man did not willingly kill his sister. The decision was made for him out of society's will."

I now looked toward the defendant. "The person standing in front of you is a nice and gentle person. He is polite and respectful and enjoys poetry and literature. In his heart he is not a violent man. He loved his sister. He was only two years older than her, and they had a lot in common. They shared a bedroom, they went to school together, they played together, and they loved each other dearly."

Suddenly the young man let out an enormous cry. Banging his head repeatedly against the edge of the cage in which he was held, he broke down. All of the court's attention was on him as he continued to slam his head into the bars until he drew blood.

With blood pouring down his face and his cries filling the courtroom, he let rip a piercing cry. "*I'm sorry!*" he screamed. "*Please forgive me! Please forgive me! I'm sorry!*"

The judge was startled by such an outpouring of emotion. It was very clear that this incident had greatly affected my client.

Knowing that this scene was doing enormous damage to his case, the prosecutor stepped in. "Your Honor," he said, "this is nothing more than an acting show. Please put an end to it."

But before the judge had a chance to answer, I knew that I had to interject. "Your Honor, please allow me to tell the court a well-known story that clearly illustrates just what a horrific situation my client has found himself in, and why he now suffers so greatly."

After the judge indicated that I should continue, I went on to tell the court the story of Khalifa.

Before Khalifa Haroon al-Rasheed had ruled Iraq, he had grown up with the prime minister's son, Jafar, who was from the powerful al-Barahmika tribe. The two became firm friends, and when they grew older Khalifa was delighted when Jafar announced that he wanted to marry Khalifa's sister, al-Abassa.

However, one day Khalifa heard that Jafar al-Barahmika's tribe was plotting a revolution that would remove him from power. Knowing that he had to strike quickly, Khalifa ordered all of the heads of the tribe be killed, including his close friend and now brother-in-law, Jafar.

After the killings had taken place, Khalifa's distraught sister, al-Abassa, stormed into the palace to confront her brother. When she entered his bedroom she was surprised to find her brother crying inconsolably.

"How can you have killed Jafar and now cry for him?" she shouted.

"I had no choice," Khalifa sadly replied. "Maintaining my kingdom and the peace of my people is more important than my closest friend."

After I finished recounting this story, I bellowed at the court, "If a renowned ruler such as Khalifa can kill someone close to him and cry like a child, then why shouldn't my client also be capable of the same? He was forced to kill his sister. The pain is killing him, and his tears today are the greatest proof of it. I leave the fate of this young man in the merciful hands of the court."

After thanking the court for its time, I took a seat. My speech had clearly struck a chord with most people in the room, and I wanted to quit while I was ahead. However, owing to the barbarity of the crime, even I had to acknowledge that it was still likely that the young man would have to serve a significant amount of time behind bars. So be it. It was better than hanging.

I had expected to be waiting outside the court for several hours while the judges reached their verdict, but when we were called back inside after less than an hour of deliberating, I did not take it to be a good omen. In my gut I felt that my client would be facing the full twelve-year stretch.

When I walked back into the court I looked over at the young man who peered back at me despondently from inside his cage. Although his face had been cleaned of blood, he still looked terrified. I wasn't sure if such a gentle boy would be able to cope with prison. A twelve-year sentence could be tantamount to an execution in his case.

As the president of the court began to recount the facts, I really did fear the worse. And it appeared that so did my client, as he could not stop whimpering. Try as he might, he just could not stifle his tears as they streamed down his face. I felt terribly sorry for him. These were circumstances entirely beyond his control. Whatever decision he made would have put his life or liberty on the line.

Slowly but surely the president proceeded to inform the court of the sentence. "The court accepts that this was an honor crime, and as such we understand the pressure the defendant was put under," he began. "Subsequently the court accepts this as a mitigating circumstance and sentences the defendant to serve one year in prison, which he has already spent in detention. Accordingly the defendant is now free."

The defendant is now free! I couldn't believe my ears, and neither could the young man, who slumped to the floor and began praying to Allah. Never in my wildest dreams did I think that he would walk free from court that day. As the cage door opened, the young man ran toward me, fell to his knees, and tried to kiss my hand.

"Do not thank me," I said to him. "Thank your grandfather. I would not have taken the case if it were not for him."

Suddenly his grandfather, father, and uncle were surrounding me. While I shook the grandfather's hand and accepted his good wishes, I turned my back on both the father and the uncle. They both understood that I knew the truth.

With that this case came to an end. I may have fulfilled my duty to my client, but I was very uneasy with the idea that the perpetrators of the crime had escaped punishment. It was far from my idea of true justice, but in this circumstance my duty had been to protect my client from the death penalty, or a prison sentence, and I had done that. God knows what the father and uncle did, and I have no doubt that He will see that they pay for their crimes in this lifetime or the next.

10.

BREAKING THE LAW

"Justice without force is powerless; force without justice is tyrannical."

—Blaise Pascal

IT WAS CLOSE TO MIDNIGHT. The usually bustling Baghdad district of Mansour was quiet. The air was humid and still, the mood relaxed. Nothing suggested that within moments there would be a hail of bullets that would propel the defendants and me onto the front pages of Iraq's newspapers.

While the night may have been quiet, night guards continued to zealously patrol the area, keeping a look out for any sign of something untoward. So far the night had been uneventful. Yet still they kept their fingers on the triggers of their guns. In Baghdad you never knew when the silence could erupt into anarchy.

Keeping a watchful eye as they walked the streets a taxi suddenly careened past one of the guards, bouncing and weaving along the uneven road and spraying dust behind it as it went. Suddenly, the taxi came to a stop. Raised voices raged from inside. A fist slammed against the condensation-lined window. Momentary silence. Then the car jolted forward, moving slowly, then quickly, then slowly, until it came to another stop twenty yards down the road.

A night guard tentatively walked toward the car, crouching low on his tiptoes to avoid making noise. Straining his eyes to see through the condensation on the windows, he made out what appeared to be a woman's leg frantically kicking up and down. Sensing danger he ran toward the taxi, but as he did so the car moved forward again: slow, quick, slow, quick, slow, quick. The night guard tried to keep up, but the car suddenly veered onto the wrong side of the road and sped away. He blew his whistle, frantically signaling for the taxi to stop, yet it did nothing of the sort. Instead it flew around the corner and out of sight.

Hearing the shrill sound of the whistle pierce the night air, another night guard who was on patrol three blocks away saw the taxi and fired a shot into the air to try to get it to come to a halt. If anything, this only seemed to encourage the driver to go faster.

Nearby another one of the night guards heard the sound of the whistle and the 'gunshots' just as the taxi raced erratically down the street he was patrolling. Having heard the shots, the guard feared that the taxi's passengers had been shooting at the guards, so he frantically flagged down a police car.

"A taxi is shooting at the night guards," he told the officers in a panicked tone. "We ordered it to stop, but it got away."

The police set out in search of the renegade taxi, scouring the area fruitlessly for over five minutes. However, it seemed to have disappeared into thin air. But then, just as they were about to give up, they saw it parked at an angle on the side of a road. Putting on their flashing blue lights, the police approached the taxi from behind. Yet just as the officers had stepped out of the car, the taxi once again screeched away, despite one of the officers shooting his gun into the air.

A number of police cars soon became involved in a dramatic chase through the streets of Baghdad, the sound of gunshots filling the night air. Despite being pursued by as many as six cars, the taxi still would not stop; in fact it did everything it could to evade capture. Mounting the sidewalk, it weaved through pedestrians before spinning across the street and down a dark warren of alleyways, all in an effort to shake the police cars off its tail.

One police car decided to leave the chase and raced down a side road in an effort to head the taxi off. Upon reaching the far end of the street, the officers jumped out of the car and pointed their guns toward a dark alley. Moments later the headlights of the rogue taxi flashed in the darkness, barelling directly toward them.

Aiming at the taxi's tires, and engine, the three police officers opened fire, sending bullets rocketing toward the vehicle. A sound of hissing, crunching of metal, and then a plume of smoke followed before complete silence. The taxi was finally at a stop.

One of the officers nervously walked toward the wrecked vehicle and apprehensively opened the driver's door. Meanwhile, the other two officers stood with their guns pointing directly at it, not wanting to take the chance that their foe was still in a fighting mood. But they need not have worried. As the door opened, the driver dropped out onto the street. He was dead, as was the passenger next to him.

Hearing groans from inside the car, the officers looked into the back seat. There they saw two men whose shirts were soaked with blood.

"Don't shoot! Don't shoot!" one of the injured men pleaded.

Taking a closer look, the officers could see that the men were naked from the waist down. One was wounded, but the other appeared to be dead. Splayed across them was the body of a half-naked woman. She had been shot in the chest, but the gargled sounds coming from her mouth indicated that she was still alive.

As an ambulance was called for the survivors, a search of the taxi was carried out but nothing untoward was found, not even a gun. So just how had the passengers been shooting at the police, as had been thought, when there was no gun? And why had they been so desperate to avoid capture?

It transpired that when the police had fired into the air to warn the taxi to stop, other officers had thought the shots were coming from the taxi itself. When the chase ensued, the police cars, which were on either side of the taxi, opened fire, effectively shooting at each other. At no point had anyone in the taxi actually been shooting at the police.

When the survivor recovered, he confessed that the men had indeed been involved in a crime. He admitted that after a few drinks they had picked up a prostitute and were taking turns having sex with her in the car. Then, when the police arrived, he said that they had panicked and drunkenly decided to try to evade capture rather than stop. They had effectively been in breach of the law but not to the extent where they deserved to be shot.

It was a mess, and soon it was all over the front pages of Baghdad's newspapers. Before long, it turned into a major scandal, with the police's conduct under intense scrutiny.

While this debate raged, I was extremely busy in my law office. I was snowed under in fact, up to my eyes in files. I was working eighteen-hour days by this stage to try to keep on top of things. As such, a few weeks after the car chase and ensuing scandal, I was still at my desk at 8:00 p.m., with no end to my working day in sight. My secretary also continued to work diligently outside my office, with express orders not to disturb me unless absolutely necessary.

As I tried to get through everything that needed to be done, I heard the sound of the office door opening. Then I heard shouting, which proceeded to get louder. Good, I thought. My secretary is doing just what I told her.

However, just as I got my head back into my papers, my secretary tentatively entered my office.

"I told you I am too busy to see anyone tonight," I scolded, annoyed at being interrupted.

"I'm sorry, Mr. Aris, but these men claimed that you would definitely want to see them."

Suddenly, in marched a big man in an army uniform flanked by two police officers. I saw what my secretary had meant. This man was certainly not someone you could ask to come back at another time. After all, General Taha was the head of the Iraqi police.

"General Taha, please come in and take a seat," I said, gesturing with my hand toward the sofa in the corner of the room while my secretary scurried away.

"I have a case I want you to defend," he said gruffly, forgoing pleasantries, as he marched across the room and sat down.

"You are normally the one who prosecutes cases. What case could you possibly want me to defend?"

He pulled a newspaper out of his suitcase and thrust it into my hands, pointing to the front page. It was a story about the recent charges of homicide that had been made against the three officers who had opened fire on the taxi.

"You want me to defend these men?" I asked, glancing up from the newspaper in shock. The general nodded. This was serious stuff. I already knew a lot about the case from the media, but there were still some questions that needed to be answered.

"Were the officers given an order to shoot at the taxi?" I inquired, to which the general shook his head.

"Listen," he began, "this is a hugely important case. I need you to save not only these officers but also the reputation of my police force. Of course it is an unfortunate incident, but if these officers are convicted, it will send a very dangerous message to the criminals of Baghdad, as well as to my officers. Why should they risk their lives to stop criminals if in turn the courts make them criminals?"

The case certainly wasn't a trivial matter. And while I was already extremely busy, I knew it was something that would need my full attention.

"I will do my best," I smiled, standing up to shake the general's hand.

"I hope so, Mr. Aris," the general replied, with my hand still locked firmly in his grasp. "Because I will be in court watching."

The general was true to his word. On the day of the hearing he was sat in the middle of the front row in full military regalia. It seemed he had also ordered most of the Iraqi police force to attend as well, as the courtroom was packed with officers. Unsurprisingly, representatives from all of the top media outlets in Iraq were also present.

As I took my seat, the general leaned over the barrier.

Putting his hand on my shoulder, he said, "All of the police officers in Iraq are depending on you today. Don't let us down."

I shook my head and smiled. The pressure was on, and the odds were against me, just the way I liked it.

Soon the three officers were brought into the courtroom, and the trial was underway.

After the defendants pleaded not guilty to all of the charges, the prosecutor set about his task. It was all pretty standard stuff. There were certainly no surprises. The line of questioning proved that the officers had not received any orders to fire on the taxi, the passengers had no weapons on them, and the only crimes they were guilty of committing were drunk driving, prostitution, solicitation, and not stopping when ordered to do so by the police, all of which the prosecutor told the court were hardly crimes that warranted unauthorized shooting across the streets of Baghdad.

While all of this was expected, it was still very unhelpful to our defense. On the face of it the three officers looked to be in serious trouble. I knew our chances were slim, but still I held out hope that my defense strategy could win over the three judges.

It is always a special feeling when you have the eyes of the court on you. Some lawyers can't handle it and retreat into themselves, like a turtle into its shell. I, on the other hand, have always thrived on it. My palms would become slightly sticky, my heart would race, adrenaline would surge through my body, and then I would be ready to put on a show. And that was just what my defense needed in this instance, a show of epic proportions.

"Your Honor," I started, as I stood up to address the court, "the case today is a very serious matter, not only because of the facts set before us but also because it involves the measures the police are allowed to take to procure security in society."

Behind me I could hear General Taha grunt in agreement. It seemed his approval of this part of my speech spurred his officers to also make approving sounds, which encouraged me to continue.

I went on to tell the court that everything the prosecutor had said was correct. I would not argue with the facts. But there was more to this case, much more. For a start, I informed the court that I had taken a professional photographer with me to photograph the taxi at every angle, which I now admitted into evidence.

"As the court will see," I said while holding up some of the photographs, "these photographs document eighty-two bullet entries in the taxi, which was hit from all directions. The officers here today each held a revolver that carried six bullets in the chamber. Therefore, the maximum number of shots they could have fired was eighteen. And as we know, the officers before us today were directly in front of the taxi, so they could have only shot at it from that angle. If that is the case, then the vast majority of shots that hit the taxi were not shot by these officers. So why then are they the only ones charged with these offenses?"

I knew that this would cast doubt on whether these officers could be charged with the homicides if it could not be proven that they had fired the decisive shots. Yet for this case I needed to do much more than that. As General Taha had made abundantly clear, I was also fighting for the reputation of the Iraqi police force.

Taking a sip of water, I allowed the judges to inspect the pictures before I then embarked on the second part of my strategy.

"Your Honor, it is clear that no order was given from central command to shoot to kill. That is not in dispute. However, an order was given to stop the taxi. So when officers shot in the air to warn the taxi to stop, and it still continued to drive at speed erratically through the streets, what conclusion could they reach other than that the passengers were hell-bent on avoiding arrest as they were fleeing a serious crime?

"If these officers are found guilty today, then any officers in the future will think twice about reaching for their guns when faced with what looks to be a serious crime. This case is unfortunate, but more often than not, these circumstances would lead to serious criminals being apprehended by these exact methods."

Now came my coup de grâce. Picking up a copy of the Iraqi criminal code that I had placed on the table in front of me, I turned to face the court. I knew that what I was about to do was technically against the law and could get me into serious trouble if it backfired, but under the circumstances I felt it was worth the risk.

"This is the book of law," I intoned, facing the judges. "But while it contains the law, it is useless without police officers willing to put their lives on the line to defend it."

To emphasize my point, and to the shock of the court, I suddenly tore the book in half. "May the court forgive me for tearing this book," I said, to the gasps of the spectators and one of the judges, "but I just want to prove that the book of law has no power without the likes of the men who stand before you today, men who willingly put their lives on the line in dangerous situations to ensure that the laws in this book will be adhered to. Without them, the book of law is helpless. It can be torn by anyone. It can be violated by anyone."

Such was my passion in making this point that I began to lose my voice. I hoarsely finished off by saying, "This case will be remembered within the police force for many years to come. I hope that your decision today sends out a message that the court supports the police and that they can continue in their duties defending the security of society."

As I finished, General Taha rose to his feet behind me. There was complete silence in the room as he did so. What was he going to do? Suddenly he put his hands together and started to applaud. Then every other officer in the room stood and did likewise. It was an exhilarating moment. It was up there with anything I have ever felt in a courtroom. There was no more I could have done. And I was certainly relieved that the general and his officers seemed to feel the same.

Following my defense we broke for a recess while the judges came to their decision. We were outside for less than an hour before we were called back to the courtroom. I felt this was a sign that my defense had been either a rousing success or a calamitous failure.

Taking my seat, I really didn't know which way the verdict would go until I saw the head judge look at me. He smiled and very subtly nodded his head. No one else in the room probably noticed, as it was very quick, but I knew then that I had done my job. Seconds later this was confirmed: Not guilty.

When I went to visit my mother later that night, she told me that I looked tired. I smiled. "For once I am not tired from work," I said. "I am tired from shaking almost every hand in the Baghdad police force."

11.

THE DAWN OF SADDAM

"The immutable principles of justice are to make way for
party interests, and the bonds of social order are to be rent
in twain, in order that a desperate faction may be sustained
at the expense of the people."

—Abraham Lincoln

IRAQ UNDERWENT AN ENORMOUS CHANGE during the 1970s after President Ahmed Hassan al-Bakr and his vice-president, Saddam Hussein, had stormed to power in 1968. Some of the changes they made were good. Some of them were not.

Perhaps the new government's most popular move came in 1972 when they nationalized the Iraq Petroleum Company. For many years the Iraqi people had been very critical of the fact that so much of the country's oil revenues had been diverted to foreign companies, and Saddam and al-Bakr had realized that not only would it be a very popular move to rectify this but also, more importantly, it would be tremendously profitable. With complete control over the country's oil, hundreds of millions of dollars suddenly started to pour in.

Wasting little time, the government embarked on a huge welfare program that was unprecedented in the Middle East. Among other initiatives it provided housing for the poor, modernized the public health system, and initiated a compulsory free education scheme. Land and machinery were also given to peasant farmers to help free them from the chains of poverty.

This newfound prosperity also allowed the country to fund a series of major infrastructure projects. Not only did this improve the standard of living, but also it meant that lots of work was readily available. Before the Ba'ath Party came to power, roughly two-thirds of Iraqis had been peasants, a statistic that dropped dramatically during the 1970s, as most could now find employment. Such was the development boom that at one point there were actually more jobs than there were available workers, which led to over two million migrant workers flocking to the country to fill the gap.

While working-class Iraqis were generally very happy with these developments, they also benefited those of a higher social standing, as government contracts were made available for all manner of projects. This was an area that certainly helped my legal practice, as I was soon appointed to act as legal counsel for some of the world's largest construction companies who were executing major contracts in Iraq.

The money I earned from the foreign companies was considerable. I remember a director of a French company once asked me to attend a meeting with him to discuss a new project with a government department. It was a request I sadly had to decline, as lawyers were prohibited from attending such meetings. Undeterred, the director still insisted that I go along and sit in the lobby, just in case he needed me. This didn't sound like the most exciting job in the world, so I quoted him a fee of $10,000 for my time, a figure I was surprised to find he was more than happy to pay.

With the people generally content and oil money boosting the economy, it finally looked as though Iraq was pulling its weight on the world stage. For a moment, the future looked incredibly bright.

But beneath the surface, not everything was so positive. As Saddam built up his intelligence agencies and networks of informants, Baghdad suddenly became a dangerous place to live if you held an opposing opinion to the regime's.

Political discussion was never very high on my agenda anyway, but during this time it definitely became a strict no-go area. Saddam and al-Bakr had stated their intent to purge Iraq of any dissenting voices as soon as they had come to power, and they went about their business with ruthless efficiency. In an unprecedented swoop, they settled old scores—and potential future problems—by rounding up communists, Western-oriented businesspeople, former politicians, and those Ba'ath Party members who were deemed not to be 100 percent loyal. Overnight thousands disappeared and were never heard from again.

Everyone soon learned that you could not risk criticizing the Ba'ath Party in any way whatsoever. Even the softest criticisms were leapt upon and dealt with swiftly. An air of paranoia swept the country, and before long we all realized that if we wanted to stay out of trouble, we had to keep our mouths shut.

This was a situation that almost got a future employee of mine, Dr. Yasmin, into deep trouble. Before Dr. Yasmin came to work for me, he served as a secretary for a government committee that dealt with economic issues. Saddam was the head of the committee, and one day, after he had finished a particularly long speech, he turned to Dr. Yasmin and said, "Did you get all of that down?"

Dr. Yasmin innocently replied, "I have made a summary of all of the main points."

His response was met with an incredulous silence that ended only when Saddam stormed out of the room.

While Dr. Yasmin did not appreciate the gravity of his offense, his colleagues were horrified. "Go home now!" they urged. "Say goodbye to your family. Saddam will throw you in jail for this!"

Dr. Yasmin was unperturbed. He could not see how such an act could get him into trouble. With nothing untoward happening he returned to work the next morning only to find that his office had been completely emptied. Bemused, Dr. Yasmin tried to ask his colleagues what had happened, but everyone ignored him. For the remainder of the day, no one said a word to him. He had no choice but to sit in isolation.

This continued for a couple of days until finally Dr. Yasmin could stand it no more. Confronting his manager, he asked if there was a problem, to which his manager replied, "Leave now and just be thankful that this appears to be your punishment."

Thankfully, Dr. Yasmin came to me for a job, and I eagerly employed him, despite his brush with Saddam, as his reputation as a lawyer of high repute was well known.

However, with Saddam in charge of the army as well as agencies such as the People's Party and the Mukhabarat (Iraq's version of the CIA), on July 16, 1979, he took full advantage when he removed the elderly al-Bakr from power and became president of Iraq. It seemed that al-Bakr had been so concerned about attempted coups from within the army that he had failed to notice that the man who controlled them had been secretly plotting to use them against him.

Over night, thousands of posters, portraits, statues, and murals were erected in honor of Saddam all over Iraq. Wherever you went, you could expect to see his picture emblazoned on the sides of office buildings, schools, airports, and shops. There was no doubt in anybody's mind that Saddam was very much in charge.

Life under Saddam, as under al-Bakr, wasn't all bad though. I remember that there used to be a government hotline that anyone could call to address any problems they might have. Saddam himself even used to answer the phone sometimes and would deal with issues personally. Indeed, there was an occasion where I was extremely thankful for this.

A couple of times a month a group of my friends, consisting of lawyers, doctors, judges, and army officers, used to visit the home of a retired lawyer to play poker. One evening, as we were playing, the doorbell rang. A servant went to answer only to quickly return, ashen-faced. "The police are at the door," he blurted. "They want to conduct a search of the house."

Our host went to investigate only to be told by one of the officers, "You are conducting an illegal gambling casino here. We are confiscating all of the proceeds of the crime, and we are arresting every one of you."

This caused an uproar, especially when the officers stormed into the house and tried to handcuff one of the judges. Everyone started to shout and complain, but I knew that it would do us no good. The officers were just following orders.

Amid all the commotion, I managed to slip out of the room and find a telephone. Calling the Presidential Palace hotline I was put through to an army general. I quickly told him my name and the names of those I was playing with and insisted that it was nothing more than a private game in the house of a well-respected ex-lawyer. The general was familiar with most of the names I mentioned, and he also knew me, since my law office was situated in one of the most prominent areas of Baghdad. As such he told me to fetch the officer who was in charge.

When I walked back into the room, I told the officer in charge that the office of Saddam Hussein was on the phone for him. At first he didn't believe me, yet he knew that he could not take the risk that I was telling the truth. Nervously, he followed me into the adjacent room and picked up the phone. Sparing formalities, the general began to tear into him.

"Leave the house immediately and have a report prepared for the office of Saddam by the morning," I heard him shout. "If it is found that you have raided the house without legal justification, you will face the consequences."

As the general continued lambasting the officer, I noticed that the phone started to rattle in the man's hand. He was shaking with fear.

With the assault on his ears at an end, the officer fell to his knees and begged for our forgiveness. Moments before, he had been arrogantly throwing his weight around, but now he was reduced to a blubbering wreck.

However, while the hotline helped me on this occasion, it almost got me into serious trouble with Saddam himself.

I was in my office one afternoon when I received a phone call from a friend who owned a workshop next to my cigarette paper factory.

"Sabah, there is a problem," he told me in a worried tone. "Someone at your factory has called Saddam to complain."

"What do you mean?" I cried.

"Saddam is at your factory right now. He is talking to your workers," the man replied in a panicked voice. "Run, my friend. They are talking against you. He will arrest you and throw you in jail!"

For half an hour I barricaded myself in my office as a million thoughts swirled around in my head. Who had complained and why? Should I run? What was going to become of me? Suddenly the phone rang. Tentatively I picked it up, fearing the worse.

"Mr. Aris," said a voice I immediately recognized as belonging to a woman named Shamsa who worked for me. "Saddam has been to the factory speaking to the workers. He has just left."

"Is it safe to come?" I asked.

She whispered, "I think so."

I made my way to the factory and gathered my thoughts so that I could get to the bottom of things. Once I was there Shamsa told me that one of my workers who was always creating problems had called the hotline and complained about the wages and conditions.

After Saddam had arrived at the factory to a rapturous welcome, he had apparently asked the men about their working conditions. The men told him that they all received above minimum wage. On top of that, they also confided that I paid them a transportation and medical allowance, something that was very rare.

Despite Saddam telling the workers that they were very lucky to have such a job, some of them continued to complain, to which Saddam shouted, "Does Mr. Aris keep you here against your will?"

"No," they replied.

"If Mr. Aris were here now, would you be able to raise these complaints with him, as you have done with me?" he asked.

"Yes," they answered.

"Then you are privileged to work for such a man who also happens to provide you with good conditions and pay. Do not waste my time when many would swap with you tomorrow."

And with that Saddam left, having admonished the few workers who had made complaints.

That night as I watched the news on TV, there was a segment showing Saddam visiting my factory. To my intense relief, he said very nice things about it. I thanked God that it had met with his approval. Otherwise I might have been spending that night, and maybe even the rest of my life, in jail.

Despite this incident, I had an excellent relationship with the men who worked for me, and most never had cause for complaint. In fact, to this day, I am still in contact with some of them and count them among my dearest friends.

During this time, Saddam was present in virtually every area of public and private life. Indeed, his leadership also had an effect on my work as a lawyer, as he established a new court called the "court of revolution" that dealt with cases of special importance, whether political, economic, or otherwise. The decisions passed by the court were final and could only be changed by Saddam himself. In effect, Saddam became the final court of appeals.

Perhaps the best example of Saddam's influence where I was concerned occurred when I acted for a woman who was the general manager of the River Transportation Authority. By the time I was instructed to act, she was waiting to stand trial for receiving a $10,000 bribe from an Indian company in exchange for a ship building contract. This was an extremely serious offense that carried the death penalty.

There was, however, no doubt about it; she had received $10,000 from this company, and she did not deny it. She said that the man in charge of the company had left an envelope for her, and without realizing what it was, she had put it away in a drawer. When she did eventually open it and found money inside, she fully intended to return it to the man the next time she saw him, but she was arrested before she had the chance to do so.

At trial I explained how the envelope had come to be in the woman's possession and also stressed that every contract she had signed had been in the best interests of Iraq. There was not a single contract that could be said to have been given solely on the basis of a bribe, as all of the contracts were actually extremely beneficial to Iraq, and it was very clear that she was a talented negotiator.

The president of the court was sympathetic, but he stressed that my client had still received $10,000. While he did not sentence her to death, he did sentence her to twenty years in prison. Under the circumstances I felt that this was as good as we could have hoped for.

Yet the woman's family were understandably devastated. They begged me to write a letter to Saddam on their behalf concerning the case, in the hope that he would be merciful. When writing to Saddam, I knew that there was no point in writing more than eight lines, as no matter how long your letter was, an assistant would summarize it to that amount before it reached him. In my letter I succinctly stressed how a woman, who had served Iraq admirably for a number of years furthering the country's interests, was now in jail owing to an innocent mistake. I asked that he consider granting this woman clemency so that she could be freed from jail and continue to serve Iraq.

Days later, Saddam's office called my client's daughter and ordered her to appear at the palace immediately where she would get her chance to present her case to Saddam himself. At the palace and before Saddam, she stressed that what her mother did in principle was wrong but that she had never harmed the interests of Iraq or Saddam's presidency.

I had been out that night and was not aware of any of this, but when I returned home I received a call from my client. I told her that I was surprised that the prison warden was allowing her to call me so late at night.

"What prison warden?" she replied, "I am free." Within three hours of her daughter meeting Saddam, he had quashed the conviction and had ordered her freedom.

Saddam's concept of justice was usually firmly in tune with the Qur'an, which states that crimes should be punished with "an eye for an eye." To illustrate this, I remember a story where one of Saddam's cousin's had failed an exam at his university. Enraged by his own failure, the cousin ordered his bodyguard to break his professor's hand, which his bodyguard did with a baton. Following this assault, the professor, who was Egyptian, wrote to Saddam and informed him of what had occurred, without ever expecting a reply.

However, a few days later a car arrived at the professor's house, and he was unceremoniously ordered to get in; Saddam had requested his presence at the palace. When the professor arrived, he was terrified, particularly when he saw that Saddam's cousin was also in the room. Without hesitation Saddam demanded that the professor tell him the whole story. After listening to the professor's recitation of events, Saddam asked his cousin if it was true, to which the cousin meekly nodded his head.

"Do you have your baton with you?" Saddam asked his bodyguard, which prompted the guard to pull it out. "Give it to the professor," Saddam ordered.

Now addressing the professor, Saddam said, "The guards will hold my cousin down. I want you to break his hand, just like he had done to you."

The professor was shocked. He didn't know if it was a trick, and at the same time he really didn't want to break the cousin's hand. Realizing that the professor was too afraid to act, Saddam instead ordered his bodyguard to carry out the punishment.

Despite knowing what was going to happen, the cousin stood rooted to the spot as the guard grabbed his hand and beat it until it was clearly broken.

Saddam then turned to the professor and said, "You came to this country to teach. Justice is a part of knowledge, and no knowledge can prosper without justice. You have just witnessed the justice of the Islamic doctrine. He broke your hand; now his hand is broken. An eye for an eye."

Saddam's concept of justice certainly changed my world, and it took me a while to adjust. But I soon found myself dealing with a case where, without Saddam's involvement, I may have faced a lifetime of regret, as for the first time in my life I knowingly helped to send an innocent man to jail.

12.

THE JUDGE'S DAUGHTER

"Injustice anywhere is a threat to justice everywhere."
—Martin Luther King Jr.

HOW CAN A MAN CHOOSE between his duty to his friend and the truth? It is an almost impossible choice, yet one case left me facing this exact dilemma. If I lost the case, my friend would be publicly disgraced. If I won, then an innocent man could face seven years in jail.

The case came to my attention as I was working yet another all-nighter. While I sat at my desk, swamped by papers, my secretary interrupted me to say that there was a man outside who was insisting he had to see me straight away.

"Who is he?" I wearily asked.

"He won't tell me," she answered. "And I can't tell who he is because he is wearing a hat and covering up his face."

I was always happy to see people in my office, but behavior such as this concerned me. As a criminal lawyer in Baghdad who had fought against many dangerous criminals in the courtroom, I always faced the danger that one day one of these individuals would seek vengeance. Yet while this was a possibility I was also intrigued.

"Send him in," I told my secretary.

Shortly after she left, the door slowly opened and a man appeared hiding his face, just as my secretary had described.

"Who are you and what do you want?" I asked.

"Sabah, it is me," the man replied as he took off his hat.

I recognized the man immediately, "My God, what are you doing here?"

"I'm sorry, Sabah," the man said, as I embraced him in a warm hug. "I could not let anyone see me entering your office. After all, it is technically illegal for me to be here."

He was right. It was illegal. The man was an acting judge, and it was forbidden for any judge to visit a lawyer's office.

Taking the judge's hat and coat, I offered him a seat. As we sat down the judge picked up an old picture of my father from my desk and smiled. He remembered him well. He had actually presided over a case that had made my father very happy. It had been a trial where I had represented an old family friend, a woman named Salma, who had been wrongly dismissed from her job because her manager wanted to replace her with a younger and more attractive secretary. I won the case that day, which made my father very proud, as Salma and her family had been very kind to him when he first came to Iraq. He saw it as finally paying her back after all the kindness she had shown him.

Putting down the picture, the judge smiled as we talked about Salma's case as well as other cases that we had both dealt with throughout the years. Yet despite enjoying the chance to reminisce, I was eager to hear what the judge's current visit was about. However, for now it was clear that he wanted to ease himself into the subject. It was obviously going to be something very important, considering he had come to my office in disguise, so I did not want to push him until he was ready. Finally, after twenty minutes of talking there was a short silence.

"We have spoken of the past," the judge started tentatively, wringing his hands together, "but I now have a problem in the present. A big problem."

Asking him to share his problem with me, he started to outline the reasons for his concern. He told me that his daughter had married a very successful doctor and that they both lived in a big house that required the employment of a number of servants. One of the servants, whose work was always impeccable, was a young Sudanese man who lived in a guesthouse in the garden.

One day the husband came home from work and heard screaming. Rushing to the guest house, he found his wife crying, her hair messed up and her dress ripped. Sobbing uncontrollably, she claimed that the Sudanese servant had tried to rape her. As the husband cradled his distraught wife, she explained that she had been calling for the Sudanese servant to help her, but when he had not answered she had gone to the guesthouse to find him. She said that when she got to his front door, the servant had forced her inside, and that is when the assault took place.

Following this event the servant was arrested and charged with attempted rape. Yet there was a twist. The judge told me that the servant was now claiming that the judge's daughter had in fact tried to rape him! He had told the police that when he had rejected the daughter's advances, she had ripped her own dress and had then cried rape when her husband arrived home.

As the judge told me this, I laughed. "Is he serious?"

"Deadly serious," the judge replied. "The case will now go to trial. I am confident in my daughter's story, as why would she want to sleep with an ugly servant? But if we do not win this case, then my family's honor will be destroyed. I will have to step down as a judge."

Placing my hand on the judge's shoulder, I told him to leave it with me. It was preposterous that anyone would believe that his daughter would wish to sleep with such a man, let alone that she would make up such a story. Any court on earth would be able to see through the servant's disgraceful cover-up story. Moreover, it was the servant's word against that of a respected judge's daughter. The case was as good as won.

"Thank you," the judge smiled, as I told him I would take on the case. "I will remember your kindness always."

A few days later the daughter and her husband came to see me before the trial got underway. When I asked her about her relationship with the servant, she claimed that she had caught him looking at her a number of times and felt that he was attracted to her.

"Why then did you go to his guesthouse alone?" I asked, already anticipating the question any defending lawyer worth his salt would ask in court.

"He is our servant," she said bluntly. "He did not respond when I called, so I had to find him. Even if I thought he was attracted to me, never did I think he would try to rape me in his master's house."

As the daughter spoke, I noticed that the husband was very quiet. Something was clearly on his mind, but I wasn't sure what. I put it down to nervousness. No man wants to discuss with another man the circumstances surrounding the attempted rape of his wife. What was of more concern, however, was the wife's demeanor. Unlike rape victims I had represented in the past she didn't seem damaged by the experience at all. She looked me directly in the eye, didn't need to stop to compose herself, and also didn't look for her husband's support. It could be said that she was merely being strong but I felt somewhat troubled. And that gut feeling was exacerbated when, a few days later, I was provided with a witness statement from one of the other Sudanese servants. In it the servant claimed that the defendant had previously told him that the judge's daughter had made a move on him. Furthermore, he also claimed that the daughter was known to flirt with the defendant. There was of course no concrete evidence of these assertions; they could be easily dismissed in court as one friend creating a story to help another, but still I had a very uneasy feeling in my stomach. I knew I would get this man convicted for the crime and save my friend's honor in the process, but what if the man was actually innocent?

On the day of the trial my uneasiness grew when the defendant entered the courtroom. Everyone I had spoken to had claimed that he was nothing but an ugly servant, but those assertions could not have been further from the truth, as he was actually incredibly handsome. At over six-feet tall, he was very well built and had a graceful walk, dark brooding eyes, and a strong jaw. He was one of the best-looking men I had ever seen. He could have been a movie star.

Of course, the appearance of the man didn't change the case. It was still a servant's word against the word of a judge's daughter. However, when I looked towards the daughter, as the servant was brought into the room, far from looking upset, angry, or traumatized, I saw her happily talk with her husband. Again, this was not the reaction I would have normally expected from a rape victim when confronted with their attacker.

However, now that I was in court, with the eyes of my friend watching from the gallery, I knew I had to wipe out any conflicting thoughts and deliver what I had promised. I was the prosecuting lawyer. My job was to present evidence to the court that the defendant was guilty. Then the fate of the defendant would be left in the court's hands. That was all I had to do.

After the judge's daughter confidently told the court her version of events, the defendant took the stand. Despite feeling that he might be innocent, I set out to do my job to the best of my ability.

"On the day of the incident, did you try to rape the victim?" I started bluntly, immediately putting him on the back foot.

"She tried to rape me," the man shot back.

"Did you fight her off?"

A pause. "No."

"You claim she tried to rape you, but you did not fight back?"

"I had no time. I . . . "

"No. There was time. But you have clearly told the court that you did not fight back. So how can you accuse this woman of a crime as serious as rape when you admit that you didn't fight back?"

"She came on to me."

"And why should we believe you, a servant, rather than an upstanding member of the community? According to Islamic law, when a woman claims she has been raped, she is to be believed unless the man can produce concrete evidence to the contrary. Can you provide any such evidence?"

The man looked at me. He was helpless. He knew it. I knew it. There was nowhere left for him to go.

"I am innocent," he pleaded, first to me and then to the court. "I am innocent. God help me. I am innocent."

"So innocent that you accused a respectful woman, who is the daughter of a respectful father and the wife of respectful husband, of trying to rape you?"

The defendant said nothing. Neither did I. I had done what I had aimed to do.

When the defendant's lawyer began his defense, I actually felt sorry for him. He had an impossible job on his hands. All the evidence was in our favor. And while I knew the defendant would be facing jail, there was something deep inside me that almost wanted the lawyer to do something miraculous.

However, it was not to be. Rather than come up with anything new, the defense lawyer tried the only tactic available to him: pleading for the mercy of the court.

"My client is extremely unlucky today," he said, looking forlornly at the judge. "He is unlucky that he came to work in the house that he did. He is unlucky that no one saw the wife come on to him. And he is unlucky that in court he is up against Mr. Aris, one of the most accomplished lawyers in Iraq. However, my client is innocent. He did not commit this crime. He has been set up by the wife, who is taking her revenge after he rebuffed her advances. She ripped her own dress, and she is the one in the wrong. I realize this is an unusual case, but I beg the court to look deeper into the allegation before passing the decision."

That was that. There was nothing more he could have done, but I knew it would not be enough. And I was proved to be right. Just over an hour later the court returned a guilty verdict with the defendant sentenced to serve seven years in jail.

Following the verdict, my friend, the judge, was ecstatic. Hugging me he told me that I had saved his family's honor. Of course I was glad to have done so, but in the process I wondered if I had just harmed my own honor by sending a man I thought was innocent to jail?

For the next few days I was unable to shake this thought from my head. Even when I slept I dreamt about the case. It got right under my skin and haunted my every moment. But now it was too late. The man was in jail. What could I do about it?

Almost two weeks after the trial, my secretary came into my office and said that there was a Sudanese man waiting to see me. Cautiously I told her to send him in, despite knowing that he could be seeking vengeance on behalf of his friend. But it wasn't vengeance this man was after. It was my help.

Handing over a letter, he said that the defendant had written it to me. As I went to open it the man said that if I wanted to speak to him further, he had left his phone number with my secretary. Then, as quickly as he had arrived, he was gone.

Fingering the envelope, I worried about what lay inside. I knew that whatever it was, it had the potential to open a huge can of worms. Perhaps it would be best if I didn't open it. What was done was done. Reasoning that this was the best solution, I threw it in the bin.

However, as I tried to get on with my work, curiosity pinged at my conscience. Surely, after everything that had happened, I owed it to the defendant to at least read what he had to say? Picking the envelope out of the bin, I tore it open and began to read it before I had second thoughts. This is what it said:

> Dear Mr. Aris,
> Please know that I hold no grudge against you. I know you were just doing your job as a lawyer, and I know that the woman's father is your friend. But now that the case is finished, I must tell you that I am innocent, yet I am behind bars. I know this is an unusual request, but please help me if you can. I believe you are the only one who can get me out of here. May God forgive you for what you have done to me.

The last sentence of the letter hit me hard. "May God forgive you." Would God forgive me? Could I forgive myself if I didn't do something?

I spent the rest of the day in a quandary debating within myself about what to do. I had many lawyers working with me at that time, but for now I kept my thoughts to myself. I did not yet want to admit that I had had such a serious lapse in judgment. Finally, at the end of the day, when most of my staff had gone home, I sent for one of my lawyers who I knew would give me excellent counsel, Sadiq al-Khudary, who before working for me had been one of the best judges in Baghdad.

Asking him to join me in my office I proceeded to tell him everything, from the judge's first visit to the letter I had received that very afternoon. Taking all of this in, Sadiq was very quiet.

"Do you want to do something for him?" he finally asked.

"I think so," I answered. "I was thinking of sending him some money to help make things easier for him in prison."

"I don't mean sending him money," Sadiq said, shutting the door to ensure we could not be heard. "I mean, do you want to try to get him out of jail?"

In my gut that was exactly what I wanted to do, but how could I do it without disgracing my friend? Thankfully, Sadiq had the answer.

"Why don't you draft a letter to Saddam?" he said. "Explain the circumstances of the case and have the defendant sign it himself. Saddam will not know it is from you, and the defendant will have had you draft his defense for him. Plus the judge will also not know you have intervened in any way, so he saves face!"

Yes! That was the answer. I could do my bit for the defendant, which would clear my conscience, without disgracing my friend.

With that in mind I immediately drafted an eight-line letter to Saddam. Once it was finished I sent for the Sudanese man who had delivered the defendant's letter to me. I told him to take my letter to the defendant, have him sign it, and then return it.

Not wanting to have any link to this whatsoever, I then arranged for a friend of mine who had links to the palace to ensure that the letter was delivered to Saddam. I knew this could be a long process, so while we waited for any sort of response, I sent the defendant money every few weeks to help make prison life as bearable as possible for him.

Three months passed, and there was no further news. My efforts looked to have failed. I knew I had tried to do something, but that was still no consolation. I had put an innocent man behind bars. I just hoped God would forgive me, even though I struggled to forgive myself.

But just as I had given up hope, my secretary came into my office one afternoon and told me there was a group of Sudanese men outside who wanted to see me. "One of the men is disabled," she said. "He's walking on his knees."

"Is the man who brought me the letter with them?" I asked, to which she nodded. "Please send them in then."

Moments later the door opened. Just as my secretary had described, a man entered walking on his knees. When he looked up, I couldn't believe my eyes. It was the defendant! Pulling him up off the floor, I took him in my arms. Tears were rolling down his cheeks, and I have to admit that I was also very emotional.

"When did you get out?" I asked.

"This morning! Thanks to your letter, Saddam has pardoned me. I am a free man. Thank you. Thank you. I am forever grateful to you."

"What will you do now?" I asked, thrilled at the news.

"I will return to Sudan. There is nothing but bad memories for me here."

Nodding my head, I went to my safe, turned the combination, opened it, and took out a wad of cash. Putting it in an envelope, I then gave it to the man.

"What is this?" he said, taken aback.

"Compensation. For the time you had to wrongly spend in jail. I am sorry, but I hope this will give you a chance at a better life back home."

"You don't have to do this," he stammered, clearly moved, holding the envelope carefully. "You were just doing your job. You have done more for me than anyone else has."

Placing my hand on the envelope, I gently pushed it back toward him. "Please, it will help me clear my conscience."

The man embraced me, unable to say anymore, but no words were needed. The tears in both our eyes said all that needed to be said between us. It was a very sincere moment. As I watched the man leave my office and set off for a new life, I thought of an old Arabic proverb that seemed especially true in this case: "Life is nothing but a debt and its repayment." And a case I dealt with soon after emphatically proved that if you don't repay a debt, then justice will inevitably be waiting.

13.

THE ROAD TO JUSTICE

"I'm for truth, no matter who tells it. I'm for justice, no matter who it's for or against."

—Malcolm X

DOCTOR?"

"What is it?" I hesitantly answered, still getting used to the title, the result of me passing my doctorate exams in Lebanon earlier that year, where I was one of only two from a class of 152 students to do so.

"I have a very serious bribery case that I need your help with."

The person asking for my help was my good friend Suran, who I had met during my doctorate studies in Lebanon, where we had spent more hours together in the casino than in the lecture hall. Regrettably, unlike me, he did not pass the exams. Despite this, he was still a very capable lawyer who was now back working in Baghdad. So when he came to my office to discuss a case, I was more than willing to help him out in any way I could.

"Do you have the file of the case with you?" I asked, which led to Suran placing it on my desk. As I picked it up and flicked through the pages, Suran waited patiently to hear my thoughts.

My immediate thought on perusing the file was that the case was doomed to fail. Suran had been asked to defend a man who had already confessed to trying to bribe an officer at the tax office in order to reduce his tax liability. Worse still, the officer was high up in the Ba'ath Party.

In other words, if a man such as that accused someone of a crime, then that person needed to have a very good defense if he was going to avoid serious incriminations.

And that wasn't all. The case was also going to be heard at the court of revolutions in front of a judge who was not only a very high-ranking member of the Ba'ath Party himself, but also renowned for dealing with cases very harshly. So great was his reputation that most lawyers refused to plead cases before him, no matter the financial inducement to do so, for fear of not just losing the case but also being on the wrong end of his wrath.

Knowing all that, when Suran asked me what I thought, I placed the file on my desk without ever intending to pick it back up again and said, "This is a waste of time. The defendant has no chance."

"I knew you would say that," Suran smiled before placing a witness statement in front of me. "But I have spoken to the defendant's wife."

Intrigued, I picked up the witness statement and scanned over it, not wanting to waste any more time than was necessary on a case that I felt had already been decided. But as I read the statement, I started to focus on every word. Far from being a hopeless case, I soon realized that if I didn't act quickly, then a gross miscarriage of justice might be about to occur.

"So? What do you think now?" Suran asked, as I raised my eyebrows at what I had just read.

"I think we need to go to the tax officer's street and see if there is any truth to the wife's story," I replied.

And that is exactly what we did. Within half an hour Suran and I were parked outside the tax officer's house, where we saw him sitting on his front porch with two women, enjoying a drink. With him not realizing who we were, we now had to focus on the most important thing of all: had the defendant's wife been telling the truth?

As Suran discreetly made some door-to-door inquiries, I took a penknife from my pocket and knelt down onto the ground. Remembering the wife's statement, I cut into the road and prised out a chunk. While I carefully placed the chunk into a box Suran ran over to me.

"The wife's story is true," he said, panting and wheezing through his excitement. "The neighbors have confirmed it."

Although we now had a strong defense, I was still worried about the case. Suran had asked me to act in court, and I knew I was going to have to call a high-ranking Ba'ath Party member a liar and a crook in front of a judge who normally would not stand for such remarks. It was a big risk for very little reward, as Suran had already told me that the defendant couldn't afford to pay our fees in full. But how could I turn away when it was clear to me that a Ba'ath Party member was abusing his position against a normal, law-abiding member of society?

On the day of the trial I knew I had to tread very carefully. Any remark or accusation out of line could see me in serious trouble. This was a case for tact, patience, and my extensive experience. However, all my planning went out the window when I was confronted by circumstances that left my blood boiling.

After the prosecution had examined the tax officer the judge asked "Does the defense have anything to add?"

"I would like to cross examine the tax officer if I may, your honor?" In the circumstances this was a perfectly reasonable request, but to my horror the judge said that this would not be allowed. I was stunned. 'But your honor,' I began, trying to argue, "This is the crux of our..."

"You may not cross-examine the tax officer. I have told you this," the judge shouted. "Now, do you have anything else?" Shocked at this turn of events, and unable to reason with the judge, I did the unthinkable, I turned my back on him. "Dr. Aris, is there anything else you want me to consider before I make my decision?" the judge bellowed again.

"No, your Honor. No further questions," Suran answered in a panic, hoping this would placate the judge, who was now boring a hole into the back of my head with his raging eyes.

"Dr. Aris," the judge boomed, not satisfied with Suran's response, "I am talking directly to you. It is not the proper behavior of a lawyer to turn his back when the judge is speaking to him. Do you have any further comments on what the witness has just said?"

Turning around I took a moment to glare angrily at the judge. I tried to compose myself, but in the mood I was in I knew that would be impossible. "If I was present in this court, I would answer you," I replied.

"Is this a riddle?" the judge replied, confused by what I was saying.

"No," I said. "This is no riddle. As you won't allow me to legitimately produce evidence that shows that what the tax officer has just told the court is a lie, then I may as well not be present in this courtroom. I resign from the case."

I could see that this remark made my client panic. He knew that without me representing him, he faced life in prison. However, I had no real intention of walking away. I just needed to do something to highlight that this was a gross miscarriage of justice. Yes, it was a maneuver that could have gotten me into serious trouble, but by this stage I was beyond caring.

Following my comment the courtroom went quiet. Even Suran, who was usually chattering away by my side, looked at me as if I had lost my mind. For a moment the judge and I just stared at each other, daring to see who would break first.

"Very well," the judge finally said. "I will recall the witness for questioning. However, if you are unable to prove he is lying, I will refer you to the Disciplinary Committee at the Bar of Lawyers where I will push for the harshest punishment. Is that understood?"

"It is, your Honor," I answered, praying I could now lay bare the true facts of the matter.

The first time the tax officer had taken the stand, he had been full of himself. In his head he thought this case was already decided. Now he looked nervous. His walk was slower. His shoulders were hunched. His eyes flicked this way and that. He knew that if I did my job properly, he was facing the abyss.

Taking the stand he swore on the Qur'an as well as on the Ba'ath Party that he would tell the court the truth. Now was my chance to prove that so far he had not said a word of it. To the contrary, he was a liar of the worst kind, the kind who abuses his position to try to benefit economically at the expense of an innocent man.

"Sir," I began, "has your street recently been covered in a layer of sub-base?" I knew this question would baffle the court, but it went straight to the root of the case.

"No," he replied.

"Sir, I'll ask you again: has your street recently been covered in a layer of sub-base?"

"No."

"You are lying to the court," I shouted, struggling to contain my anger.

Looking up at the judge, the officer pleaded, "I am a much respected Ba'ath Party member. Please defend me from an attack from this cheap lawyer."

Just as the judge was about to speak, I took a step forward. "The cheap person is the one who commits a criminal act and then frames someone else."

Producing a Perspex box, I pulled out the black chunk of sub-base I had removed from the road during my visit to his street.

"I personally visited your street," I continued, to the tax officer's obvious dismay, "and I removed this piece of sub-base from the road with my bare hands. I even saw you sitting outside your house as I did so."

"This has nothing to do with the case," the tax officer cried. And to most people in the courtroom, that seemed true, but I knew differently.

"Dr. Aris," the judge suddenly intervened, "the witness is correct. I fail to see what the witness's road being covered in sub-base has to do with the current case."

"Your Honor, before I reveal why this is so vital a fact, I must first establish that the witness's road has recently been covered in sub-base. If the court does not accept the evidence I have now, then I would invite you to travel to the witness's road so that you can see for yourself."

Not wanting to undertake any such excursion, the judge turned back to the witness. "Answer the lawyer, is your road newly covered in sub-base or not?"

The officer clearly didn't want to answer the question. He knew where this was going. But he was trapped. And as soon as he admitted that his road was covered in sub-base, then I could reel him in.

"Yes," he finally murmured, wincing as he did so. "It is covered in sub-base."

Pulling some papers from my bag, I approached the judge and handed them to him.

"Now that the witness has admitted that his road is covered in sub-base, I respectfully invite the court to please consider the following witness statements my colleague took from his neighbors when we both visited his street."

Taking the bundle of statements from my hand, the judge started to read through them.

"As you will see, your Honor," I continued, "the witness's neighbors have all stated that the defendant in this case laid the sub-base in their street. All the witnesses can be called for direct questioning if you feel that is necessary."

The tax officer was now quiet. He had nowhere to go. Once this piece of evidence was accepted, then all that was left was for me to deliver the final crushing blow.

Glaring at the tax officer, the judge asked, "Will it be necessary for me to call your neighbors to attend this court, or can you verify that the defendant was responsible for laying the sub-base on your street?"

"He laid it," the tax officer softly answered, after taking an age to respond, all the confidence in his voice and body long gone.

Now was my final shot, my chance to wrap everything up. "Thank you, your Honor. Now that we have established that the sub-base was laid by the defendant, I can tell the court the true story of what actually took place here."

For the next few minutes I told the court how the defendant had previously visited the tax office to finalize his tax return. While he was there, he met the tax officer, who, knowing that the defendant was a contractor, asked if he would be able to lay sub-base on his street if they could agree a price, as at this moment in time the street merely consisted of mud. After this request, the defendant stated that he could do the work for 2,000 dinars, to which the tax officer replied that he would first need to collect the money from his neighbors before the work could begin.

A few days later the tax officer called the defendant and informed him that he had managed to collect 1,500 dinars from his neighbors and asked if that would be sufficient. The defendant subsequently agreed and immediately commenced work.

With the sub-base laid the defendant visited the tax officer in order to pick up payment for the work. When he entered the office, the tax officer produced an envelope containing the money and placed it on the table in front of him, telling the defendant it was for him. However, as soon as the defendant picked up the envelope, the tax officer called security. Upon being asked by the security guard if the money in the envelope was his, the defendant confirmed that it was, still not sure what was happening. As soon as the defendant said this, he was arrested and taken for questioning. Only then did it become apparent that he was being accused of trying to bribe a public official.

It seemed that the tax officer's plan had worked. His road was now covered in sub-base, he had pocketed his neighbors' money, and the only person who knew all of this was the defendant, who now faced life in jail after his innocent confession.

As I informed the court of this, there was understandably anger and shock. Despite this, the tax officer continued to try and abuse his position. "I am a high-ranking Ba'ath Party member," he said. "Do you believe the words of this cheap lawyer or of a man who stands side by side with you in the party?"

"*Silence!*" the judge shouted at the top of his voice. Addressing the officer of the court, he then said, "Place the witness in detention so that I can refer him for a criminal investigation."

Grabbing the tax officer by the arm, the officer forcibly dragged him away, much to the delight of the defendant, who stared at me, smiling in disbelief. I nodded my head at him. My job was almost complete.

"Your Honor," I said, trying to get the judge's attention while the court was still in uproar. "Now that you have heard the true story behind what occurred here, I would ask that the charges against the defendant be dropped."

At this request I half expected the prosecutor to jump in, but even he knew the game was up. Indeed, his own sense of justice actually made him support my request. All that was left for us in this case were the judge's final words, which soon came: "Case dismissed." We had done it!

My good friend Suran, who had seen the need for justice in this case before even I had, put his arm around my shoulder and smiled. Justice always felt good, but this time it felt even better because Suran had played such a vital role in it with me.

However, my time at the court of revolution was not yet over. Soon I would return for the most important case of my life, a case I dared not lose, for if I did it would destroy the life of my greatest friend.

14.

THE BRIBE

"True freedom requires the rule of law and justice, and a judicial system in which the rights of some are not secured by the denial of rights to others."

—Jonathan Sacks

SINCE MY DAYS IN LAW school I had continued to forge a very close friendship with Khalid, the fellow student who had diligently provided me with all of his notes for the lectures I was unable to attend. After graduation I tried to repay the favor when I hired Khalid to work in my law firm and also manage my cigarette paper factory, which he did for nine years. Away from work we were also very close, especially when my father died, and Khalid did everything he could to lift my spirits, including writing a very touching poem in my father's honor.

However, after nine years of working in my factory, Khalid had decided that it was time for a new challenge. As such, he took up a very well-paid legal advisory role with a Japanese company which was based in Baghdad. I was very sorry to see him go yet still wished him all the best.

Despite Khalid not being present at my factory, we continued to socialize regularly. Indeed, we particularly enjoyed meeting at the Maroosh restaurant that overlooked the Tigres River, where we would relish long lunches and talk fondly of the past as well as our plans for the future. Usually these lunches were lighthearted affairs, and we would both spend the whole time laughing and joking. But when we again met at the restaurant for our weekly catch up I could tell something was troubling him.

"What is it, Khalid?" I asked as he chewed on a toothpick. "You are not yourself today."

"I have a problem and need your advice," he replied hesitantly.

"Anything you need, just tell me."

"I need your help to bribe the Registrar of Companies."

Hearing those words, I almost choked on the bread I was eating. Such a statement was most unlike Khalid. He was one of the most honest, courteous men I have ever known. I knew that for him to even contemplate it he must be in deep trouble.

"Why do you need to do such a thing?" I inquired.

He proceeded to explain, under his breath, that after some sort of dispute, the Registrar had suspended the Japanese company he was working for from operating in Iraq. This was, of course, disastrous. After seeking out legal advice, Khalid had come to the conclusion that the only option now available to the company was to try to bribe the Registrar, a man who was known to be open to such incentives.

"Sabah," Khalid said, looking into my eyes, "will you help me do this?"

While Khalid was my greatest friend, this was not a path I wanted to take. "Khalid," I responded, speaking slowly and deliberately so he could not mistake my words, "you came to me for advice, so I am going to give it to you. Do not go through with this under any circumstances. If you are caught, you are looking at doing serious jail time, and your career will be over. It is not worth it."

Khalid slowly nodded his head before slumping back in his chair, thinking over what I had said. I hoped that my words had pulled him back from the brink. He still remained quiet during the remainder of our lunch, no doubt going over the turmoil in his head, but I really thought he had decided not to go through with it.

However, a few weeks later Khalid's brother contacted me with terrible news.

"Sabah," he cried, "it's Khalid. He has been arrested by the Security Police!"

My heart sunk. I instantly knew that despite my warning Khalid had gone ahead with the bribe. It soon transpired that Khalid and the manager of the Japanese company had traveled to Geneva along with the Registrar of Companies, so that they could pay him the bribe from a secret bank account. The Registrar had apparently kept the authorities updated on these developments, and upon landing back in Baghdad, Khalid and the manager were arrested.

On hearing this news, I immediately set into action and did everything I could to get Khalid released on bail, but it was no use. Bribing a public official was an extremely serious offense, and Khalid had been caught red-handed. Getting him off on such a crime was going to be extremely tough, especially in the court of revolution. Things were made tougher when I wasn't allowed to see Khalid until the day of the trial itself. I now had no real way of preparing a defense.

However, one night, during my weekly poker game with some of the most prominent lawyers and judges in Baghdad, I found that one of my good friends, Jar Allah al Alaf, who we called Abu Amar, would be the judge in Khalid's case. This was obviously very good news.

The next day, when I mentioned to my mother that Abu Amar would be judging Khalid's case, she begged to be allowed to be present at our next poker game, which would be at my house. She loved Khalid and had never forgotten his support after my father had died.

On the night of our next poker game, my mother came to my house and cooked us all a big meal. Later, with the cards and the eating at an end, she asked if she could see Abu Amar in my office. I have to admit, I was a bit on edge. I had asked my mother not to put Abu Amar under any undue pressure, as not only would it be wrong ethically but also it could land her in serious trouble.

But despite my warning, as soon as Abu Amar entered the room, my mother blurted out, "Please, Abu Amar, I know you are judging the trial of our good family friend Khalid. Please look on him with kind eyes."

Abu Amar took my mother's hand in his and said, "I respect you like my own mother. I will do what I can."

It was not the response I had been expecting, but it was certainly one that pleased my mother. It also made me think that perhaps Khalid wouldn't receive the maximum possible sentence, which was certainly a high probability owing to the gravity of his offense.

Soon the day of the trial was upon us and I could finally meet Khalid. He was always a happy-go-lucky character who made the best of a bad situation, but I was shocked by the figure who greeted me. After three months in detention, he was unrecognizable. He had lost so much weight that his cheekbones seemed in danger of piercing his parchment-like skin, and the skin around his eyes was black.

"I'm sorry, Sabah," he mumbled, struggling to get the words out. "I should have listened to you."

"Do not worry about that now," I replied. "We need to put all of our focus on your case."

"Can you get me off?" he pleaded, staring at me desperately.

"I am not sure," I said truthfully, knowing that Khalid could see right through me if I tried to sugar coat his situation. "But I promise I will defend this case like no case before."

Khalid smiled. "Thank you, Sabah. With you representing me, I know I am in the best possible hands."

However, as we were about to enter the court, something extraordinary caught my attention. Scanning the witness list I saw that the Registrar had not been called to give evidence. I thought that there must have been some mistake. He was obviously the most crucial witness, and someone I had wanted to question. I knew that he had quite a reputation in Baghdad for taking bribes, and my research had found that more often than not it was he who actually initiated the idea. One of the cornerstones of my defense was going to be that this was a case of entrapment. However, if I could not cross-examine the Registrar, then this was going to be almost impossible to prove.

Marching into the court, I intended to put this oversight right as swiftly as possible. Approaching the bench, I saw Abu Amar, the president of the court, with two judges flanking him on either side. I was happy to see that one of the judges was a general in the army who I also knew very well. I nodded my head at the general, and Abu Amar in acknowledgment, but while the general nodded back, Abu Amar completely ignored me. I knew that in court we had to separate our friendship from our professional duties, yet in all the previous cases where we had met, we had still exchanged this polite courtesy. In my stomach I felt something was wrong.

Shortly afterward, with the prosecutor standing to commence his case, I quickly spoke up. "Your Honor," I said, addressing Abu Amar, "it has come to my attention that the Registrar has not been notified that he should be in attendance. I would therefore respectfully ask that we postpone the case so that the only witness we have in this matter can accordingly be present."

To my great surprise, Abu Amar shot me down. "Your remark is out of order," he bellowed. "Take your seat and we shall proceed."

I was completely stunned. This was not a response I would have expected from any judge, let alone someone who was my friend. I sat down in turmoil, as Khalid looked on at me, also in astonishment. Without the Registrar being present for questioning, I knew our case had just been dealt a fatal blow.

As the prosecutor began to outline the case against Khalid, I quickly got my head back together and again made an objection, clinging on to all we had left.

"Your Honor, the alleged crime in this case took place in Switzerland, therefore . . . "

"*Sit down, Dr. Aris, or I will have you arrested!*" Abu Amar suddenly screamed, cutting me short.

Again, I took my seat, confused by Abu Amar's attitude toward me, my head now awash with doubt. My objection had been a perfectly reasonable one, yet I had been threatened with arrest. What was going on?

When the prosecutor finished his case against Khalid, I asked for a fifteen-minute break so that I could regroup with two fellow lawyers who formed part of my defense team. To my surprise, Abu Amar granted me this small request.

Reconvening outside, I was in a terrible mood. I so desperately wanted to do all that I could to help Khalid, but I felt the court was acting in a terribly unjust way, particularly as my requests were perfectly legal, and understandable.

"What can we do?" I asked one of the lawyers, who was a former officer in the army. "It is clear the judge is against us."

"There is little you can do," he replied. "The normal procedures of the court are being violated, but this is the court of revolution. The judge can do as he wishes."

This was true. The court of revolution was not required to apply the well-established rules and regulations of the Iraqi courts. Yet most judges chose to apply them anyway to ensure that justice would be done.

"I'm going to resign from the case," I said in a fit of pique, knowing that this was a hollow threat, as Khalid would never understand why I had left him during the hour of his greatest need.

As the lawyers calmed me down, I suddenly realized what I needed to do. "Someone get me a pad of paper and a pen," I asked, with both quickly thrust into my hand. I then wrote a withering assessment of the procedures of the court, as well as the conduct of Abu Amar, outlining in particular how he had unreasonably denied a request to have the main witness provided for cross-examination. I pulled no punches and ended by stating that the court, and its subsequent judgment in this matter, violated the constitutional laws of the country.

When I had finished writing I handed the memorandum to my fellow lawyers to sign, but they looked at me as if I was mad. "Are you crazy?" one of them cried. "We cannot sign this. We will all be thrown in jail!"

"Very well," I replied, snatching back the paper. "I will sign it alone."

"Please, Sabah," they pleaded. "You are angry and not thinking straight. Please don't do this!"

Nevertheless, despite their warnings, I signed the memorandum and went to present it to the officer of the court, who I knew from previous cases. "Please pass this on to the judges," I said, handing over the memorandum. The officer quickly glanced at it before stopping.

"Please, Dr. Aris," he said, trying to hand the memorandum back to me, "you will get in real trouble with this."

"I don't care," I answered, pushing the paper back into his hands. "Please take it to Abu Amar immediately."

After staring at me as if I had lost my mind, the officer turned away and did exactly as I had asked. Then, just a few moments later, we were all called back inside to recommence the case.

Reentering the courtroom I braced myself for a ferocious argument with Abu Amar, but nothing happened. It was very strange. I wondered if the officer had decided not to hand him the memorandum after all.

In any event, with the trial recommencing I had to focus on matters at hand, especially with Khalid on the stand being examined by the prosecutor. As the prosecutor ripped into Khalid, my friend admitted paying the bribe, although only after the Registrar had induced him to do so.

Frustrated, I clawed inside my brain for something to cling onto, but no magic solution presented itself. Without the Registrar being available for questioning, and with Khalid admitting to paying the bribe, there was nothing I could say or do except plead for mercy. Unsurprisingly, long before Abu Amar read his judgment, I knew that we would lose the case.

When the judgment came I was prepared for the worst, but the severity of the sentence shocked me, as Abu Amar condemned my great friend Khalid to ten years of hard labor, double what had been expected. The sentence was devastating. Throughout my career I had successfully represented clients I barely knew, but now, when my friend was relying on me, I had failed.

Before I left the court I asked if I could spend a few moments with Khalid before he was taken away. When we saw each other we both broke down. Taking him in my arms I wept, "I am sorry I could not help you."

He broke away from my embrace. "You told me not to do it," he stuttered through his tears. "I have no one to blame but myself."

With that the guard approached Khalid and took him away. All I could do was look on through my tears as my great friend disappeared from sight to begin a ten-year prison sentence.

Things became harder that evening when I went to visit my mother, who was very eager to hear the news. As I had always been successful in court, and after her conversation with Abu Amar, my mother had fully expected Khalid to be coming home with me. Yet when I arrived alone, she immediately knew that I had failed.

"Ten years," I muttered. "He must do ten years."

My mother was absolutely devastated.

There was also to be no respite from Abu Amar, as just three days later it was time for our regular poker game, which this time would be hosted by a good friend of mine, Abu Abdullah, who owned one of the biggest building contractors in Iraq. Abu Amar did not attend every week, and therefore I prayed that he would not be present. While

I hoped to get an explanation from him at some point, I knew that the wound was still too raw to meet with him now.

However, when I entered the house and asked Abu Abdullah if Abu Amar was present, my heart sank when he replied, "Yes. He is here."

"Then I won't play tonight," I answered, as politely as possible, turning back toward the door.

"Wait," Abu Abdullah shouted, grabbing my hand. "You are not in his house; you are in mine. Please do not dishonor me by leaving now." As much as I didn't want to see Abu Amar, I also didn't want to upset Abu Abdullah, who was always an excellent host.

Reluctantly, I followed Abu Abdullah into the room where everyone was gathered and made a point of shaking everyone's hand apart from Abu Amar's. When the cards were dealt Abu Amar suddenly stood.

"Please, my friends," he announced, "allow me to say a few words." I knew he may try to embarrass me in front of everyone, so I was half-expecting what was to come.

"Sabah did not shake my hand because we had a professional difference of opinion," he began. "He attended my court representing a friend of his who was caught red-handed giving a bribe. I had no choice but to sentence the man to ten years, but Sabah thought I should have been lenient because he was his friend. He also submitted a memorandum savaging my court and my procedures! He should get down on his knees and thank God I did not pass it to the Security Police, as otherwise he would now be serving a longer sentence than his friend."

As Abu Amar took his seat, all eyes in the room switched to me. "What you have said is partially correct," I said, also now standing. "I did present the court with a very critical memorandum, but I was, and still am, ready to stand by it and accept any consequences, as what I stated was a fact. Your court was unjust and contrary to the rules of the land. Khalid may have committed a crime, but you committed a violation of justice by overseeing an unfair trial. I did not expect you to be lenient to Khalid because he was my friend. I expected you to give him a fair trial because you are a judge!"

The room was silent. No one had expected such a scene, particularly as before this Abu Amar and I had always been close. The atmosphere was now uneasy, as no one knew what to do.

I broke the silence by saying, "Anyway, we are here to play poker, so let's play!"

Everyone was grateful to return their attention to the cards and avoid more ackowledgment of the fact that Abu Amar and I were on very bad terms.

During the break, Abu Abdullah tried to get Abu Amar and me to make up. Abu Amar eventually offered his hand toward me and said, "I have nothing against you, Sabah. We are friends, but in court we are judge and lawyer."

While I did not want to shake hands with him, I knew that there would be nothing gained from continuing this feud. As such I shook his hand, but from that moment onward our friendship was completely destroyed.

As the years passed, Khalid served his sentence, and I tried to visit him as often as possible, but every trip broke me. He looked a shadow of himself and was extremely remorseful. Sadly, even though he only served six of the ten years, he died of a heart attack not long after his release. This matter had completely destroyed his life. Khalid was a generous, kind, and clever man who never got the recognition his talents deserved, particularly in poetry, where he excelled. He really was the best of friends, and I took his passing very hard.

A few years after Khalid's death, Abu Amar left the court of revolution. Our paths had crossed many times in the intervening years, but things were never the same again. However, after he had stepped down as a judge, I was surprised to find him visiting me one day at my office. With all boldness he said that he was now ready to work as a lawyer and would be happy to work for me.

"I am sorry, Abu Amar," I said, remembering how poorly he had treated Khalid as well as his views on procuring justice, "but we have no room for any more lawyers." He understood then that he was not welcome.

I was not the only lawyer Abu Amar had upset during his tenure as a judge. Many others also had violent disagreements with him, with one lawyer even swearing at him during a case. Indeed, years later, when Abu Amar passed away in the city of Mosul, I asked my friend and colleague Fawsi to attend the funeral on the firm's behalf, as despite our differences I still thought it was the right thing to do. However, I will never forget Fawsi's response: "Sabah, if you order me to go to the funeral of a dog I will go, but I will not go to the funeral of Abu Amar."

In this case everyone concerned lost something. I lost my great friend. Khalid lost his freedom, his reputation, and eventually his life. And Abu Amar lost his sense of justice. It was a case that sent me into a dark depression, as I questioned if life as a lawyer was really for me. Thankfully, someone soon pulled me back from the brink.

15.

ALL IS FAIR IN LOVE AND WAR

"The course of true love never did run smooth."
—William Shakespeare

WHEN ARE YOU GOING TO find a nice girl and settle down, Sabah?" It seemed that every time I saw my mother, this was the first question she asked. She was desperate for me to get married and have children. Yet at the time I was far too busy running my law firm and looking after my other business interests to even think of such matters. And I was having a lot of fun too. As a regular on the Baghdad social scene, I spent a lot of time in the casino and in the best restaurants and clubs. Getting married and raising a family were things I wanted to do, but just not right now. Besides, love looked to be nothing but hard work.

For example, I remember one day a very distressed woman in her mid-thirties came to see me at my office. She looked as if she hadn't slept in a month. She had bags under her eyes. Her skin was gray. Her hair was unkempt. Something was obviously seriously wrong. When she told me that she wanted to divorce her husband, I assumed it was for one of three reasons: the man had beaten her, he had been having an affair, or he was not providing for the family financially. In the matrimonial cases I had worked on from time to time, these complaints were always the most common grounds for divorce.

However, I was surprised when she said that her husband was guilty of a far more serious crime.

"What is it?" I asked, wracking my brain to think of what it could possibly be.

Lowering her voice, she answered, "My husband is a sex maniac."

At this I almost laughed. It was hardly on a par with being beaten or cheated on.

Yet despite my reservations she soon explained why this was so terrible. Instead of having an ordinary sexual appetite, her husband seemed possessed. She claimed that he demanded sex up to ten times a day and still wasn't satisfied. It had got to the point where he wanted to have sex every single second they were alone. Just by looking at her it was clear she was exhausted. Her husband had taken her to her breaking point.

But was a husband's addiction to sex with his wife really grounds for a divorce? I wasn't so sure. Additionally, if I were to raise such a case in the courts I knew I would be laughed out of the courtroom. The other lawyers and judges would have a field day.

"If your husband calmed down, would you still want to divorce him?" I asked, hoping to try to find a middle ground and save a marriage in the process.

"My husband is a good man," the woman reluctantly admitted. "But I have tried everything. He just won't stop. It's an illness."

It was certainly a unique predicament, one that I had not encountered before or since. And there didn't really seem to be any way that I could help in a legal sense. Then an idea struck me. I called my secretary and asked her to retrieve the number of an herbal chemist I had represented some years earlier. With the number in my hand I then called the chemist and explained the situation to him.

"Send her to me," he said. "I think I may be able to help."

Handing the chemist's address to the woman I said that if she really wanted to give her marriage one last try, then she should see this man. And that was that. Eager to give it a go, the woman left my office and set off to see the chemist. I hoped he would be able to help, as she was clearly desperate.

A few months passed, and the woman did not return, so I soon forgot all about her visit. Then one day my secretary sent in a man and a woman who had made an appointment to see me. My mouth dropped open when I realized that this was the woman who had come to see me about her husband's sex addiction. And now she was in my office, with her husband alongside her.

Not quite sure what was going on, I regained my composure and pretended that I had never met her before, and she did likewise. As her husband spoke I started to relax a bit. It turned out they hadn't come to see me about his sex addiction but just wanted some legal advice on a property they wanted to buy.

After half an hour of discussing this property, the man asked if he could use the restroom. As soon as he left the room, the woman grabbed my hand.

"Thank you," she said. "You have saved my marriage."

I laughed and asked what had happened.

Pulling a small bag that looked to contain a mixture of herbs from her pocket, she smiled. "Your friend the chemist gave me this. I put it in my husband's food every day, and it kills his excess need for sex."

While I was glad to have helped save her marriage, and they both seemed very happy, cases such as this certainly didn't provide me with a good inducement to settle down. Indeed, even the simple act of falling in love looked to be nothing but trouble.

I had once dealt with a case where a young man was so infatuated with a woman that he would do anything she asked of him. Despite the fact that he was doing very well studying for a degree in engineering, the woman demanded that he drop out and apply to become a police officer. For months the woman harangued her boyfriend and even threatened to end their relationship if he did not follow her wishes.

So, faced with this ultimatum, the love-struck man did the next best thing to actually becoming a police officer: he pretended to be one. Telling the woman that he had been accepted in the police force, he then went to the market and bought a police uniform, which he wore when he was with her. The woman was so pleased that she took her boyfriend to meet all of her family and friends so that she could show him off which only exacerbated the man's lie.

Upon meeting the woman's father he was asked if he would show him his police ID. In a panic, the young man explained that he had forgotten to bring it, but the woman soon demanded to see it as well. Faced with the exposure of his lie, the man went another step further and forged a police ID, including the signature of the head of the Iraqi police.

Completely infatuated with this woman, the man could not face the prospect of losing her, so he would set off at night pretending he was on police duty, in full uniform and carrying his forged ID. However, one night a real police officer thought the man looked suspicious and arrested him. Now he was facing not only his lie being exposed to the woman he loved but also life in prison.

When it came to defending him, I knew that normal legal arguments would not suffice. But I had a suspicion that both the judge and the chief of police may be susceptible to the defense I planned to submit, that love had made my client insane! Indeed, I knew that both the chief of police and the judge had in the past endured very difficult relationships with their wives and that they may have some sympathy for this approach.

Thankfully, as there were no real victims in this case and the court could clearly see that my client meant no harm, he was sentenced to time already served. His girlfriend even agreed to marry him, despite his lie, as she could see the lengths he had gone to to satisfy her.

Again, I was happy to have won the case, but after observing at close hand the insanity that love had inspired and seeing the pain it had caused very well-regarded men such as the judge and the chief of police, I hardly thought that engaging in a serious love affair would improve my life. Indeed, I had already witnessed how a love affair could bring down a respected man.

The president of the supreme criminal court in Baghdad was a very well-regarded judge. He was well informed, articulate, and able to manage the courtroom like no other. However, there was one weakness in his armor: he was an incorrigible womanizer. If there was an attractive woman around, he just couldn't help himself, despite the fact that he was married. This behavior eventually destroyed his career and his life.

Dealing with a case where he was set to sentence a defendant to a long term in prison, he was visited in his office by the defendant's attractive girlfriend. The judge was, of course, always open to the visit of a pretty woman, even if the visit was most irregular under the circumstances. Well aware of this, the girlfriend put on all her charm, and pulled out every trick in the book to see if she could persuade the judge to let her boyfriend off. However, the judge wanted more than charm. Knowing he was in a position of power, he told the woman that if she really wanted to "discuss" the case, then she should visit him at his farm that weekend.

While the girlfriend was willing to charm the judge into being lenient toward her boyfriend, this was a different matter altogether. Confused by this turn of events she eventually decided to inform the Security Police of what had transpired. They offered her a deal. If she took a hidden recorder to the meeting at the farm and this led to conclusive evidence of the judge acting improperly, then they would use their influence to have her boyfriend's case dropped.

Subsequently, the woman contacted the judge and arranged to meet him at his farm that weekend. Upon arriving she gave the judge a present—a radio—which he was happy to receive. What he didn't know was that the radio was also a recorder, and the Security Police were listening to his every word, which included him telling the woman that if she had sex with him, he would let her boyfriend go free.

Armed with this evidence, the police stormed the farm and arrested the judge. He had been caught red-handed. Subsequently he was sentenced to fifteen years of hard labor. Not only was his career at an end, but also life for a judge behind bars was unimaginably painful. Nearly every day the prisoners, some of whom the judge himself had sentenced to jail, beat him. Such was the severity of the attacks that one of the judge's legs was left permanently paralyzed.

While this case was ongoing, I had been out of the country on business. Upon my return I was saddened to hear about what had happened to the judge, but I can't say that I was surprised. It seemed that he had always left himself open to something like this. However, did he deserve to be beaten every day by violent criminals? No. In my eyes he had more than suffered for his crime.

Wasting little time, I wrote an eight-line letter to Saddam and had the judge's wife sign it. In the letter I claimed that the judge had fallen prey to a human weakness, as seen in the story of Adam and

Eve. I stated that the bribery charge was unclear and that the life of a previously reliable member of the court had been ruined. It seemed that Saddam, someone who was also said to be a victim of human weakness of this nature, agreed, as within two months the judge was freed and placed on early retirement.

After dealing with so many cases that showed the bad side of love, I was wary of exposing myself to it. I was happy to lead my free life and have relations with the most beautiful women without binding myself to any commitment of marriage. But just as I had settled down into the life of a bachelor, I was struck by love when it was the last thing on my mind.

I had hired a new secretary named Aida, but I soon found myself falling head first for her traditional olive-skinned Iraqi good looks. She was not only beautiful but also kind and had a strong personality, which I admired. I knew that I had met my match.

I pulled out all the stops in courting her. Aida eventually couldn't resist my charm—she is only human after all—and with my mother's happy approval, we were soon married in a lavish ceremony. Shortly afterward she gave birth to my first son, whom we named Tariq, the Muslim name I had acquired when working as a contractor in the Shi'ite city of Karbala. Little more than a year later, Aida bore me a second son, who I named after my beloved father, Edward.

While I had seen the bad side of love so often during my work as a lawyer, my relationship with Aida and the boys reminded me of the greatest love affair I had ever witnessed, that of my mother and father. It is no wonder I held off from love for so long, as I never thought I could ever replicate the immense affection they had for each other. Thankfully, having Aida and my two sons in my life made me remember just how magnificent love can be.

With a wonderful wife and family I was immensely proud of, life had never been better. But just as I started to enjoy family life, I came face to face with love's polar opposite: war.

16.

THE IRANIAN WAR

"Justice must always question itself, just as society can exist only by means of the work it does on itself and on its institutions."

—Michael Foucault

WITHOUT WARNING, ON SEPTEMBER 22, 1980, just as dawn was breaking, Iraqi fighter jets bombed ten Iranian air bases while armed forces crossed into Iran's Kurdistan provinces in the north and south. Tensions with Iran had been at a breaking point for some time, and there had been plenty of war talk filling the shisha cafes of Baghdad, but I never thought it would come to this.

The seeds of this war had first been sown when the British had controlled Iraq after the First World War. During this time the British government had demarcated the borders of the country, and while it granted Kuwait its independence, the government decided, in its wisdom, that Kurdistan should remain a part of Iraq. This simple act set in motion a conflict that raged for decades.

During the 1970s the conflict became particularly brutal, especially when the Iranian army backed the Kurds in their quest for independence. This intensified matters to a whole new level. Thousands of Iraqi soldiers were killed, and slowly but surely the cost of the conflict began to have an adverse effect on the economy. There was little doubt that the matter needed to be swiftly addressed.

In early 1975, Saddam and the Shah of Iran met in order to try to hash out a peaceful solution, which eventually became known as the Algiers Agreement. In hindsight, Iran got the better end of the deal, as while it agreed to withdraw its support for the Kurds, it also got the Iraqi government to acknowledge its claim to the vital Shatt al-Arab waterway. This was one of the few waterways that both Iraq and Iran could use to transport oil, and therefore it was strategically very important for both countries.

In the short term this agreement was very positive for Iraq, as without the Iranian army's support, the Iraqi forces were soon able to suppress the Kurds. The bloody conflict that had raged for years seemed to finally be at an end. However, it was blindingly obvious to everyone that without the use of the Shatt al-Arab waterway, Iraq would struggle to export oil in the vast quantities that it wished.

For five years the Iraqi government tried in vain to reach a new agreement with the Iranian government over the waterway, but it was to no avail. As a result Iraq remained virtually landlocked. However, when Saddam came into power in the late 1970s, he was presented with a situation that turned this volatile situation on its head.

A revolution in Iran had seen a Shi'ite Muslim regime, led by Ayatollah Khomeini, take power. An Islamic fervor suddenly swirled around the Middle East, as Ayatollah Khomeini urged a Shi'ite uprising in Iraq. Saddam and most of his regime were all Sunni Muslims, but over 60 percent of the population of Iraq were Shi'ites, and they had long campaigned for a bigger slice of power. It was therefore obvious that the Iranian revolution just across the border represented a real threat to Saddam's grip on power.

Although Saddam reached out to the Shi'ite Muslim community, he also brutally disposed of anyone who spoke against him. Thousands of Shi'ites were subsequently arrested or killed while he desperately tried to keep a lid on things.

Complicating matters further was the fact that the new regime in Iran proceeded to ignore the terms of the Algiers Agreement. The most significant breach of the agreement was that the Iranians started to once again back the Kurds in their quest for independence from Iraq. Saddam sensed that a storm was brewing, and he soon realized it could play right into his hands.

With the Iranians in blatant breach of the agreement and with tensions intensifying, Saddam came to the conclusion that a brutal strike on Iran not only would stop any uprising but also could give him control of the Shatt al-Arab waterway once and for all.

Thus, in September 1980, a horrifying eight-year war began that permanently scarred both nations. Over a million lives were lost on both sides as the war descended into trench warfare, the likes of which had not been seen since the First World War. Officers ordered wave upon wave of human bayonet charges that were quickly quelled by machine gun fire. No matter the colossal loss of life, the orders for the charges continued.

However, those of us who lived in Baghdad were all blissfully unaware for quite some time of the carnage. This was of course before the days of the Internet, and therefore the only news we heard was the news that the government wanted us to hear, and the only pictures we were allowed to see of the war were either of dead Iranian soldiers or of Saddam posing triumphantly at the front. As far as we were all concerned, we were comfortably winning the war and Saddam was very much in control.

Although I knew we were at war, it did not initially affect my family or me. Business continued to be good in both the cigarette paper factory and my law firm, and the economy looked strong. Government spending continued to rise on a vast array of projects, food was easily available, and at this point the Iranian fighter jets had been unable to reach Baghdad. As far as I was concerned, the war was going in our favor, and we would largely remain unaffected. Unfortunately, things rapidly took a turn for the worse.

Aida's cousin, Jamal, was in the Commandos, where he saw plenty of hand-to-hand combat as he fought on the front line for over three years. He was a vastly experienced soldier, and while we knew that he was in danger, we were comforted by his intensive military training and the fact that he actually wanted to fight for his country. It was his choice. He believed in the war and what it stood for.

While Jamal fought for his country, his younger brother, Ayad, remained in school. Ayad was determined to make a career for himself in business and, unlike Jamal, he had no intention of fighting on the front line. He was a sensitive and kind soul whose disposition was not suited to a war such as this.

Yet despite Ayad's best intentions, he failed two of his exams and was forced to abandon his studies. This turned out to be disastrous. All of those who were of fighting age and who were not in school were immediately subjected to a compulsory military draft. Against his wishes and to his family's horror, Ayad was sent to the front line.

As I said, Ayad was young and gentle, yet a twist of fate meant that he now had to fight in one of the bloodiest wars in Iraqi history. Aida and her family were beside themselves, but at this time we really weren't aware of the sheer brutality of the fighting. I just prayed that he would be able to keep out of harm's way.

If only that had been the case. . .

Within twenty-nine days of arriving at the front, Ayad was killed in combat. When his body was returned to Baghdad in a black box, it scarcely seemed believable. Aida and her family were inconsolable, as was my elder son, Tariq, who had idolized Ayad and could not comprehend that he was never going to see his uncle again. In the most brutal fashion imaginable, the war with Iran had suddenly smacked us all across the face.

Having lost Ayad, Aida's family now turned their attention to ensuring that they didn't also lose Jamal. But no matter what they tried, there was no way of getting him out of combat. With casualties mounting up to the hundreds of thousands, it seemed inconceivable that a soldier would be able to survive the whole bloody conflict unharmed. Jamal's luck was surely going to run out at one stage.

But just as we were beginning to give up hope, a solution presented itself. As I sat in my office contemplating our options, I was called by a friend who was the head of the army's legal department.

"Can you come and see me right away?" he asked urgently. "I have something I need you to take a look at."

Wasting no time, I set off for the Ministry of Defense where on my arrival my friend took me into his office. Forgoing the formalities he got straight down to it.

"General Adnan Khairallah has asked for your help," he said to my surprise. Instantly I knew that this would not be a trivial matter.

Not only was General Adnan the Minister of Defense but he was also Saddam's cousin. It was well known that the two of them had been brought up together as brothers in Tikrit, and Saddam had even married Adnan's sister, Sajida.

When a person in General Adnan's position asks you to do something for him, you dare not refuse. So what did he want with me?

"Regretfully," my friend said, "the general's bodyguard, Peter, visited a cabaret club recently where he had a bit too much to drink. In the end he became so drunk that he was unable to open a door, so he shot at it with his gun. Unfortunately, a belly dancer was standing behind the door, and she was killed. Now Peter is on trial for murder. General Adnan wants you to defend him."

"Did he ask for me by name?" I inquired, wondering how he could have heard of me.

"No, but he asked me who was the best criminal lawyer I knew of, and I told him it was you," my friend replied.

I was flattered to receive such a compliment, but at the same time it had brought me far closer to the regime than I had wanted to be.

For days I thoroughly prepared for the trial, leaving no stone unturned. I needed to ensure that I did my job to the best of my ability and that I lived up to the reputation I had in court. After all, General Adnan would be watching, and I certainly didn't want to get on his bad side.

One day, as I was immersed in researching the case, I was disturbed by my phone ringing. Upon answering it, and annoyed that my train of thought was disrupted, a deep voice on the other end of the line announced, "This is Adnan."

Aida had a brother named Adnan who would call me from time to time, so naturally I assumed that it was him. "Come on, Adnan," I replied jokingly. "Stop messing around. Why do you sound so serious?"

"This is General Adnan, the Minister of Defense," came the stern reply. I almost dropped the phone.

Struggling to regain my composure, I hurriedly explained that I had thought that it was my brother-in-law, who was also called Adnan. Thankfully, the general found this extremely funny.

"Please think of me as your brother," he said cheerfully.

"Thank you, general," I replied, ensuring that I sounded suitably humble.

The general asked if I could send him a copy of the case file before the trial commenced. I knew that under normal circumstances this would not be possible, as the court would not release it. Nevertheless I said that I would see what I could do. As I predicted, the court initially refused to provide me with a copy, but when I told them whom it was for, they swiftly changed their minds.

When the day of the trial came around, I was understandably very nervous. Behind me in the packed courtroom were many well-known army officers as well as General Adnan himself. The pressure was on. Having worked hard on my defense I told the court that the death of the girl was a very unfortunate accident that could not have been foreseen. Peter had no criminal intent when he had shot the gun, as not only did he not expect the bullet to penetrate the door but he also did not think that anyone was behind it. It seemed that this was enough to satisfy the court, as Peter was acquitted. I was relieved. I had won the case, and hopefully I had pleased General Adnan.

That night when I returned home, I was delighted to see that Jamal was on leave and had come to visit us. My delight, however, soon turned to horror when he told us of some of the gruesome scenes he had endured on the front. He told us that just days before he had almost been killed when his gun had malfunctioned and he was forced to fight a man to the death with his bare hands. Jamal was a very tough man who was used to action on the battle field, but I sensed that even he was deeply affected by some of the things he had seen. I knew that we had to get him out of there quickly. Time was of the essence.

The next day, when my friend from the Ministry of Defense called to settle my legal fees, I informed him that rather than have my fees paid, I would prefer it if he could do something for me.

"Anything," he replied.

"My wife's brother Jamal has been fighting on the front line with the commandos for over three years now," I told him. "Many times he has almost lost his life. In fact, 90 percent of his colleagues have already met their fate on the battlefield. Sadly, his brother also recently died in the war, and as you can imagine, we are all terrified that Jamal could be next. Is there any way Jamal could be taken from the front and placed in an administrative position?"

My friend was quiet for a moment before saying, "I'll see what I can do."

Less than twenty-four hours later I received some good news. General Adnan himself had ordered that Jamal be stationed in an administrative position in Baghdad. It is an understatement to say that my family and I were overjoyed. But the matter did not end there.

Jamal was so highly rated as a soldier that his commander at first refused to release him. While Jamal continued to engage in missions, we waited in agony for further news. Eventually, the commander was informed that the transfer of Jamal was no ordinary request; it was an order that had come directly from General Adnan himself. Faced with such an order, the commander had no choice but to agree to it. Shortly afterward, Jamal was back in Baghdad. His fighting days were over.

It turned out that I had acted just in time. Jamal later informed me that within a month of his release, his entire battalion was wiped out. I thank God that He helped me to spare Jamal's life.

Before the war came to an end, it became very clear that Iraq was really starting to struggle financially. Not only was the war effort costing Iraq in excess of $1 billion a month, but its oil reserves, which the country depended on, also took a hit as pumping stations in Basra and Mosul were severely damaged. Indeed, Iraq also struggled to export its oil as without control of the Shatt al-Arab waterway, coupled with the loss of its other key port, Abadan, followed by the crippling decision by Syria to shut the Mediterranean pipeline, it became very hard to deliver it to other countries.

Slowly but surely Saddam realized that he couldn't continue to prop up the economy and fight a war at the same time. Before the war Iraq had boasted foreign reserves of over $35 billion, but by 1983 these were down to just $3 billion. Cuts were made wherever possible, and this unsurprisingly had a dramatic effect on morale. Every Iraqi was now very much aware of the true cost of the war.

With Iraq overcome in debt, Saddam made a public appeal for all Iraqis to donate whatever they could to the war effort. With a sense of national loyalty, everyone answered the appeal as enthusiastically as possible, with peasants donating their life savings and the rich giving away their jewelery and other items of value. The fact that I owned a very successful cigarette paper factory and law firm meant that I also wanted to do my bit. As a result I offered to pay the salary of a general in the army until the war came to an end. My contribution actually came to the attention of Saddam himself as he invited me and two guests to meet him at a reception at one of his palaces, which led to my mother and my wife also joining me.

While I was honored by the invitation, I also felt very wary. I do not wish to boast, but at this time I had reached the pinnacle of my career, where I was now regarded as one of Iraq's top criminal lawyers. Most men in my position were cherry-picked by the regime to work for the government, and this was something I dreaded. My interest in politics was minimal. I didn't want to become involved in it in any way. Yet there was no way I could turn down an invitation to the palace. I vowed that while I would be polite and respectful, I would also try to remain as inconspicuous as possible.

When the day of the reception came, we were not told where we would meet Saddam, as he moved from palace to palace on a daily basis in order to avoid being targeted by the Iranians. This meant that Aida, my mother, and I, along with other invited guests, gathered at a designated meeting place in downtown Baghdad with none of us having a clue where we would be going. When a bus eventually arrived, and we were all unceremoniously ordered to get in it.

As we sat on the bus I noticed that all of the windows were completely blacked out so that we couldn't see the route we were taking. For over an hour we weaved our way through the streets of Baghdad before we came to a stop and were ordered to get out. There before us stood a grand white building that I didn't recognize.

Before we could go any further, we were told to put everything that we were carrying, from watches and jewelry to fountain pens, into a white envelope held by one of the officers. It was clear that they were not taking any risks as they didn't want any object being taken into the palace that could in some way be disguised as a weapon. Aida was very reluctant to take off her diamond wedding ring, but in spite of this I told her to do as we were told.

With all of our personal items deposited in an envelope and left behind with an officer, we were all escorted into a huge hall. It was an awesome sight. Diamond chandeliers and gold furnishings decorated the room, and on the walls hung various pictures of Saddam in victory poses. Without warning, Saddam, dressed in a green military uniform, suddenly strode into the room.

He started to make his way down the line of guests who had stood to attention and thanked them one-by-one for their contribution to the war effort. Everyone, without exception, seemed to have come prepared with some warm words to say to him. This was not something I had thought about. I had planned to shake his hand, smile, and answer any questions, but I certainly hadn't prepared any words.

As he came closer to me I wracked my brain for something suitable to say. Most people were reciting a verse from a famous poem or from a book, and although I love poetry, my mind was now a blank. When Saddam was just one person away from me, Shakespeare saved the day.

As the president shook my hand firmly, I greeted him with, "Your Excellency, may you always be the northern star."

This made him stop. While still holding my hand in his firm grip, he raised one bushy eyebrow and inquired with a hint of menace, "What do you mean?"

"It's from the Shakespeare play *Julius Caesar*," I nervously replied. "The northern star is the one that shines more than any other, so that the other stars may take from it."

This answer seemed to please him, as a broad smile swept across his face. "Thank you for your kind words, and thank you for your contribution," he finally said before moving away. I breathed a sigh of relief.

With the meet and greet out of the way, my mother, Aida, and I were invited to have a picture taken with Saddam. My mother was extremely proud. She had come to Iraq in the 1930s from Syria with very little, and now here she was standing next to the president. To this day I still have the picture on my mantelpiece so I can enjoy seeing the pride on her face.

When the day came to an end, I was relieved to get out of the palace unscathed. However, I was perhaps most relieved to find that when we got back on the bus, the envelopes containing our valuables were returned to us untouched. If they hadn't had been, I dread to think what Aida would have done!

Eight years after the war had begun, with over a million people dead and billions of dollars squandered, the fighting finally came to an end on July 18, 1988, with no outright winner. In the end Saddam was helped to victory when powerful countries such as the United States, France, the Soviet Union, and other Gulf states opted to back Iraq rather than Iran. They had all feared an Iranian revolution sweeping the Gulf and the hard-line stance Iran would then proceed to take. Faced with little option, they all helped Iraq's war efforts in whatever way that they could.

Bombardment after bombardment rained down on Iran until finally Ayatollah Khomeini agreed to negotiate a ceasefire. Despite being in the ascendency, Saddam knew he had little option but to accept, even though he had to give up his claim to the Shatt al-Arab waterway. Iraq's economy and morale could take no more of this bloody war.

At the end of the 1970s, Iraq had been a shining light in the Middle East. Its potential knew no bounds. Now, at the end of the 1980s, hundreds of thousands of young Iraqis were dead, our oil money was seriously depleted, and we were also crippled by debt. The war had decimated our country. Our morale was crushed. What had once seemed a bright new dawn for Iraq had turned into a nightmare. It seemed that things could not possibly get any worse, but we were wrong. So very wrong. However, before my country again faced the abyss, I would have to deal with a series of cases that would take me into the heart of the regime itself.

17.

THE LION'S DEN

"Justice is sweet and musical; but injustice is harsh and discordant."

—Michel Foucault

BARZAN AL-TIKRITI: A NAME THAT once struck fear into the heart of every Iraqi. Not only was he Saddam's half-brother but he was also the head of Iraq's version of the CIA, the Mukhabarat. His job? To track down those who were said to be traitors to the regime.

As you can imagine, Barzan, backed by Saddam, was feared almost as much as the president himself. He was certainly not a man you wanted to get on the wrong side of. So, when a case came along involving Barzan and the Mukhabarat, I was extremely nervous.

An old lawyer friend who was now a leading legal adviser to some of the top political figures in Iraq came to see me one day and said that he had a case for me.

"Very well," I said. "What is it about?"

"A very important man is accused of killing his brother-in-law. I want you to defend him," he replied. When he told me the name of the man, I was shocked. As far as I was aware, he was just the owner of a well-known restaurant in the affluent Kurkh area of Baghdad. With dark, film star good looks and a charming manner, he was well known on the Baghdad social scene, but was he "important"? Not to my knowledge.

"Why is it so vital to you that I represent this man?" I asked, confused by the fact that someone in my friend's powerful position was prepared to help someone who appeared to just be a restaurant owner.

Leaning closer toward me he said under his breath, "He is Mukhabarat."

I was shocked but on reflection not too surprised. The owner of a restaurant that some of the leading business and political figures in Iraq frequented was the perfect informant. Right in the hub of everything, he heard all of the gossip and saw who was meeting with whom.

However, if he was a member of Mukhabarat, why did he need my help? It had always seemed that people associated with that agency were immune from prosecution. Confused, I asked my friend this very question.

"This is a murder charge," he replied. "It is a serious offense. We want to hire a good lawyer and then let the courts decide."

This answer satisfied me. I had no wish to be involved in any charades of justice.

Without hesitation I made my way to the police station where the defendant was being held. Rather than be kept in a cell, I was surprised to find that he was being held in a special room where he was being treated very well, far better than any usual murder suspect. It was clear that the police knew that he was connected. When I entered the room the defendant broke into a big Hollywood smile, revealing his perfect white teeth. He was delighted to see me. Not only did he recognize me from his restaurant, but he also knew that with me involved, the regime was taking his case seriously.

The case and his defense initially seemed simple enough. He told me that shortly after he had visited his brother-in-law at that man's apartment, the brother-in-law had shot himself. A suicide note was subsequently found at the scene. Case closed. Or so I thought.

"OK," I said, a little confused. "If there is a suicide note, then why have they arrested you?"

Looking at the floor while nervously rubbing his hands together, he slowly lifted his head and replied, "There is no gunpowder in the wound."

I wasn't quite sure what he was getting at. Sensing my confusion, he explained. "When people commit suicide in this manner, they usually hold the gun no more than 30 centimeters away from their head. When they do this, the gun is so close to the head that when it discharges, the bullet also leaves traces of gunpowder in the wound. In this case there was no gunpowder present, which means that the police think the shot must have come from a gun that was over 30 centimeters away. In other words, a shot from someone else."

"Were you the last person known to have seen your brother-in-law alive?" I asked.

"Yes," he quickly answered, "and regretfully we had an argument that led to me storming out." Things were now getting interesting.

I inspected him intently as he spoke. During my career I had developed an excellent intuition for when somebody was lying, but in this case I couldn't really tell. He looked me directly in the eyes when he spoke, he didn't twitch or get defensive, and his emotions seemed in balance. Yes, the evidence appeared to be damaging to his case, but there was the presence of a suicide note that could form the bulk of a defense. This would surely get him off the hook.

"What about the note?" I asked, hoping that it would be useful.

"It was just on a scrap of paper and said 'Sorry,'" he quietly replied.

This was hardly the conclusive piece of evidence I had hoped for.

"Was it in your brother-in-law's handwriting?" I pressed, hoping that at the very least this would be of some assistance.

"The tests are inconclusive," he muttered, recognizing that this wasn't much use to me.

After discussing the case a little more, I decided that the only thing that could help was for me to brush up on my firearms knowledge. For the next few days I devoured every book I could find on the subject. Some of the lawyers in my office were also very knowledgeable in this area, but no matter where I looked I could not find anything of any help. Every source said the same thing: in cases where a gun is fired at close range it invariably leaves some traces of gunpowder on the target. I was stumped.

After spending another day poring over books, hoping that I could find something to cling to, I was disturbed by my phone ringing. Answering the phone the voice on the other end announced, "This is Barzan al-Tikriti. I wish to discuss the case that our mutual friend brought to you the other day."

As soon as I heard the name, I knew just whom I was dealing with. Trying to sound as confident as possible I replied, "Usually I cannot discuss a case with someone who is not involved in it, but I understand this man worked for you."

In a brisk tone, carrying the thick accent of his hometown, Tikrit, Barzan replied, "He is a close friend of mine, and I don't want to see him come to any harm." I knew that this was just terminology for confirming that the restautant owner was in fact a Mukhabarat agent.

"How is the case coming along?" Barzan asked. If I were to be brutally honest, I would have said that at this moment in time we didn't have a chance in hell of an acquittal, but I decided to be a bit more diplomatic than that.

"It is difficult," I replied, as I went on to tell him that while we had the presence of a disputed suicide note, we also had the facts that the restaurant owner was the last person to see his brother-in-law alive and that there was no gunshot powder in the wound.

Something that had also dented our defense was that the victim's mother had submitted a highly damaging witness statement in which she had said that the defendant was the only person she knew who would have had a motive to kill her son, as they had argued the day he had died. In short, things were not looking good.

"Do you want me to visit the mother?" Barzan casually asked, which I knew was an offer to persuade her to change her story.

"No, there is no need for that," I quickly answered. "I can deal with this."

"Very well, doctor. I've heard good things about you. I hope I won't be disappointed." With that our conversation was over.

Time was short. The trial was now just days away. I had nothing to go on, and now I also had the head of the security forces watching me. I don't mind admitting that I prayed that night for inspiration to strike. But then, as I lay in bed considering my options, I realized that I may have been missing something.

With this in mind I asked that the coroner be present at the trial, as it was his assertion that this was a homicide and not a suicide. As the trial commenced, under the watchful eye of many onlookers whom I suspected had links to the security forces, the coroner took the stand, where he was questioned by the district attorney. As expected, the attorney merely confirmed that he thought this could not be a suicide because there was no gunpowder present.

When it came to my turn to speak, I took one of the biggest gambles of my legal career. Pulling a Colt revolver from my briefcase, I aimed it at the coroner. Stunned silence washed over the courtroom as the coroner cowered backward, absolutely terrified.

Relishing the look of shock on his face, I said, "Based on your assertion, if a man commits suicide with a gun, then he will leave gunshot power in the wound. Is that correct?"

Still wincing at the sight of me brandishing the weapon, the coroner replied, "Yes."

"On what do you base this belief?" I quickly followed up, still aiming the gun at him.

"Because to commit suicide, a person would be holding the gun himself, and therefore it is very likely that he would not hold the gun any more than 30 centimeters away from his head. Shots from this distance always leave behind gunshot residue."

With this evidence before the court I laid my client's only possible defense on the line. "So what you're saying, doctor, is that it is not really possible for this man to have shot himself by holding the gun more than 30 centimeters away from his head?"

Taking his time to consider my question, he finally replied, "That is correct."

After asking for the judge's permission to approach the coroner, I continued outlining my theory. "Very well. I am going to show you just how easy it is for a man to shoot himself with the gun more than 30 centimeters away from his head." Holding what everyone assumed was a loaded gun I could see that the coroner was frightened as I stepped toward him.

"Please keep your distance from me," the coroner said as he shrank behind the stand.

"It is OK, sir," I replied. "You are serving justice." This response earned some laughter from the gallery.

Finally, when the coroner was convinced that I did not mean him any harm, he let me approach him. Putting the gun to my temple at a right angle, as you would expect someone to do if he were committing suicide, I pulled the trigger. A wave of gasps washed over the courtroom as I did so, followed by exhalations of relief that I remained standing. "Doctor, is this how you would imagine most people would kill themselves with a gun?" I asked.

Still very nervous, he softly replied, "Yes."

Holding the gun in my right hand, I strained my arm as far away as it would go while also straining my head in the opposite direction. Turning the gun toward my head, I fired another shot, after which I looked at the coroner and this time asked, "Is it not possible that if someone was committing suicide that he might be so scared that he might choose to hold the gun farther away from his head and lean away from it?"

"I suppose it is possible, but it is unlikely," the coroner replied.

"Nevertheless, it is possible?" I prodded.

"Yes, it is," he admitted.

Holding a meter ruler, I then measured the distance of the gun from my temple. It was easily in excess of 30 centimeters.

"As you can see, doctor, the gun is more than 30 centimeters away from me. If I shot like this, is it possible that no gunpowder residue would be left in the wound?" I asked, hoping that he would concede the point.

"Yes," he confirmed to my relief. "If it was fired from that distance, then it is perfectly possible that no gunpowder residue would be present."

I knew that I had managed to cast some doubt on the homicide theory, but a substantial obstacle still remained: the mother's testimony.

Bracing myself for a tough ride, I was shocked when on the stand the first thing that she said was, "I've already lost a son. I don't also want to lose a son-in-law. I drop what I said before. I was hurt and angry."

I certainly didn't want to dig any further, but I immediately had my suspicions that she was scared to testify.

The day had gone far better than I had dared to expect. When I came to sum up the defense, I made it clear that not only was a suicide note present but also the coroner had confirmed that it was possible for a person to shoot himself without leaving traces of gunpowder behind. Furthermore, there was nothing to tie the defendant to the supposed murder other than the fact that he and the victim had argued shortly before the victim's death. Was it not possible that the victim had been so upset at the argument that he had killed himself? In such a case, based on the evidence, I said that there had to be significant doubt as to whether a homicide had in fact taken place. To my relief, after weighing up all of the evidence, the judge agreed and ordered an acquittal.

As soon as I returned to my office, Barzan was on the phone.

"Very good, doctor," he praised. "Very good indeed."

I was relieved that he was pleased, but I was also keen to end our relationship, on friendly terms, as quickly as possible. When he asked about my fees, I told him that I was just happy to be of service and that payment would not be necessary.

I thought that would be the end of the matter, but the next day one of the office boys burst into my office shouting, "Doctor, there are people outside with several large crates of whiskey for you!"

I certainly hadn't ordered it, as I didn't even drink whiskey, but when I went to investigate, I found twenty-four crates of the finest whiskey that money could buy stacked up to the ceiling in reception. It was from Barzan. For weeks I was handing out bottles of whiskey like Santa Claus to friends, family, and colleagues.

However, when the dust had settled on this case, I still had trouble sleeping at night. For some reason, something just didn't feel right. After another restless night, I could stand it no more. The next morning I visited the victim's mother and asked if she could take me to the room where her son had died. I don't know what I was expecting to find, but I just hoped that it would bring me some closure.

For a few minutes I walked around the room and tried to imagine the scene. Yet as I glanced around I noticed two holes in the wall. Inspecting them further I found that there was still a bullet lodged in one of them. How could this be? In a suicide surely only one shot would have been fired?

Pondering all of the possibilities, I reasoned that perhaps the man had panicked when he had tried to shoot himself. Perhaps he had initially missed before finishing the job? But wasn't the more likely explanation that someone had shot at him and missed? I didn't say anything to anyone. I felt sick to my stomach. Had I just been involved in a gross miscarriage of justice?

After a few days the defendant came to visit to thank me for my help. I wasn't too pleased to see him, but I did my best to be as pleasant as possible.

When he came to shake my hand, I gripped it firmly and said, "I don't know if you pray or not, but if you do, then you should pray to the soul of your brother-in-law so he may forgive you."

The defendant was silent. He knew what I was saying. With that he left, and I never saw him again.

To this day it makes me feel sick to think that this man may have escaped justice. My job had been to defend him. I had done that to the best of my ability. I am not God. I do not decide who is guilty and who is not. Yet still the feeling of injustice hurt. I hoped I would never experience that feeling ever again.

For a long time this case left a bad taste in my mouth. I hoped this would mark the end of my acting on behalf of members of the regime, but soon I became involved in a case that left me in the middle of a fight between two of the most feared men in Iraq, Barzan al-Tikriti and Uday Hussein, the son of the president.

18.

THE LESSER OF TWO EVILS

"An unrectified case of injustice has a terrible way of lingering . . . like an unfinished equation."

—Mary McCarthy

PSYCHOPATH. SOCIOPATH. PAEDOPHILE. MURDERER. TERRORIST. THE DEVIL. All of these words have been widely used to describe Saddam's eldest playboy son, Uday Hussein. Iraqis may have feared Barzan al-Tikriti, but Uday was in a different league altogether when it came to instilling terror.

Although Barzan worked for the security forces and only unleashed his unsavory methods on those he felt were a danger to national security. Uday just enjoyed torturing people. He was a maniac.

As head of the Iraqi Olympic Committee and the Iraqi Football Association, Uday would not tolerate failure. If any of his teams lost, then they were all subjected to his wild temper and some of the most brutal punishments you can imagine. This was something he also carried into his personal life, where he seemed to take great pleasure in terrifying people, even those who had done nothing wrong.

Flashy suits, Cuban cigars, palaces, and a fleet of luxury cars were Uday's rewards for such behavior. Stories of him misbehaving in the rooftop discothèque at the Melia Mansour Hotel were legendary. Perhaps the most famous incident at a disco occurred when Uday murdered an army officer after he had made an objection to Uday harassing his wife. Whatever Uday wanted, he took. If anyone stood up to him, or even gave him a funny look, then the consequences could be dire.

Barzan al-Tikriti was, of course, an extremely powerful man. Not only was he the head of the Mukhabarat, but also he was Saddam's half-brother. Yet even he was scared of Uday, particularly, as in the early 1980s, a rift had developed between Barzan and Saddam after Saddam had decided that his daughter, Raghda, would not marry Barzan's son as originally had been agreed. This was seen as a grave insult. After many arguments Saddam eventually removed his half-brother from his role in the security services, effectively sidelining him for a time.

One day, as I worked in my office, I heard my secretary telling a man in a brisk tone that I was not available. I tried to concentrate on my work, but I suddenly heard the man announce that he was Barzan al-Tikriti. I could not get to the door quickly enough.

As I opened the door I noticed the look of fear on my secretary's face. She had not recognized Barzan, but she certainly knew his name.

"Barzan," I announced, "you know, you don't have to ask for permission to see me. Please treat my office as your home. You are welcome to come and see me whenever you wish." This seemed to placate him, as he smiled, shook my hand, and entered my office. Before I closed the door behind us, I saw tears roll down my secretary's face. She was terrified.

Looking at my library of books, Barzan commented on a few of them and surprised me with his knowledge. For ten minutes we sat and chatted, and it was clear that Barzan was actually very well educated and was not just the thug he was portrayed as. Well dressed in an immaculate, designer navy suit and with a well-groomed moustache, he also looked very impressive.

Getting down to business, Barzan started to tell me about a case he wanted me to look into for him. As he was no longer involved with the Mukhabarat, it didn't surprise me to learn that it was a personal matter. On the surface it all seemed relatively simple. Barzan was renowned for owning one of the finest stud farms in Iraq. Consequently, sheiks from throughout the Middle East paid enormous sums to have one of their stock breed with one of his.

However, Barzan had found that someone, under false pretenses, had sold three horses that were purported to be descendants from his most famous horse. It turned out that they were in fact nothing more than mules. Nevertheless, the seller of the horses had continued to falsely claim that they were bred from Barzan's horse, a claim that was now doing enormous damage to his reputation as a champion horse breeder.

In short, Barzan wanted me to commence proceedings against the seller of the horses. This all seemed easy enough, until he told me that the seller was Uday Hussein's best friend. Not only was I very aware of Uday's psychotic nature but also I knew that at this moment in time Barzan was something of an outcast from the regime. Acting for Barzan was risky enough, but doing so in a case where the son of Saddam himself was going to be involved carried enormous risks. I was well aware that if I was going to emerge from this matter unscathed, I was going to have to tread very carefully indeed.

On paper the case was a no-brainer. I struggled to see what the defense could say. But of course, when members of the regime were involved, absolutely anything was possible.

In court, with Barzan sitting alongside me, I made my case with the minimum of fuss. First, there was absolutely no evidence that the horses in question had been bred from Barzan's stable. Second, this fraud had caused immense damage to his reputation in the horse-breeding world. I even made the point that if the defendant could so recklessly commit a fraud against a man such as Barzan al-Tikriti, then he was capable of anything.

It turned out that there was in fact no real defense. The defendant's lawyer even said as much as he told the judge in a threatening manner that this trial was a complete waste of time and had no legal grounds while insinuating that his client was a good friend of Uday Hussein.

Tensions between Barzan and the regime were obvious as Barzan leapt up and started to bellow at the lawyer and then at the judge. It was clear that he was not used to being spoken to in such a manner. For a time both Barzan and the defendant's lawyer caused quite a scene. I could see that the judge, a small woman, was too scared to intervene. She knew that she was also in a very vulnerable decision and that one way or another, her judgment was going to upset someone she really didn't want to upset. Finally, I lost my temper.

"Barzan, sit down and shut up otherwise I will walk out of here," I shouted. Amazingly, he did as he was told, and I was left to question my sanity for being so brazen.

Despite the defendant's arrogant stance and clear threats, even the judge could not easily dismiss the evidence she had before her. Though she did not dare to impose a stringent sentence, she did order more than I had hoped for, namely a six-month suspended sentence and a fine. Barzan seemed happy enough. It was obvious that he was just pleased to prove that the inferior horses had nothing to do with him. Although we had won in court, I did recognize that Uday may get his justice outside the courtroom, which was a terrifying thought.

As soon as the case was over, I asked the court clerk to provide me with a copy of the judge's handwritten judgment so that I could put it on file. The printed copy would be available in a few days' time, but I always liked to also have the judgment that was written at the time of the sentence. In this case, I was right to be so diligent.

Just a few days later, I again visited the court and asked the clerk if he could provide me with the printed copy of the judgment. When he gave it to me, I was shocked. The sentence had been changed. There was now no mention of a suspended prison sentence, and the amount of the fine had been lowered. I was livid. It seemed that Uday had indeed got his justice.

Furious, I stormed into the judge's chambers and confronted her. But her appearance stopped me in my tracks. She was pale, drawn, and extremely nervous. It was very clear to me that she had been threatened and had had no option but to water down her verdict. Feeling sympathy for her predicament, I took the copy of the handwritten verdict from my suitcase and gave it to her so that no one would ever know what had occurred. She thanked me profusely for my understanding. I recognized that it was an impossible situation.

That afternoon I asked Barzan to come and see me. I was dreading telling him what had happened, but when I did tell him that the verdict had been changed, a smile formed on his lips. He didn't seem angry or even shocked. It was almost as if he was expecting it.

I apologized profusely, but Barzan merely said, "Do not worry your-self, doctor. You did a good job. I am just pleased that you have proven that those mules had nothing to do with me." In the end it seemed that all parties were happy with the verdict, none more so than me, as I knew that I had enjoyed a lucky escape.

It would seem that the relationship between Barzan and Uday was now beyond repair. Yet I soon became embroiled in a case that involved them both as well as the most feared of them all, Saddam.

19.

THE DEVIL'S ADVOCATE

"The administration of justice is the firmest pillar of government."

—George Washington

WILL YOU ACT FOR UDAY HUSSEIN?"
The request itself was a shock, and so was the identity of the person who was asking me to do so, Barzan al-Tikriti. After their previous disagreements I would have thought that Barzan would have been the last person on earth who would have wanted to help Uday, especially now that the president's son was about to be put on trial for murder.

"Is it just you who is asking me to do this?" I asked Barzan, who was now pacing my office.

"No," he sternly replied. "I told the family that you are one of the best lawyers in Iraq. His mother has given her blessing for me to speak with you."

This set my mind racing. If Uday and the rest of his family had requested my services, then there was no way I could say no, yet in this case the prosecution would be led by the last person on earth I wanted to cross, Saddam Hussein. It was the epitome of a catch-22 situation.

"Does Saddam approve?" I inquired, to which Barzan shuffled his feet.

"We've persuaded him that Uday should at least be allowed a chance to state his defense," he finally answered. This was hardly the most reassuring of answers. And this also raised another important question: did I actually want to play any part in trying to save Uday from execution?

As I said previously, Uday was very unpopular in Iraq. If there was ever any chance of him getting his long-overdue comeuppance, then I certainly didn't want to get in the way. However, how could I refuse? To do so would bring the harsh spotlight of the regime straight onto me. I had little doubt that if I turned down the family's request, then they would find a way to make me change my mind. There was also something else to consider. If I turned it down I wouldn't be putting just myself in danger but also my wife and two children. It was an impossible choice. Whatever option I chose, I was at risk.

Sensing my apprehension, Barzan tried to calm my fears. "Don't worry yourself, doctor," he said as he stopped pacing my office for a moment. "I can guarantee your safety."

"But will it be a fair trial?" I shot back.

"Of course," Barzan replied. "It will be heard in a special criminal court. No one will be allowed to interfere. Saddam knows that the nation will be watching, and he wants to use this to improve confidence in our judicial system."

This was good news. While I hated the thought of representing a monster such as Uday, I was willing to be involved if the case was going to show that Saddam could allow justice to stand, even when it involved his own son. Deep down I wanted Uday to finally pay the price for his actions, but I also wanted to ensure that he would receive a fair trial. Justice, I felt, would then naturally take its course.

"OK," I said, after giving it some thought. "I will do it."

A smile broke across Barzan's face, and with that he gave me the background to a story that had scandalized Iraq and has since been told in the film *The Devil's Double*.

While Saddam liked to portray himself as the ultimate family man, most Iraqis knew that he had enjoyed a number of affairs. Kamel Hana Geogeo, Saddam's favorite bodyguard, was his fixer in such matters. He was responsible not only for helping to arrange his boss's dalliances but also for helping cover them up. Everyone in the family knew that this went on, but no one dared to cross either Saddam or Kamel for fear of the consequences.

Kamel had served Saddam for a number of years, so the two had developed a close relationship, and Kamel also knew just the type of women his master liked: tall, blonde, and articulate. Bearing this in mind, Kamel ensured that a steady stream of such beauties was always close at hand.

One such woman who caught Kamel's attention was Samira Shahbandar, the wife of the director general of Iraqi Airways. Wasting little time, Kamel arranged for Samira and Saddam to meet in a house he used for affairs in the upmarket Mansour district of Baghdad, where the two soon commenced an intense relationship.

Yet news of this soon reached Saddam's wife, Sajida. Devastated at hearing of the seriousness of the affair, Sajida broke down and became consumed by jealousy, particularly after Saddam took Samira as his second wife, which he was permitted to do under his religion.

In the past Sajida would have called on Barzan to intervene, but at this time he was acting as an ambassador in Geneva. Faced with nowhere else to turn, she asked her eldest son, Uday, to put an end to the matter by telling him that his father's relationship with Samira could seriously jeopardize his inheritance. Uday loved his mother very much and hated to see her upset, but the thought that this new woman would share in his inheritance really set him into action.

That night Uday made his way to a party that was being held on the Island of Pigs, a small area of land situated in the middle of the Tigres River, just a short distance away from the Presidential Palace. The party was a very important affair, as following the disastrous war with Iran, Iraq was doing its best to improve its relationships with other Arab countries. Nearly all of the top members of the regime were present as well as prominent politicians from Egypt and other Middle Eastern nations.

Drunkenly entering the party, flanked by his bodyguards, Uday marched straight up to Kamel and beat him mercilessly over the head with a club. Some tried to intervene, but they were held back and threatened. All they could do was stand and watch as Uday continued to beat an unconscious Kamel over the head until his skull was crushed.

Covered in blood, Uday brushed himself off and walked out as if nothing had happened. As far as he was concerned, it was just another day at the office.

In the past Saddam had turned a blind eye to Uday's madness, but on this occasion he went berserk. Not only had Uday murdered a valued employee at a very important party, but he had also defied Saddam. For once, Uday was not spared the full force of Saddam's rage.

And if Saddam had wanted to cover up the story, that soon became impossible, as it was splashed across the Arab press. Not that this mattered. Saddam was said to be determined to punish his son, not only because of what he had done but also because he recognized that the Iraqi people may lose faith in him if he did not act.

To the shock of the nation, Saddam appeared on state television and made a statement publicly denouncing Uday. Astonishingly, he also said that Uday would be put on trial for murder. It was an extraordinary moment. Finally Uday was going to get punished. For days the streets of Baghdad were full of gossip concerning this matter. Was Saddam really going to put his son on trial? And if Uday was found guilty, would he really allow his son to be executed or sentenced to life in prison? It was at this moment that Barzan came to see me.

As we continued to discuss the case, Barzan said to me, "In order to lighten the load, you can appoint two lawyers from other firms to assist you." This was a relief, as I knew that I would need all the help that I could get. Wasting little time, I immediately called the first two names that came to mind. One was a senior doctor of law who was highly regarded in Iraq, while the other had actually represented Saddam in the 1960s when he had been accused of treason by President Arif. Both of the men jumped at the chance to be involved, and soon we got together to discuss our line of defense.

It was immediately clear that we were really up against it. It would take all of our experience and ingenuity to avoid the death penalty, let alone get an acquittal. Despite our request to meet with Uday so we could gain a better understanding of his side of the events, Barzan told me that this wouldn't be possible. Saddam had locked him in isolation, and he wasn't allowed to meet with anyone.

We all soon agreed that our only option was to plead manslaughter. In order to pull this off, I knew that I would have to know every single statute and legal precedent on the subject back to front. I recognized that it was very unlikely that I would win this case, yet in the name of justice I wanted to be as well prepared as possible.

While I diligently put together the defense for the biggest case of my life, Saddam was being pressured from all sides to drop the charges. Not only did his wife, Sajida, beg him to put an end to the matter but also he was approached by Geogeo's father, who asked Saddam to spare his son's murderer's life, according to his tribe's traditions.

Upon reflection and now having calmed down, Saddam reasoned that it was his own philandering behavior that had led to this situation. He also did not want to be responsible for the death of his son, no matter how horrific his crime. Saddam subsequently asked the Minister of Justice to use his rights to postpone the case indefinitely, an order that was very rare yet still swiftly carried out.

When I learned that there was to be no trial, I was relieved but also disappointed. Obviously, I was pleased that I would not have to be involved with Uday and would also not be up against Saddam, but at the same time I thought that this was an ideal opportunity for Saddam to send a message that no one was above the law. Unfortunately this was not a message he wanted to send out.

Although Saddam saved Uday from going to trial, he wanted his son out of his sight as quickly as possible. Arrangements were swiftly made for him to join up with Barzan in Geneva, where he was supposed to act as a diplomat. However, it appeared that he still had not learned his lesson, as after a few weeks he was deported following an altercation with a Swiss policeman.

Back in Iraq, and with his father's attention soon on another war, Uday continued to terrorize the streets of Baghdad. Finally, in 1996, he suffered some sort of retribution for his reprehensible behavior when he was the subject of a failed assassination attempt. While cruising the streets in his Porsche, an assailant fired at him eight times. Although none of the shots were fatal, one bullet lodged itself into Uday's spine, which left him partially paralyzed.

As for Barzan, I didn't see him much after this case. He continued to call from time to time, but I ensured that I kept my distance. While he always treated me with respect and was very polite and pleasant, I knew that underneath the smooth veneer lay a man who had committed many atrocities.

I was certainly lucky to emerge unharmed from my brushes with the regime. And luck would again prove to be an extremely valuable commodity not long afterward, as without it I may have been caught in a war zone.

20.

LUCK

"I find that the harder I work, the more luck I seem to have."
—Thomas Jefferson

MANY TIMES DURING THE COURSE of my life I have been called lucky. I've been told I was lucky to escape death, to get a license to manufacture cigarette papers, to win cases, to have a beautiful wife, to have two wonderful sons, to have everything I have. And yes, I recognize that luck is a very valuable commodity. But over the years I have learned something else: you can make your own luck.

For as long as I live I will always remember my childhood trips with my family to Lebanon where we would sometimes stay for up to three months at a time in order to avoid the oppressive summer heat of Baghdad. On these annual trips, as I grew older, I started to venture out at night into Beirut, where there was a huge casino. I always liked to play roulette, blackjack, and poker and found that the more I played, the more I improved, rubbishing the suggestion that these games were predominantly down to luck.

However, while practice played a big part in creating luck, the famous Greek shipping tycoon Aristotle Onassis also showed me that there was another way to do it. Onassis walked into the casino one night and caused a stir when he set himself up at the roulette table and placed a huge bundle of cash in front of him. A rope was put around the table so that he could play by himself, but that didn't stop a large crowd from gathering to watch him engage in some high stakes action.

I vividly remember him exchanging all of his cash for chips, which he then placed in front of him, before saying to the casino manager, "I will play for one hour only. I will place my chips on the table, and you will spin. During that hour, you don't change the dealer, you don't change the ball, and you don't touch my chips."

I was fascinated watching him play like this, and for the life of me I couldn't work out why all of this was so important to him. Yet within the hour he had won over $100,000 and, as promised, he got up from the table, collected his winnings, and left.

It was only later that I realized the genius of his strategy. When you are gambling on roulette and jumping from one spin to another, you are multiplying the odds against you. However, the way he played that day, he gave the casino only the normal odds of 2.7 percent against him. With a bit of luck he was able to overcome them that night. It was only a very small change in the percentage of odds, but it was enough. In life sometimes you only need a very small edge, which most people can't see, in order to make some "luck."

In my later years I fulfilled a dream of mine when I took part in the World Series of Poker in Las Vegas alongside my two sons, Tariq and Edward. The tournament was at the Rio Hotel, just off the Strip, and all of the biggest names in poker were taking part. The most famous player of all time, two-time world champion Doyle Brunson, was also playing, and I was lucky enough to speak with him.

Doyle has been playing poker for over fifty years, and despite people saying it is a game of luck, he has consistently emerged as a winner. When I asked him about the reasons behind his success, he merely explained that he had helped to ensure luck played a small role. He had studied how to learn a player's tells, observed how they bet, calculated odds, and put opponents on "tilt" to ruffle their feathers. As he said to me, "this all helps me make my own luck."

When I look back on some of the cases I have dealt with in my career, I can also see that there have been times when luck has played a huge part in how I approached a case or how a defendant came to be before the court. Indeed, in one such case my gambling hobby actually proved to be very useful when determining the role of luck.

In the 1970s Baghdad welcomed the first major casino to Iraq. As you can imagine, for a man who enjoys roulette, poker, and blackjack, I was delighted. Located in one of the finest hotels in the city, the Baghdad Hotel, the casino soon became my favorite haunt.

The casino was run by an ex-army officer named Abu Mazin who now worked for the Iraqi Tourism Department. As Baghdad was short of suitably qualified dealers, Abu Mazin brought dealers from Lebanon to train the Iraqi staff. All seemed to be working like clockwork until one of the Lebanese dealers approached me outside of the casino one night. The dealer's name was George, and I knew him well from my time at the tables. He had always been polite and good humored, not to mention a lucky charm, so when I saw the stress on his face, I was immediately concerned.

"Dr. Aris," he said in a nervous, faltering voice. "I need your help. Four dealers have been arrested by the police and charged with cheating the casino."

"Cheating the casino? How?" I asked, intrigued by the story behind the charges.

"Abu Mazin has told the police that the Lebanese dealers are taking bribes from the players so that they can hit certain numbers when playing roulette."

I almost laughed at the absurdity of the claims. How could it be possible that a dealer was able to stop the roulette wheel on an exact number? But while the claims were absurd, the charges were extremely serious. As I said, the casino was run by the Tourism Department, so the dealers were also being charged with stealing money from a government department.

"Meet me back here at ten tomorrow night," I told him.

"What are you going to do?" he replied.

"Show Abu Mazin that if he allows this case to go to court, he will be a laughing stock."

The next day I went to visit the investigating judge, who I knew from previous cases. He was someone who had been to the casino before, so I hoped even he would see that these charges were completely unfounded. Thankfully I was right. Taking out the file and reading it over, he was not impressed. When I suggested that he meet us later at the casino with the four imprisoned defendants to discuss these charges with Abu Mazin, he agreed.

As had been arranged, the judge arrived at the casino at ten o'clock along with the four handcuffed Lebanese men. They were extremely nervous. Abu Mazin had been quite aggressive toward them, and even I was aware that he probably wouldn't take kindly to us walking into his casino together. I was right. As soon as we walked through the door, he marched over, his face red with rage, his tone laced with aggression.

"Get out. Get out," he bellowed, looking at me. "If you don't leave now, I will ban you for life."

"Abu Mazin," I calmly answered back, "please contain yourself. Tonight I am not here as a member but in my capacity as a lawyer."

At this point the investigating judge stepped forward. Speaking with authority he told Abu Mazin that this visit was a necessary pretrial survey of the scene of the crime, and if he wanted to continue with the case, it was imperative that he lead us to the roulette table.

"What do you want with the roulette wheel?" Abu Mazin demanded.

"Please, Abu Mazin," I answered. "If you lead us there, I will show you."

With the investigating judge looking on, Abu Mazin was unable to refuse us. So, against his will, he took us to the table. However, such was his anger he didn't think to take us to a roped off roulette table where no one could see. Instead he took us to the most prominent table in the whole casino, which allowed onlookers to gather around us. This suited me fine. I wanted everyone to know just how preposterous Abu Mazin's charges were.

Standing by the wheel, I picked up the small roulette ball. "Please place the ball on the wheel," I told him. "Tell us what number you want it to fall into, and then carefully drop the ball from the top of the wheel into that number without spinning the wheel or the ball."

Abu Mazin snatched the ball from my grasp before confidently grunting, "Zero." Placing the ball on the wheel he dropped it down above the number 0. But the ball cannoned off a divider and instead nestled into the number 5.

Disgruntled, he picked up the ball and tried again. And again, and again, and again. But still he could not get it to fall into the 0 divider.

By now most of the people in the casino were looking on. They not only found the experiment amusing but also laughed at Abu Mazin, who got more and more irate with every failed attempt. It all looked so simple. Neither the wheel nor the ball was moving, yet still he could not do it. Finally, after countless attempts, Abu Mazin gave up.

"How is it," I began, talking loudly so everyone could hear, "that you cannot even simply place the ball into a fixed number without the ball or the wheel being spun, yet you think these men can do the same, with the wheel being spun at a pace to the right, and the ball moving to the left?"

"They are cheats," Abu Mazin stuttered, grasping at straws, unable to admit that he had been wrong. "I don't know how they did it, but they are crooks."

At that moment the director general of the Tourism Department stepped forward. He was Abu Mazin's boss, and I had not known he would be in the casino that night. "The Tourism Department is dropping the charges, and these men may come back to work immediately if they wish," he announced, much to Abu Mazin's dismay but to the delight of the Lebanese men.

The next night I went back to the casino not as a lawyer but as a member. I was pleased to see that the Lebanese men were all back at work and that Abu Mazin had resigned from his post. Taking a seat at the table, one of the Lebanese men shook my hand, smiled, and said, "I will remember you every time I spin the wheel and throw a ball. God only knows where it will land."

And he was right. In some cases you can manipulate the odds in your favor and make your own luck. But sometimes in life, and in roulette, only God can determine your fate.

While God has blessed me with more good luck than bad, I will always remember a case where a defendant I was representing had been cursed with the worst luck imaginable.

On my way out of the courtroom one afternoon, I saw a well-built young man with tears rolling down his cheeks. He was flanked by two police officers and was obviously in some distress. Suddenly he shrieked and began to bang his head against the wall. Unnerved, I immediately approached him.

"Why are you here?" I asked.

Turning to face me, he looked me up and down, wiped away his tears, and desperately asked, "Are you a lawyer?"

"Yes. Do you need help?"

The man suddenly gripped my wrist. "I have had some bad luck," he said.

Encouraging him to tell me his story he proceeded to tell me that he was a soldier who had been in charge of guarding other soldiers accused of crimes. One day he had been ordered to transfer a soldier from one camp to another, which involved a trip across Baghdad. Carrying a machine gun with him, the man handcuffed the prisoner and took him in a car to his destination.

During the journey the prisoner told the soldier he was going to be locked in the camp for a very long time and didn't have a shirt to wear, so he would be forced to wear the itchy shirts the camp provided. Taking pity on him, the soldier said that they could stop quickly in order to buy the man a shirt.

Spotting a shop, the soldier parked the car and escorted the handcuffed prisoner inside. Upon finding a suitable shirt, the prisoner wanted to try it on but couldn't do so as the handcuffs were restricting him. The prisoner seemed a quiet, timid man, so the soldier saw no harm in momentarily taking off the handcuffs from one of his hands so the man could quickly try on the shirt. However, this small act of kindness was to prove to be a huge mistake.

With his free hand the prisoner swung at the soldier, knocking him to the floor, before running from the shop and down the busy street. Quickly regaining his senses the soldier picked up his machine gun and chased after him, petrified of what would happen to him if the prisoner escaped. Shooting into the ground, the soldier hoped that the noise would scare the prisoner from continuing to flee. Tragically, rather than stop the prisoner, the bullets bounced off the concrete and hit four people who were standing nearby.

As the civilians collapsed onto the ground, wailing in agony, the soldier spotted the prisoner running onto a double-decker bus in the distance. Knowing that if the prisoner managed to get on the bus, he would escape, the soldier shot a bullet into the air to again try to warn him to stop. Yet the shot caused more tragedy, as it hit and killed an old man on the top deck of the bus. Confronted with a prisoner on the run, and a soldier accidentally shooting people, the street soon broke into anarchy, which allowed the prisoner to escape.

Later that day, the prisoner was found, but by that stage the soldier had been arrested. Now he faced the death penalty and didn't have a lawyer to defend him.

"Will you defend me?" he pleaded.

Without thinking twice, I said that I would. It seemed the soldier needed a bit of luck in his life after everything that had happened.

When the trial commenced a few weeks later, I knew it was going to be very difficult because at the end of the day an old man had lost his life as a result of my client's actions. However, I decided that while the facts were against us, perhaps the judge might show some mercy if I outlined just how unlucky the defendant had been.

"What is a crime?" I began, addressing the court. "Is it not a willful act committed to violate the law? Even in reckless acts, there is a will behind them, although the consequences are not envisaged. A person deciding to drive fast commits a willful act of violating the speed limit, even if not envisaging hitting and killing a person on the road."

Looking up toward the stand where the soldier stood, I continued. "This man before you today had no malicious thinking of any sort when he awoke the day of the alleged offense. He was ordered to escort a prisoner and was given a machine gun, with the indirect implication being to use it should the prisoner escape. When the prisoner did escape, he was possessed by fear and sadly that may have affected his judgment in shooting in a busy area."

Then my defense addressed the bad luck that had played a huge part in the soldier's destiny. "The prisoner only escaped because of my client's act of kindness. In hindsight, was it foolish? Perhaps. But should a man be punished for showing a glimpse of kindness when so much of the world is hard and brutal? And then, when his act of kindness was repaid by the prisoner running away, how unlucky can the defendant be that his shots of warning hit a man on the top deck of a bus and rebounded off the ground and hit bystanders?

"Perhaps this man is too kind, too soft, to be a soldier. Perhaps he showed too much mercy. And it is beyond question that he was extremely unlucky in all of this. So how should we punish his act of kindness and bad luck? By sending him to the gallows?"

I knew the best we could perhaps hope for was life in prison, but it seemed my speech finally gave the soldier a bit of good luck, or as much as he could hope for in the circumstances, as he was sentenced to serve seven years and was actually released in six, which was a great success considering he had killed a person and shot four others.

Luck can be random. It can be elusive. Or it can all come at the same time. But any man who has luck is blessed. And as I have always said, "If you don't buy a lottery ticket, you can never win the lottery prize." You may be lucky if you win the lottery, but you made your own luck by buying the ticket. And without knowing it, my decision to apply for British citizenship in the mid-1980s was perhaps the biggest slice of luck I would ever have.

21.

THE GULF WAR

"Justice is like a train that's nearly always late."
—Yevgeny Yevtushenko

THE SECOND DAY OF AUGUST 1990 was the day that plunged Iraq back into the dark ages. Conflict between Iraq and Kuwait had been bubbling beneath the surface for quite some time, but the war with Iran had really exacerbated tensions. With Saddam growing frustrated by the catastrophic state of Iraq's postwar economy, matters weren't helped by the fact that other nations, who were fellow members of the Organization of Petroleum Exporting Countries (OPEC), such as Kuwait, were exceeding their oil production quotas. This drove the price of oil down at a time when Iraq drastically needed to raise as much money as possible to rebuild its infrastructure.

Saddam saw Kuwait's refusal to lower its oil production as a direct attack on Iraq's economy. Indeed, he was particularly frustrated by the fact that he thought Kuwait should have been under his rule in any event. As said previously, Kuwait had actually once been part of Iraq, but when the British had taken control of the country after the First World War, they had demarcated the borders, making Kuwait a country in its own right. This was a decision that would lead to substantial conflict and dialogue over the years. Not only did Kuwait have a very well-developed coastline, in contrast to Iraq, but it also had substantial oil reserves, notably in Rumaila. Obviously these were both highly sought-after assets. Successive Iraqi governments had subsequently threatened some sort of action over this but ultimately to no avail. That is until now.

Growing more impatient by the day, Saddam issued Kuwait a list of impossible ultimatums if it wanted to avoid repercussions. These included Kuwait's stabilizing the price of oil, wiping out Iraq's debt, and helping to finance reconstruction work in the country. The price for noncompliance was dire: all-out war.

The Kuwaitis knew that this was not an idle threat. Despite the fact that Iraq's economy was in a perilous state and the country had just endured eight years of war, they were aware that Saddam had continued to invest heavily in defense. They were also aware that he would have no qualms about using deadly force, as by this stage Saddam was spending over half of Iraq's yearly oil revenues on the armed forces and had assembled the fourth-largest army in the world.

Knowing that Saddam would not hesitate to attack, Kuwait reluctantly agreed to his ultimatum. However, this did not placate Saddam. It seemed that he had already made up his mind to attack, no matter what. What Saddam really wanted was to bring Kuwait back under Iraq's control. Not only would all of his ultimatums then be satisfied without question but he would also have access to more valuable oil reserves and the ocean.

Thankfully, at this time, I was in the UK city of Cardiff attending my sister, May's, fiftieth birthday celebrations. While most Iraqis I spoke to that night knew tensions were close to the breaking point, no one expected Saddam to be so reckless as to start another war, especially when the country was still picking itself up from the previous conflict. Yet the night of August 2, 1990, as we slept in Cardiff, over 100,000 troops, backed by 300 tanks, seized Kuwait.

When I awoke to this news, I immediately called our friends and family back in Iraq, but no one could tell us anything more than we knew already. With such little information, we had no option but to keep watching the TV for any further updates. It was an agonizing time, but I thanked God that my family and I were safe in the United

Kingdom. I had no doubt that the international community would not respond well to this unprovoked invasion.

Finally, after hours of waiting, British Prime Minister Margaret Thatcher, and U.S. President George Bush made a joint statement from Colorado that was broadcast throughout the world. I listened with bated breath as President Bush imposed an economic embargo against Iraq, froze all Kuwaiti and Iraqi assets that were held by American banks, and also suspended all movement of goods and people in and out of the country. I couldn't believe it. My family and I would not be able to return home until the conflict was over.

Although this was frustrating, as I was still overseeing my law firm and cigarette paper factory, I recognized that under the circumstances I was very lucky. While we were in the United Kingdom my wife and two children would be kept out of harm's way, and we were surrounded by fellow Iraqis who were in a similar situation. It was far from ideal, but we endeavored to make the most of it.

Indeed, we were extremely fortunate that just a few years previously I had been granted British citizenship after advising a number of UK law firms on Iraqi law. I did not know that I would need to depend on it so soon afterward, but it turned out to be vital, as we could make our home in Cardiff while we waited to see how things would turn out.

As we settled into our new life, we continued to be glued to the news for any positive developments. Unfortunately, things only continued to escalate. With Saddam showing no signs of backing down, on August 28, 1990, he announced that Kuwait was now the nineteenth province of Iraq. At this news over 300,000 Kuwaitis fled the country.

It didn't matter that most of Iraq's Middle Eastern neighbors and the vast majority of the Western world violently disapproved of the invasion. Saddam felt that it was justified and rebuffed all diplomatic overtures to resolve the situation.

Finally, on January 16, 1991, the Allies' patience was at an end. In response, they subjected Iraq to one of the most devastating aerial bombardments seen in modern warfare, now known as Operation Desert Storm. For six weeks I watched in horror as Iraq burned to the ground. Wave after wave of air strikes saw key targets in Iraq and Kuwait destroyed. Such was the intensity of the attack that the Iraqi defense forces were completely overwhelmed. If Saddam didn't surrender quickly, then I feared that there would be nothing left of my homeland to return to.

It was strange watching the reports of the war while in a foreign country. During the Iranian war, no matter how dire things were, Saddam always ensured that the Iraqi people were told that everything was going to plan. But this war was different. Baghdad was being bombed day and night, and the Iraqi people were really suffering.

Reading the newspapers and watching the news in the United Kingdom left me in no doubt as to just what damage was being done to my country. I could really see that things were very bad and the Allies would not stop until Saddam retreated from Kuwait. I prayed he would do so before Iraq was destroyed.

Eventually, Saddam's positive rhetoric to the Iraqi people wore off. Even he couldn't hide the fact that Baghdad and other Iraqi cities were without running water and electricity. He also had no choice but to ban the sale of fuel to help with the war effort, which saw Iraq grind to a standstill. Travel also wasn't helped by the almost total destruction of roads and bridges.

Yet with Saddam still refusing to back down, President Bush gave him until February 23, 1991, to vacate Kuwait or else Iraq would suffer the consequences. I prayed that Saddam would finally see some sense and swallow his pride. Sadly, it was not to be. On February 23 the Allied ground forces, led by General Norman Schwarzkopf, descended on Kuwait. Within forty-eight hours the Iraqi army was routed, with the Allies taking over 20,000 prisoners of war, destroying 370 tanks, and wounding close to 100,000 men. Saddam now had no choice but to order a humiliating withdrawal.

Finally, on February 28, the conflict came to an end when the Allies were satisfied that they had taken control of Kuwait and dealt a fatal blow to the Iraqi armed forces. In little more than a month the Allies had captured over 50,000 prisoners of war and the number of Iraqi casualties totaled 150,000.

Although the war itself inflicted enormous damage, the aftermath was just as damaging. Following the military victory the Allies pushed through UN Security Resolution 687, which imposed stringent sanctions on Iraq while it continued to be under Saddam's rule. Among other things, the sanctions stated that Iraq must fully disclose to the United Nations all of its chemical and biological weapons, return all Kuwaiti property, and compensate foreign nationals and companies who had suffered as a result of the occupation. Imports and exports were also banned, apart from certain medical supplies and food products. Most devastatingly of all, however, was that Iraq was banned from selling oil on the open market. It was the most draconian sentence imaginable.

Although the sanctions were intended to make life difficult for Saddam, what they really did was harm ordinary Iraqis. The sanctions meant that because Iraq was unable to sell oil, it struggled to raise funds to repair the country's infrastructure, which had been damaged in the war. As a result, water and electricity came on and off haphazardly, which led to mass disease and malnutrition. With limited imports available, food was also scarce, which saw prices rise by over 2,000 percent. Everyone in Iraq started to suffer. Life as we had all once known it had changed forever.

Under the circumstances, there was no way I could take my family back to Baghdad. We had no choice but to remain in Cardiff, where we enrolled the boys into a new school, where they had to learn a new language as well as a new way of life. In the meantime I did all that I could to oversee my law firm and cigarette paper factory from afar. However, it soon became apparent that due to the aftereffects of the war, and with being stationed in the United Kingdom, keeping my cigarette paper factory open was going to be impossible. With a very heavy heart I had no choice but to close it. Still, I continued to work on legal matters whenever I could, with my in-country lawyers ably running the firm while I was away.

It was all a big change, but as a family we adapted well and soon made many close friends. Indeed, my two boys even started playing the Welsh national sport of rugby. However, I still longed for the day when we might all be able to return home as a family. I did not know that that would take ten years, and that the Baghdad we would return to would be nothing like the one we had left behind.

22.

RETURN TO BAGHDAD

"Military justice is to justice what military music is to music."
—Groucho Marx

*Humiliated in war by the West, terrorised by their own gov-
ernment, reduced to paupers, unwelcome anywhere in the
world, the Arabs of Iraq are falling to pieces. It is not simply
that with their money and savings destroyed and their goods
embargoed, their living standards have fallen to the level of
at least 30 years ago. In their own eyes, as Iraqis and above
all as Arabs, they have been reduced to nothing. I have never
seen a people so demoralised. Everybody I met, even the most
repellent Baathist thug and extortionist, felt himself a victim.*

THIS WAS A REPORT THAT I READ in *The Guardian* newspaper in 1999
about the conditions in Iraq following the war. Living abroad as my
homeland fell apart broke my heart. I had always loved Iraq and knew
the vast potential that its land and people possessed, yet I didn't need
to read the newspapers to know that life there was now unbearable.

On my haphazard visits to Baghdad throughout the 1990s I saw mis-
ery and distress everywhere I turned. Parts of Baghdad that had once
been renowned for their prosperity were now slums. It seemed that

with the country's economy on its knees and sanctions biting hard, everyone was struggling to make a living.

Some lawyers and judges I knew, who had once been very successful, were now reduced to living like peasants as the legal practices they had built up over the years were destroyed. When some of my old friends from my legal days heard that I was back in Baghdad, they would come and visit me at my office. Some of the stories they told me were horrifying. Many had had to sell their most valuable belongings to get by. They were lucky they had things to sell. Many did not. And those who may have had money in the past found that their investments and savings had been reduced to nothing. Before sanctions were imposed, the exchange rate amounted to $3.20 for one dinar. After the war, it plummeted to $1.00 for 3,200 dinars. The Iraqi currency had been completely annihilated. Furthermore, in 1985, the average monthly salary for a professional in Iraq had been $250. By the late 1990s, it had plummeted to $10, a sum that made it virtually impossible to survive.

With little food, poor sanitation, and the city rife with disease, many people became ill and were left for dead. Even the UN's Oil-for-Food Programme, which was initiated in 1996 and was designed to help provide medicine and food to ordinary Iraqis, was a disaster, as much of the food was found to be unfit for human consumption.

Due to sanctions, over half a million Iraqi children lost their lives. Despite this horrendous statistic, help was still in short supply, as Western countries felt that these sorts of conditions would eventually lead to the Iraqi people forcing Saddam from power. In their eyes, the death of children was a price worth paying.

Although I sent money to my mother and ensured that she had everything that she could ask for, her life in Baghdad continued to be tough. In spite of this she was determined to stay. I was consoled that my sister, Kawther, her husband, Sabah Toniettie, and their children, Ayad and Dina, were taking great care of her, but I still feared for her safety, particularly when she was diagnosed with cancer in 1994. I knew the hospitals had been decimated by sanctions and would not have the equipment, expertise, or medicines to care for her properly, but despite this, her love for Iraq prevented her from leaving.

When I heard my mother had taken a turn for the worse, I wasted little time in making the long journey to Baghdad to be at her side. Tragically, by the time I arrived, my mother was dead. I was devastated. Whether she would have survived if she had been living with us, I don't know, but I'm certain that her chances would have been improved because the hospitals in Iraq were in a sad state of decline.

By the time we finally returned as a family to Baghdad in 2001 for a short holiday, around 1.5 million had died as a result of sanctions, with 41 percent of those deaths being children under age five. If the West thought that the sanctions would help to persuade the Iraqi people to revolt, they were wrong. People reasoned that while Saddam may have been to blame, why hadn't the West removed him when they had the chance, instead of leading the Iraqi people to a slow death? If anything the sanctions strengthened Saddam's grip on power, as he used them as a propaganda tool to turn people against the West.

While I could see that Baghdad was still suffering, I also noticed that some signs of optimism had started to sprout. For instance, although international flights were still not allowed to land or depart at Saddam International Airport, flights to and from the likes of Jordan, Syria, and Lebanon were now permitted. This helped the business community to no end, and it also meant that we could now fly into Baghdad after catching a connecting flight from Jordan. This was far more convenient and safer than having to drive the twenty-hour journey from Jordan, which involved navigating through numerous waste lands, damaged roads, and hostile military checkpoints.

The vast majority of the buildings, bridges, and roads that had been decimated during the Gulf War had also been rebuilt by this time, and as such Baghdad no longer resembled a war zone. While UN sanctions were still in place, they were now largely ignored. As a result, signs of relative prosperity had started to return to the streets. I noticed that the shops in the upscale al-Mansour district were stocked with the latest designer fashions, and the marketplaces were full of food, medicines, and electronic goods. The Baghdad International Trade Fair had also recently attracted over 1,500 firms from all over the world, with many expressing an interest in investment.

There now seemed to be a lot more hope everywhere you turned. It seemed to me that the worst of the troubles were now over. Maybe, just maybe, the Baghdad I had always dreamt of still had a chance of becoming a reality.

Yet athough there had been vast improvements, I was saddened to see the state of my old school, Baghdad College, which had once been one of the finest educational establishments in the Middle East. When I visited the decaying building, I was almost brought to tears by what I saw. The sound of laughter and the sight of American priests alongside Iraqi students rushing to lessons was no more. In its place was a shell of a building left to rot.

As no one was guarding the building, I freely walked around reminiscing about a time when American priests in Baghdad were loved and respected and the two cultures greatly admired one another. Peering through a crack in a door, I could even make out my old classroom where in the shadows, covered in dust, remained the old wooden desk where I used to sit all those years ago. I had come a long way since those days, and I paid tribute to the fact that my life may have turned out to be very different had I not received the wisdom of the priests.

That painful visit to Baghdad College inspired me to write a poem about my time there that I hoped would pay homage to the efforts extended by the Jesuit fathers and the role they played in the lives of all of the young men who were lucky and privileged to be their students:

> At Christmas time,
> I was back home,
> Where the past has slept,
> And memories roam,
> Where the Palm Trees stand,
> With Graceful pride,
> That hides the pain,
> They have inside.
> I remembered when, from the cup of knowledge,
> I came to drink,
> And of a place we know,
> I began to think,

Where the lessons of life,
I once have learned,
So, to Baghdad College,
I now returned.
The streets were dark,
Yet I could see
My withered desk
At Class, One E.
As I moved my hand, to touch the walls,
I felt the bricks, began to cry,
As neither of us,
Could say Goodbye . . .
The years will pass,
And the walls will fall,
Yet the BC Legend
Will stand up tall,
And always live,
In you and I,
For legends born,
Will never die . . .

While my visit to Baghdad College was painful, my return to the courtroom filled me with pleasure. During my time away from Baghdad I had continued to work on a few legal matters from my home office in Cardiff, but I was never one for paperwork. My main thrill came when I was before the court, speaking on a case where someone's liberty or life was at stake. The adrenaline rush I used to get at moments like that was indescribable, and since I had left Baghdad I had missed it more than anything.

On my return to the court, with two lawyers from my office, I arrived just in time to hear a verdict in a criminal case. As I sat in the gallery I envied the lawyers who were involved. That moment, just before a verdict was read out, used to be so special. You knew that you could do no more and that your client's fate was now out of your hands. It used to give me a sensation of apprehension mixed with excitement.

Listening intently to the judge, I learned that the case involved a young man who had been charged with possession of stolen materials. When he was brought into the room, his head was bowed and he looked terrified. In my eyes he certainly didn't look to be the type who would be involved in such a crime. On hearing his sentence, ten years imprisonment, he dropped to his knees and screamed, "I am innocent. I am innocent. I am innocent."

Wailing and shrieking as he was dragged away, I really felt for him. Turning to speak to the lawyers who had accompanied me, I told them that I felt that the sentence was wrong. My colleagues also felt that even if he was guilty, the sentence was extremely harsh for merely handling stolen goods. Indeed, I dealt with honor crimes where murderers got lesser sentences. Without any time to waste, I decided that I had to speak to the young man.

Along with the two lawyers, I swiftly made my way to the detention cell area hoping that I could catch him before he was taken to prison to start his ten-year stretch. After I explained that I was a lawyer, the guard allowed me to have five minutes alone with the young man, who was sat on the floor, sobbing, his head between his knees.

"Are you really innocent?" I asked.

Lifting his head up and defiantly looking me in the eyes, he replied, "If I am not innocent, may God take my life now."

I had seen enough. Approaching the bars I told him, "If you need a lawyer, I will act for you."

The young man stood up and took my hand in his. "God has answered my prayers," he stuttered tearfully. "My mother is upstairs. Please tell her that I am innocent, and you're trying to save me."

Tightly gripping his hand, I told him that I would try my best to set him free and that he needed to be strong. Shortly afterward I located the young man's mother, who sat alone outside the courtroom. Holding her head in her hands with her eyes full of tears, she looked to be in shock. After introducing myself I said that I would help her son, to which she cried, "God must have heard me."

I refused to accept any payment for my work, despite the family's offer. It was just a good feeling to be back involved in a case where I sincerely felt that my client was innocent and that my work could help set him free. It was just the sort of case that had always got my blood pumping.

Diligently I put together an appeal memorandum that I sent to the Court of Cassation. In my appeal I not only explained why I felt the man was innocent but also spoke of how I came to represent him. Sadly, I knew that I would not be able to stay in Baghdad for the duration of the case, as I was soon to return to Cardiff, but I hoped that my appeal would fall upon sympathetic ears.

For the next few weeks I waited anxiously back in Cardiff to hear of any news. One day a lawyer from my office called to say that he had received a letter from the court. The young man had been acquitted. He was free. I was ecstatic. I had helped to set an innocent man free in what turned out to be the last criminal case I dealt with in Baghdad. It was a positive end to a career I cherished and continue to miss.

Looking back on the case, it almost seemed as if it was God's will that I was destined to be in that courtroom the moment the verdict was read. If I had not been, then I am certain that the young man would have spent the next decade behind bars. I told my sons that if I accomplished nothing more on our trip to Iraq except setting this innocent man free, then my journey was well justified.

That trip to Baghdad gave me great hope that good times were finally around the corner. But just as the city was on the brink of recovery, it was hit by the most devastating attack it had ever seen.

23.

THE GHOST OF 9/11

"Revenge is a kind of wild justice, which the more a man's nature runs to, the more ought law to weed it out."

—Francis Bacon

JUST A FEW MONTHS AFTER my family and I had left Baghdad, the world was rocked by the events of 9/11. It was clear that following this atrocity we would all be entering a dangerous new dawn. But what I didn't realize at the time was that these events would also engulf Iraq.

Following the U.S. invasion of Afghanistan, President George W. Bush swiftly turned his sights on Saddam. Since the Gulf War, intelligence had indicated that Saddam had supposedly defied the West and UN Sanctions by stockpiling chemical, biological, and nuclear weapons. In Bush's mind, in this post-9/11 era, Saddam was a significant threat to worldwide security and needed to be removed once and for all.

However, before the UN Security Council would even consider any military action, it enacted Resolution 1441, which authorized the return of weapon inspectors to Iraq. Under the direction of Hans Blix, the weapons inspectors focused on finding weapons of mass destruction. Yet after a thorough four-month search, they found nothing. It seemed that the intelligence had been wrong.

While the search for weapons continued, the U.S. congress passed a resolution authorizing the use of military force against Iraq, with or without UN approval, regardless of whether any weapons of mass destruction were found. This left me very worried. Iraq had only just staggered up off its knees. Now it was facing the threat of Armageddon.

I was not the only one who was concerned. Antiwar protests broke out all over the world, with millions of people joining the largest protest in history. But ultimately it was to no avail. The U.S. and UK governments pushed ahead on their inevitable course, with the British Parliament opting to back military action by 412 to 149 votes.

And so, in the early hours of March 20, 2003, my family and I sat in stunned silence as we watched Sky News's footage of U.S. forces embarking on a shock-and-awe bombing campaign of Baghdad. For the next three weeks I could not take my eyes from the television as my homeland was once again ripped apart.

Brutal air and ground strikes tore apart the cities of Basra, Mosul, and Karbala before the Coalition forces marched into Baghdad itself. By April 12, 2003, the war was over, as Saddam and members of the regime fled. I felt a mixture of elation and worry as I watched residents of Baghdad gleefully vandalize pictures of Saddam and topple a statue of him in Firdos Square. For some it was obviously a euphoric moment, but I still felt that the troubles would not be at an end.

Throughout the centuries, Iraq—or Mesopotamia, as it was once known—had been riddled with sectarian differences, mostly between the Shias, Sunnis, and Kurds. By and large Saddam had succeeded in stopping the country from descending into outright civil war, often by employing grisly means that ensured that the minority Sunni Muslim population dominated. Now that Saddam and his regime were no more, I knew that both the Kurds and the Shias would stake their claims for the new Iraq. I wasn't sure if the Coalition was prepared for such a situation.

Almost immediately my worst fears came true. As President Bush declared "mission accomplished," vicious fighting broke out throughout the country as each religious faction fought for supremacy.

Iraq's postwar elections soon revealed just how difficult it would be to reconcile these differences. Having been under Sunni rule since the 1920s, the Shias and the Kurds had their vengeance as their candidates flooded Iraq's new parliament, with Jalal Talabani, a Kurd, being elected as president. The Sunnis were unable to accept their loss of power, which only escalated tensions.

Complicating matters further was the fact that members of Al Qaeda proceeded to cross the border and engage in fighting against U.S. forces. Suicide bombings soon became a daily occurrence, and the death toll of ordinary Iraqis started to rise rapidly.

Another situation that quickly became apparent was that food and water was in short supply. Bombing had destroyed purification and sewage facilities, and bottled water was too expensive for most Iraqis to buy. Fearing starvation and thirst, many Iraqis went on looting sprees. With very little police presence on the streets and the armed forces' resources stretched, hundreds of shops were ransacked, as were places such as the National Museum of Iraq, where thousands of priceless artifacts were stolen. Most disturbingly of all, looters even stole vials of HIV infected blood and cholera from Baghdad's Central Public Health Library, while barrels of unprocessed uranium were also taken from an unguarded warehouse in Tuwaitha.

Terror now ruled the streets. Thousands of Iraqis tried to flee the country as anarchy broke out. Thankfully, nearly every member of my family escaped the atrocities and came to stay with relatives in Canada, Sweden, and my home in Cardiff. There was no way of knowing how long they would stay with us, but that didn't matter. We were just delighted to know that they were safe and away from the daily threat of looting, suicide bombs, sectarian violence, and military action.

On December 13, 2003, American forces finally got their man when they found Saddam Hussein hiding in a hole at a farmhouse in ad-Dawr, just a short distance from his hometown, Tikrit. I remember being stunned when I saw the footage of his capture on the news. Gone was the all-powerful dictator who had struck fear into the hearts of all Iraqis. He had now been replaced by a fragile old man with unkempt, straggled hair and a gray-flecked, bushy beard. It was hard to imagine that such a man had once ruled the country with an iron fist.

What was also hard to imagine was how the Coalition would now charge and try Iraq's former president. The question brought up a number of legal and ethical questions that would all present major issues. Yet nothing I considered came close to the final solution.

24.

THE INTERROGATION OF SADDAM HUSSEIN

"It is certain, in any case, that ignorance, allied with power, is the most ferocious enemy justice can have."

—James A. Baldwin

JUDGE: ARE YOU SADDAM HUSSEIN AL-MAJID?
Saddam: Yes.

Judge: Were you born on 28 April 1937?

Saddam: Yes.

Judge: Are you the former president of Iraq?

Saddam: I am the current president of Iraq.

Judge: Were you leader of the Ba'ath party and head of the armed forces?

Saddam: Yes. Can you introduce yourself?

Judge: I am the judge of the investigative court.

Saddam: Do you represent the American coalition?

Judge: I represent the Iraqi people. . . . You have the right to examine witnesses and documents.

Saddam: Everyone here knows this is a theatre carried out by Bush the criminal to win the election.

Judge: You are charged with seven crimes [these were said to be the killing of religious figures in 1974; gassing of the Kurds in Halabja in 1988; the killing of the Kurdish Barzani clan in 1983; killing various members of political

215

parties over the last 30 years; the 1986–88 Anfal campaign of displacing the Kurds; the suppression of the 1991 uprisings by Kurds and Shiites; and the 1990 invasion of Kuwait].

Saddam: How can you charge me with this? You are an Iraqi and everyone knows Kuwait is part of Iraq.

Judge: This is not a trial. I am a prosecuting judge investigating.

Saddam: I carried out these acts in my capacity as president of Iraq.

Judge: You have a right to defence attorneys.

Saddam: According to the Americans I have millions of dollars in Geneva so I should be able to afford one.

Judge: Do you have anything else to say?

Saddam: In Kuwait I was defending the Iraqi people from those Kuwaiti dogs who wanted to turn their women into 10-dollar prostitutes.

Judge: Do not use that language in this court. Will you now sign this document listing your rights?

Saddam: No.

Judge: Let it be recorded that he has not signed. You are dismissed from the court.

The date was July 1, 2004, and the above discussion between Saddam Hussein and an investigating judge in Camp Victory, one of Saddam's former palaces in Baghdad, was one that most Iraqis never thought they would see. It finally seemed as though Iraq's dictator was going to have to answer for his alleged crimes.

Dressed in an ill-fitting gray suit jacket and an open-necked white shirt, and with a thick, gray-flecked beard, the former president of Iraq looked every inch of his sixty-seven years and more. Yet despite his haggard appearance, it was clear from this opening exchange that Saddam was not going to go down without a fight. The Iraqi government and the Coalition were definitely going to have their work cut out.

As an Iraqi and as a lawyer, I followed these proceedings avidly. President Bush had invaded Iraq on the pretense that he was freeing the Iraqi people from Saddam's dictatorship and he was now bringing democracy to the country. I sincerely hoped that Bush would use this trial as a showcase for his supposed American ideals. It was a real opportunity to show that a mix of Western and Middle Eastern justice could deliver a fair trial, even to those accused of horrific crimes. If, however, the Coalition missed this opportunity, then I feared that irreparable damage could be done to the already fragile relationship between the West and the Middle East, as well as between the various religious factions throughout Iraq.

Ramsey Clark, the former U.S. Attorney General who acted as an advisor to the defense, said the following in regard to this: "This trial can either divide or heal. And unless it is seen as absolutely fair, and as absolutely fair in fact, it will irreconcilably divide the people of Iraq."

I prayed that the Coalition would listen to these wise words.

However, even before Saddam had walked into court, I feared the worst. I say the following not to make any political statement but based purely on my legal analysis as a lawyer of many years.

When the manhunt for Saddam was still in progress, the Coalition had to consider under what laws it would try former members of the regime. As far as I could see, it had three choices: Iraqi law, its own domestic laws, or international law. However, it soon became clear that none of these options was going to be suitable.

Ideally the trial would have been held under the existing laws of Iraq, but the Coalition knew that this would be impossible. Article 40 of the Iraqi Constitution made perfectly clear that the president and members of the Revolutionary Command Council were granted immunity for any crimes they were said to have committed while in power. Another issue was that crimes such as genocide, crimes against humanity, and war crimes were not recognized by the laws of Iraq. Therefore, if the case was tried under Iraqi law, the Coalition would have no basis on which to charge the regime.

Trying Saddam and his regime under the Coalition's domestic laws for breaches of the Geneva Conventions was also unsuitable. Not only would this have meant that the trial would have had to be held somewhere like the Old Bailey in London, which would be a security nightmare, but also at such proceedings the Coalition would lose control of the composition of the judges and lawyers who would be appointed.

Something else to consider was that the Coalition craved the death sentence, a remedy that would not be available in most Western courts.

In light of the above, and in a case of such magnitude involving likely charges of war crimes, genocide, and crimes against humanity, I fully expected an international tribunal to be the most obvious option. Indeed, when former Yugoslav president Slobodan Milosevic had been charged with war crimes and crimes against humanity, his case had been before The Hague. However, the prospect of an international tribunal was not appealing to the Coalition.

A major issue for the Coalition was that in order to try Saddam under an international tribunal, it would first need to ask for a UN resolution, something it had failed to acquire before invading Iraq. If the UN now decided to grant a resolution, then it could be seen as approving of the invasion and subsequent occupation, which it clearly did not wish to do. As such, the Coalition decided against this, clearly anticipating the embarrassing situation that could ensue.

However, I don't think the Coalition ever really intended to try Saddam in an international court. It was clear that the most important thing was to retain control over the proceedings, as it needed to do everything in its power to secure a guilty verdict, otherwise severe questions would be asked about its decision to invade Iraq.

With this in mind the Coalition created the Iraqi High Tribunal (IHT), a court that would sit in the Green Zone in Baghdad. This court would have jurisdiction over those accused of committing genocide, crimes against humanity, and war crimes in Iraq between July 1968 and May 2003. It was a scenario that reminded me of something former Associate Supreme Court Justice William O. Douglas once said about the Nuremburg trials: "Law was created ex post facto to suit the passion and the clamor of the time." This was certainly the case here.

Having granted itself the power to try Saddam, the Coalition put in place rules and regulations that covered almost every possible scenario to ensure complete control of the trial. However, just in case it missed something, the Coalition also gave itself the right to overrule any ruling of the IHT that it did not agree with. Section 2 of Order 48 of the Coalition Provisional Authority stated that, should any conflict arise, between any promulgation by the Governing Council or any ruling of judgment by the Tribunal and any promulgation of the Coalition Provisional Authority, the promulgation of the Coalition Provisional Authority shall prevail.

I have given numerous examples during this book of Saddam and the regime attempting to interfere with the courts, something that the Coalition had rightly criticized them for, yet here it was doing something very similar.

Something else I found astonishing was that when the Coalition had invaded Iraq, it had immediately put into force Order 7, which suspended capital punishment in criminal cases. Yet when it came to the trial of Saddam, the use of capital punishment was immediately made available as a one-off sentence.

While the Coalition was extremely careful to ensure that every aspect of the IHT was designed to result in Saddam's guilt, it also took great steps to ensure that it could not be tried at any point for war crimes itself, as the IHT expressly prohibited any non-Iraqi being tried for such crimes that were committed during or after the occupation.

With complete control over the rules of the courtroom, the Coalition also ensured that it appointed sympathetic judges and lawyers. In order to do this it banned any lawyer or judge from presiding who had been a Ba'ath Party member. This may have seemed reasonable, as the top members of the Ba'ath Party were on trial, yet during Saddam's regime membership in the Ba'ath Party was a prerequisite for admission to judicial training. Being a member didn't imply that you supported him or the Ba'ath Party; it was merely necessary for many to commence a legal career in Iraq.

Obviously, this rule significantly narrowed the pool of available judges and lawyers from whom the Coalition could choose. In effect, it was predominantly left with judges and lawyers who had very limited legal experience and were certainly not qualified to be involved in a case of such complexity.

When the names of some of the lawyers involved started to filter through, there was immediate concern that they were not going to be suitable for such a case. Human Rights Watch, who was monitoring the trial, was even moved to state that "the level of legal and practical expertise of the key Iraqi actors in the court—trial judges, administrators, prosecutors and defence lawyers—is not sufficient to fairly and effectively try crimes of this magnitude."

The Coalition then made matters even more difficult for the defense by imposing certain safeguards. While Article 31 of the IHTS granted immunity to the judges and prosecution lawyers for anything that they said or did during the trial, this same privilege was not granted to the defense. In effect the defense team knew it had to tread carefully while the prosecution was allowed to do as it wished.

As seen in Saddam's exchange with the investigating judge, the Coalition was considering charging Saddam with seven crimes. Yet when the charges were formally announced, I was confused to find that Saddam and his co-defendants were now only charged with crimes against humanity in regard to their part in the execution of 148 residents of Dujail after an attempt on Saddam's life in 1982. I found this choice of crime very strange.

The incident in Dujail, a mixed town of Sunni and Shia Arabs some 60 kilometers north of Baghdad, occurred on a stifling hot day in 1982. Many of Dujail's men were away fighting in the war with Iran at this time, so in order to drum up support, Saddam visited the village and gave a speech.

As the presidential convoy was heading out of town, it was ambushed by a small group of men with machine guns. Incredibly, Saddam was not hurt, but many of his bodyguards were killed. Immediately returning to Dujail, Saddam made another speech where he promised to root out the "small number" of traitors in the town. Over the next few days, men, women, and even children were rounded up and sent to intelligence headquarters for interrogation.

When the trial reached the court of revolution, Awad al-Bandar, the president of the court, allegedly ordered that 148 of the suspects be executed. Over twenty years later Saddam, al-Bandar, Barzan al-Tikriti, Taha Yassin Ramadan, Abdullah Kazim Ruwayyid, Mizhar Abdullah Ruwayyid, Ali Dayih Ali, and Mohammed Azawi Ali were now all charged with crimes against humanity for their parts in this alleged "crime."

As far as I could see, the president of Iraq had been subjected to an assassination attempt, and the court of revolution had subsequently sentenced those involved to death under the laws of Iraq. Could the Coalition really prove that Saddam had committed a crime against humanity in such circumstances?

Crimes against humanity, under Article 12 of the IHTS, meant that the prosecution had to prove that he had committed a "widespread or systematic" attack on civilians. In my mind, the current allegations did not meet that charge.

In Western countries where the death penalty is an option, would it have been a major scandal if those involved in an attempted assassination of the country's president were subsequently executed? Many would argue that the Dujail verdict was a harsh sentence, but the court had applied the law of the land at that time.

Weighing up all of the above, it seemed to me that the Coalition was trying Saddam in a case that would be hard to prove. To justify a death sentence I felt the Coalition would need to provide compelling evidence not only that the trial of the accused was unfair but also that Saddam had played a major role in ordering the verdict itself. Obviously, as these events had happened over twenty years ago, finding conclusive proof would be very difficult.

As the defense lawyers tried to come to grips with the case, they were surprised to find that they were prohibited from meeting with their client, Saddam Hussein, until the trial commenced on October 19, 2005. It is a well-established principle of justice that a defendant has a right to meet with his or her lawyer before trial, but that right was denied in this instance by those who were supposedly bringing democracy to Iraq.

However, if I was concerned by the legal machinations before the trial even came to court, then what came next horrified me.

25.

THE TRIAL OF THE CENTURY

"What I perceive, is above all justice, where everyone has the same law."

—Imran Khan

IKE MOST IRAQIS, ON OCTOBER 19, 2005, I was transfixed when the trial of Saddam Hussein finally commenced. For months talk had raged in the media about the fairness of the trial and the charges against Saddam, but the time for debate was now over. Now we would really see if the justice everyone craved would be delivered in a democratic manner.

The trial took place in the former headquarters of the Pan Arab National Leadership of the Ba'ath Party, in the heavily fortified Green Zone. Saddam, holding a copy of the Qur'an, sat alongside his codefendants. Far from the dishevelled figure he had cut before the investigating judge in 2004, he now looked far healthier. He had added a bit more weight to his frame, so he now filled his dark gray suit, and his unkempt beard had been trimmed, giving him the appearance of an elder statesman.

Behind him was my old client, Barzan al-Tikriti, dressed in a khaki military shirt and wearing a red-and-white checked headscarf. Despite suffering from cancer, he looked ready for action, his gray moustache twitching in anticipation. Having seen Barzan in courtrooms before, I knew that he would not sit idly. If there was anything said that displeased him, he would erupt. This would prove to be the case.

Taking a seat alongside his four assistant judges, Kurdish Chief Judge Rizgar Muhammad Amin looked nervous as he tentatively began proceedings.

> Judge Amin: Mr. Saddam, we ask you to write down your identity, your name, occupation and address and then we will allow you to talk. Now it is time to write down your identity.
>
> Saddam: I was not about to say much.
>
> Judge Amin: We want your identity, your name, then we will listen to what you have. We are writing down the identities at this time. We will hear you when we need to listen to you.
>
> Saddam: First of all, who are you and what are you?
>
> Judge Amin: The Iraqi Criminal Court.
>
> Saddam: All of you are judges?
>
> Judge Amin: We don't have time to get into details. You can write down what you like.
>
> Saddam: I have been here in this military building since 2.30 a.m., and then from 9 I have been wearing this suit. They have asked me to take it off and then put it on again many times.
>
> Judge Amin: Who are you? What is your identity? Why don't you take a seat and let the others say their names and we will get back to you.
>
> Saddam: You know me. You are an Iraqi and you know who I am. And you know I don't get tired.
>
> Judge Amin: These are formalities and we need to hear it from you.
>
> Saddam: They have prevented me from getting a pen and a paper because paper, it seems, is frightening these days. I don't hold any grudges against any of you. But upholding what is right and respecting the great Iraqi people who chose me I won't answer to this court, with all due respect to the individuals involved in it, and I reserve my constitutional rights as the president of Iraq. You know me.

Judge Amin: These are the procedures. A judge cannot rely on personal knowledge.

Saddam: I don't recognize the group that gave you the authority and assigned you. Aggression is illegitimate and what is built on illegitimacy is illegitimate.

As Saddam continued to battle the judge, he and his codefendants were read their rights as well as formally charged. After this the judge again turned his attention to Saddam.

Judge Amin: Mr. Saddam, go ahead. Are you guilty or innocent?

Saddam: I said what I said. I am not guilty.

Appearing to sigh with relief that the ordeal was over, Judge Amin called a halt to proceedings and ordered that the trial would reconvene on November 28.

There had been concerns about the security of the defense team before the trial, with five defense lawyers already murdered. Once the trial commenced, things rapidly went downhill. The day after the opening session Awad al-Bandar's lawyer, Sa'doon Al-Janabi, was killed. Just a few weeks later a second defense lawyer, Adil Muhammad Abbas As-Zubaidi, met the same fate.

When the trial recommenced, Ramsey Clark, an advisor to the defense, attempted to raise his concerns that while the prosecution lawyers were under guard 24/7, the defense team had no such protection. Despite Clark's legitimate concerns, the judge informed him that he was not allowed to address the tribunal and could only raise his issues in writing. After a prolonged argument, the defense team walked out as Barzan stood up and bellowed, "Why don't you just execute us and get rid of all of this?"

While the court did eventually listen to Mr. Clark's concerns, it still did not provide the defense with the same level of security as the prosecution enjoyed, something which is quite astonishing given that seven people had already been murdered. The ability of the defense to represent its client without fear of reprisals is one of the basic principles of a fair trial. It was clear that this was not an overriding concern for the court or the Coalition, and before the trial was over, Khamis al-Obeidi, Saddam's chief defense lawyer, would also lose his life.

As Baghdad continued to be hit by suicide bombings and sectarian violence, the next few weeks of the trial saw the prosecution outline its case against the accused. Enraged by some of the allegations put before the court, Saddam refused to attend on some days, shouting, "I will not come to an unjust court! Go to hell!" And on the days when Saddam and his codefendants did attend, the trial descended into a farce, with the judge struggling to impose his authority and Saddam refusing to be seated. In protest at the shambles, the privately hired defense team regularly walked out.

With the courtroom descending into chaos, Chief Judge Amin stood down in January 2006 to be replaced by Judge Ra'ouf Rasheed Abdul-Rahman, someone who had never sat as a judge before this case. To make matters worse, the judge had also previously been imprisoned by the Ba'ath Party for being a member of the Kurdish nationalist movement. Incredibly, he had also publicly stated before the trial that Saddam should be executed. Normally, such a blatant show of bias would result in a judge being excused from duty, yet he was still appointed to preside over the case.

On January 29, 2006, I remember watching in amazement the scenes that greeted the appointment of Judge Abdul-Rahman. Knowing the background of the judge, both Saddam and Barzan went ballistic in the courtroom. Barzan was dragged from the room shouting incessantly before the defendant's privately hired defense team also walked out in protest. This didn't faze the Coalition; it merely appointed new lawyers for the defense who were directly under its control.

With the new, Coalition-controlled defense team in place, the prosecution was now free to enter documents into evidence with no opposition. As such, the court read twenty-three prosecution witness statements into the court record without making those witnesses available for questioning by the defense. Of those twenty-three witness statements, thirteen were never disclosed to the defense beyond having been read out in court. It was trial by ambush.

Unsurprisingly, the new defense team didn't enter any objections to such a blatant disregard for the laws of disclosure or to the fact that it was not allowed to question the witnesses. It merely sat back and allowed it to happen. When a member of Human Rights Watch asked one of the lawyers why he hadn't done anything the lawyer explained that the defense did not wish to risk a reprimand from the judge.

In protest, Barzan regularly arrived at court wearing nothing but long-sleeved white underwear, while Saddam continued to wage war with the judge.

> Judge Abdul-Rahman: First we want to hear the lawyers assigned to you. Let them come.
>
> Saddam: I decline this representation!
>
> Judge Abdul-Rahman: Alright. Alright. The court will follow the rules anyway.
>
> Saddam: This is against the law. It states that the court has to assign lawyers if the defendant is not able to assign his own lawyers. Only in this case the court is allowed to assign lawyers.
>
> Judge Abdul-Rahman: Well, where are your lawyers?
>
> Saddam: I do have lawyers! But where are they? Outdoors? In front of the TV? Do they hold political speeches? You really think these are lawyers?
>
> Judge Abdul-Rahman: They are honourable lawyers. Listen! Your lawyers are getting millions of dinars and they instigate violence.
>
> Saddam: No they don't. They are good.
>
> Judge Abdul-Rahman: Listen, Saddam. Will you listen! Your lawyers are getting millions from the state. They are not lawyers, they are arsonists. They don't want that justice enforced. But we face them and we will do justice well.

I was amazed to hear a judge speak in such a manner. Yet in spite of Saddam's protests, one of which included a hunger strike, the trial continued with more questions than answers being raised.

In order to get a guilty verdict, the prosecution had to prove that the Dujail trial was unfair and that Saddam Hussein had played a major role in ordering the defendants' execution. In order to justify these claims, the file of that trial would obviously be the most vital piece of evidence.

Yet while the Coalition had a copy of the 361-page file, the prosecution didn't refer to it in the trial. Upon al-Bandar, the judge in the Dujail case, asking for a copy of the case file to be admitted into evidence, the following amazing exchange occurred:

> Judge Abdul-Rahman: Asking for dossiers is the work of the defence but don't ask us to do it.
>
> Al-Bandar: The Americans have seized all of the documents of the Iraqi government, and the court can ask them to bring it but if you want to litigate me without knowing the truth . . .
>
> Judge Abdul-Rahman: I don't do that, this is not a special court, I am not prosecuting you without fulfilling my conscience. I won't issue a sentence on 148 within one hour. I am not this type.

Not only was the judge claiming that the Dujail trial had only lasted an hour, something fiercely refuted by al-Bandar, but also he was refusing to allow concrete evidence to be submitted into court that could clear up the matter.

It was at this point in the trial that Awad al-Bandar's son called me in the middle of the night and begged me to return to Baghdad to defend his father. As I said at the start of the book, this put me in a difficult situation. I was desperate to come to the aid of someone I had respected and who had asked for my help. Yet at the same time I also had to acknowledge that my presence was unlikely to make any real difference. Most important of all, I just couldn't risk exposing my family to any danger.

It was one of the most difficult decisions I have ever had to make. For my entire legal career I had put my health and safety on the line to fight against injustice in the courtroom, and now, right at the end, I had the opportunity to do it on the biggest stage of all. I desperately wanted to go, and if it was just my life at stake, I wouldn't have hesitated.

When al-Bandar's son called to ask for my decision, I reluctantly had to say that I could not go. He was disappointed and asked me to reconsider, but I could not be persuaded.

Frustrated at being unable to make a difference, I continued to watch the footage of the trial in the safety of my home in Cardiff. Witness after witness testified that al-Bandar had been a fair judge who had applied the law correctly.

In response the prosecution did not produce any concrete evidence that showed that al-Bandar was a corrupt judge or had not presided over a fair trial in the Dujail matter. It refused to disclose the trial transcript and merely kept repeating that the trial had lasted just an hour. It even claimed that he had tried many of the defendants without hearing their evidence.

Incredibly, the court also heard evidence that many of those who were said to have been executed in Dujail were actually still alive, while some had in fact died during the Iran/Iraq War. The prosecution was given the names and addresses of those persons but neglected to follow up.

Over the course of the trial the prosecution had questioned fifty-eight witnesses, yet after the defense had called twenty-six witnesses and still had plenty more to call, the judge abruptly brought an end to the case. His reason was that the defense had enjoyed ample opportunity to state its case and that questioning any more witnesses wouldn't make any difference to his decision.

To add insult to injury, the final statement read by the defense was not actually drafted by the defense team. It was drafted by William Wiley, who was not a qualified lawyer and who was a member of the American-run Regime Crimes Liaison Office. Basically, the prosecution drafted the defense's closing statement.

As this closing statement was being read, Saddam shouted, "A Canadian wrote this! He is a spy and the Americans told him what to write!"

On November 5, 2006, the IHT delivered its verdict. The eyes of the world were watching, but everyone already knew what the decision would be before the judge had opened his mouth.

Judge Abdul-Rahman: Stand up. We will read the verdict. Stand up!

Saddam: I cannot listen to the verdict.

Judge Abdul-Rahman: Stand up!

Saddam: No! I want to sit down.

Judge Abdul-Rahman: The court has sentenced Saddam Hussein to execution by hanging.

Saddam: Long live the people. Down with the traitors. God is great. God is great. God is great.

Judge Abdul-Rahman: The punishment is according to the law.

Saddam: Long live the people. Down with the traitors. Down with the conquerors. Damn you and your court.

Judge Abdul-Rahman: This is for war crimes and crimes against humanity.

Saddam: You are the enemies of humanity. God is great. Damn the losers. The great Iraqi people long live them. All those who retreated I say to them accept the will of the occupiers. You are servants of the occupiers. You are traitors. Life for us. Death to our enemies. Death to the enemies of the people. Long live this glorious nation.

Judge Abdul-Rahman: Take him out.

With Saddam removed from the courtroom, Barzan and al-Bandar were also given their sentences: death by hanging. While I wasn't surprised by the sentences themselves, watching the verdicts still left me in a state of shock, as Judge Abdul-Rahman had merely declared the defendants' guilt without mentioning his reasons for coming to this decision. This is virtually unprecedented. In courtrooms in the United States, United Kingdom, and even Iraq, the summary of the judgment is always read before the sentence.

However, I suspect that a more sinister motive may have been afoot. Article 27 of the IHT statute made it explicitly clear that all sentences must be carried out within thirty days of the verdict. This tight time limit would give a defense team an impossibly short period in which to try to launch an appeal. Therefore, to make matters as difficult as possible, the IHT did not actually provide the defense with the reasons for the judgment, either orally or in writing, until seventeen days after the sentence had been announced.

When the defense team did finally receive the written judgment, it must have been bewildered, as the judgment contained information that had not been raised at trial. For instance, when giving its reasons for pronouncing the death penalty, the judgment referred to the 148 people who were sentenced to death but then went on to state, "in addition to the tens who died in detention." At no point in the trial was any reference made to any person having died in detention, let alone "tens."

Among other things, the judgment also quite brazenly announced that the IHT had not considered any petition or application that the defense had submitted that referred to Saddam as "the president." It seems incredible that in a case of such magnitude, and where someone's life is at stake, this could be the case, but page 12 of the judgment made this clear:

> as Saddam Hussein has no position in front of this court but that of being the accused, the Court has decided not to make any judgment on any petition submitted with that title or description [of president] and not even to refer to those petitions in the judgment because they were not proper.

Indeed, when the judgment outlined its reasoning for finding Saddam guilty, it included the most amazing passage:

> Most of the complainants whose statements have been taken during the investigation and trial and who have laid accusation against Saddam Hussein, never saw Saddam Hussein ordering the arrest, imprisonment, torture or killing of the people of Dujail. In addition, they never saw Saddam Hussein do any of these acts personally.
>
> However, some of the complainants and witnesses testified that they heard, and saw, others stating that Saddam Hussein ordered his subordinates to carry out these acts.

It seems from the preceding consideration that there were no eye witnesses testifying that Saddam Hussein committed these crimes by himself or even ordered that these crimes be committed.

Even though the IHT had acknowledged that it had no concrete evidence to convict Saddam in this matter, it still declared him guilty, relying on hearsay evidence, which is inadmissible in most legal jurisdictions. Most damning of all, at no point in the trial did the IHT produce the names of those who said that they had heard that Saddam was responsible, let alone make them available for questioning.

The New York–based Human Rights Watch echoed my feelings on the nonexistent evidence that was relied upon to get a conviction in this case:

Overall, the case prepared by the investigative judge in relation to the events in Dujail in 1982 suffered from important gaps in terms of the kinds of evidence necessary to prove intent, knowledge, and criminal responsibility on the part of the defendants. When preparing the case, it appears that neither the prosecution nor the investigative judge paid sufficient attention to the requirements of what must be proved under international criminal law in order to establish specific, individual criminal responsibility of each defendant for the abuses that were committed against the people of Dujail.

Unsurprisingly, despite having limited time to do so, the defense launched an appeal and requested an extension of time in order to adequately produce further evidence. An extension of two weeks was granted, no doubt to the disbelief of the defense, yet in a case where a head of state has been sentenced to death, this hardly amounted to a sufficient amount of time to lodge an appeal.

In any event, the defense probably already knew that it would not matter what its appeal contained, since it would only be dismissed with no real reason being provided. And this proved to be the case when on December 27, 2006, the conviction and sentence were approved in the following judgment:

> *The accused were given adequate guarantees that was suffi-*
> *cient to provide a just trial. He was immediately informed of*
> *the charge against him and its reasons. He was given enough*
> *time to prepare his defense and was given legal assistance*
> *from among those he chose. He was given ample opportu-*
> *nity to defend himself with the assistance of his legal advis-*
> *ers and given the opportunity to question his witnesses and*
> *cross-examine prosecution witnesses. He fully used his right*
> *to defend himself and was not forced to state what he did not*
> *want to state.*

No evidence whatsoever was provided to back up any of the above, but there was nothing that could now be done. Despite falling well below the standard of justice required in such a case, the defendants would now hang.

Wasting little time, on December 30, 2006, the sentence was carried out, with footage of Saddam's execution quickly surfacing on the Internet. To no one's surprise the footage showed that even the execution of a head of state could not be conducted in dignity, with Saddam being mocked by men in balaclavas before meeting his fate.

While Saddam's execution was unseemly, it was nothing compared to that of Barzan al-Tikriti, who was hanged on January 15, 2007. With the rope the incorrect length Barzan was decapitated. Even in matters as simple as this, the Coalition could not get things right.

Awad al-Bandar was also hanged on the same day as Barzan. At no point in the trial was any evidence provided whatsoever that proved conclusively that he had played a part in any injustice during his handling of the Dujail trial. He is unique in being the first judge in history to be executed for supposedly running a sham trial.

The Coalition invaded Iraq under the pretense that it was bringing with it democracy and a bright new dawn. Sadly, this has not proved to be the case, not only in this trial but also in the events that followed it.

Sitting in my home in Cardiff over these last few years, surrounded by my loving wife and two sons, I have watched the television pictures of Iraq in horror. The streets of Baghdad have resembled a war zone, and now, at the time of writing in 2014, the terrorist organization that calls itself the Islamic State of Iraq and Syria (ISIS) has poured over the border and taken control of many of Iraq's major cities.

From speaking to my Christian friends who remain in Iraq, I know that the situation is desperate. Much like the Jews during the Holocaust, they are being persecuted and exterminated. Many have had to leave their homes in order to escape this madness.

As I watch dumbfounded, I ask myself just what the death of Saddam Hussein has actually achieved. Is the current situation any better than life under Saddam? At this moment in time, most Iraqis would tell you that it is not.

Yet while Iraq continues to be plagued by troubles, and its great cities Baghdad, Mosul, and Basra have been decimated, something gives me hope: the Iraqi people. History has shown that while Iraq has been the victim of many attacks, Iraqis have always stood tall and have come back from every catastrophe. I know that to this day, despite the troubles, there continue to be just, fair, and wise Iraqis all over the world who will eventually provide our country with the glorious future it has long been promised.

Oil will of course be Iraq's saving grace. Once it has regained control of its oil, and the country's infrastructure is rebuilt, then Iraq will rise from the ashes. With so much money at its disposal, the economy should prosper, and when such a thing happens, religious bigotry will be set aside. Of this I have little doubt, as for a short period of time I witnessed this very thing happen in the 1970s under the regime of al-Bakr.

One day I hope to return to a Baghdad that has achieved its potential, a Baghdad that has become a thriving, modern metropolis built on the ambitions, hopes, and dreams of the millions of ordinary Iraqis who desire one thing more than any other: peace. Every night I pray for this.

If I could have one wish in this lifetime, it would be to return with my family to my house on the banks of the Tigres, where we would sit on the veranda where I once sat with Abu Fahmi, the bear. Together we would look out onto the new Baghdad, and instead of hearing a cacophony of guns, bombs, and screams, we would hear sounds of laughter, happiness, and prosperity, sounds that can only be brought by one concept: justice.

26.

JUSTICE

―――――――――――――――――――――――――――

"Although the path of the law practice may be difficult and hard, with conflicting points of view, always stand with what you believe is right and never ever abandon this course."

—Edward Aris Sr.

THROUGHOUT THIS BOOK I HAVE quoted many concepts of justice that have been put forward by great men. Over the course of my career, there have been times when I have put all of them into practice, yet the words above, which were said to me by my father the day I graduated from law school, are without a doubt the most important.

From my days in Baghdad College, where I was the president of the Debating Society; to working as a lawyer in Baghdad in cases involving murderers, rapists, and pedophiles; to the present day where I still fight vigorously over trivial matters, such as an unjustified parking ticket, my father's words have always been at the forefront of my mind.

No matter the alleged crimes or the defendants' religious or political background, if I felt that they been wronged, then I would fight for them. As I have said previously, such was my passion for justice that I worked on a large number of cases for free.

I was, of course, in a fortunate position in that my factory gave me the freedom to work in law without the overriding need to make money. Despite this I still believe that even if I had been a penniless lawyer, I would still have fought for those who could not afford to hire me.

I remember a time in the early 1980s when one of my great friends and most accomplished colleagues, Fawsi, came to me with a very lucrative case. The potential client had been accused of a double homicide, and he was offering to pay us an enormous sum if we could help him beat the charges. When I looked at the case, I realized that I could probably get it dismissed on a legal technicality, but the issue remained that the man was clearly guilty. Despite Fawsi begging me to take the case, I refused. No sum of money was going to persuade me to act for a man whom I knew was guilty of such a terrible crime, especially without any mitigating circumstances present.

Did I manage to obtain justice in every case that I worked on? No. I am not God. As I have shown, there were cases where I vigorously defended clients, truly believing them to be innocent, only to find that I had been duped. I took those instances very hard. However, at the time I had worked honestly and fairly, truly believing that my client was innocent. Justice may not have been the end result, but I had been honest in my work and fighting for what I had believed was right.

Some of the cases I worked on involved torture and the death penalty, which are both very controversial issues. There is no doubt that there have been occasions when they have been wrongly applied, and that is very regrettable. Yet I do feel that, if subject to stringent regulations, there is definitely a place for them both in the justice system.

In certain violent crimes when compelling evidence is present and the accused is refusing to speak further, then I do believe that he or she should be subjected to certain pressure to reveal the truth. Of course, torture is abhorrent, but if it helps to serve the greater good, is strictly regulated, and leaves no lasting marks, then surely it must be considered as a means to an end. As I have shown in the case of the Cage Man, without the use of torture, that man would have got away with murdering and raping two little boys and would have no doubt repeated this crime. In such a case, the rights of the Cage Man were secondary. We needed justice. Without the use of torture, we would not have achieved it.

And the same goes for the death penalty. If there is compelling evidence, perhaps backed up by DNA, and the accused is guilty of a despicable crime, then he or she should be made to pay the ultimate price. I'm not saying that the death penalty should be made available for every violent crime, as I do believe that sometimes crimes are committed as a result of very unfortunate circumstances and a long spell in jail is punishment enough. However, there are some crimes that are so horrific, and where the accused has acted in a manner that cannot even be termed human, that he or she does not deserve any compassion or second chances. Death is the only justice in such a case.

I truly believe that the vast majority of judges and lawyers who acted during the time I was working in Baghdad were exemplary. Some of those working in the legal profession were among the most wise and just men I have ever encountered, and they did it all working under the most extraordinary and pressurized circumstances. I consider it an honor that I was able to work alongside such great men, and I continue to be a proud member of the Iraqi Bar Association.

One incident, that always lives in my mind, occurred when I was defending a man who had murdered his sister. My client had learned that while he was living abroad, his sister had virtually become a prostitute and as such was bringing great shame on his family. When he finally returned to Baghdad after many years away, he killed her, despite the fact she had now settled down and married.

On the day of the trial I started the cross-examination of the victim's husband by asking a perfectly innocent question under the circumstances: "Did you know of your wife's past before you married her?"

Yet the judge shot me down. Slamming his gravel against the bench, he shouted at the man, "Do not answer." I was stunned. When I asked the judge why I could not ask such a question he merely responded, "Your question is overruled. Do you have anything else?"

Wracking my brain for how I could ask the same question in a different way, I continued by saying, "When you married your wife, was she a virgin?"

Again the judge intervened. "Do not answer," he shouted, this time even louder than before.

By now I was on the verge of losing my temper. Questions such as these were to be expected in a case such as this. But the judge was not to be moved. I was told that any such questions would continue to be overruled, no matter which way I chose to ask them. For the life of me I didn't know why the judge was acting this way. Deep down I felt that he was being very biased toward the prosecution, although of course I did not say this out loud.

I went to bed that night seething. Unable to keep my counsel, I awoke at the crack of dawn and drove to the court, determined to confront the judge in private. After being granted an audience in his chambers, I asked if I could speak freely.

"By all means," he said, no doubt knowing what was to come.

Watching my words carefully, I stated, "Your Honor, I am a young lawyer at the beginning of his career. I felt I was within my rights to ask such questions of the witness yesterday. What mistake did I make?"

The judge smiled. "In the rules of the court, none at all. But in the rules of decency, you made a moral mistake."

I furrowed my brow, not quite sure what he was getting at. Realizing this, the judge explained. "You were within your rights, but the morality of justice stands up higher than the equation of right or wrong. The man married the girl knowing full well of her past. Despite this he took her as his wife and gave her his name. He tried to make a new life for her where the past was left behind. He acted with great dignity and honor when he did this. I did not therefore want him to feel ashamed of what he had done. What's more, you did not need to ask these questions of him when the girl's past had already been made quite clear by the other witnesses."

For a minute I thought of what the judge had said. In law school I had been trained to believe that the law and the court's rules were equal to justice. But this judge had just taught me my most valuable lesson, one you cannot learn in law school, that justice encompasses not only the law but also dignity and virtue. Standing up from my seat, I looked at the judge and bowed while saying, "I bow to your justice." And I meant it.

This was just one of many times I was moved to make such a gesture to a judge or a lawyer in the courthouse in Baghdad. In the most extraordinary circumstances, they were men and women of high principle and courage. Even today I bow to all that they have taught me.

And now, with over fifty years having passed since my father's death, with the help of my family, friends, and colleagues, I believe that I have fulfilled his wishes. It has often been hard, and at times a high price has had to be paid, but I can sleep easy at night knowing that I did my best.

So, as this book comes to an end, I want my last words to be to my two sons, Tariq and Edward, who are also law school graduates but who chose not to pursue legal careers and instead chose to work in the financial markets. As my father once said to me, stand with what you believe is right. You do not need to be a lawyer to do that. And if you have true sincerity, honesty, and good relations with all you meet, work with, or work for, then I am certain that life will be kind to you both.

May God bless my two sons, Tariq and Edward, and my very dear wife, Aida; I am proud of them and am indebted to them for all that I have achieved in life.

I pray that my two sons, who have already enjoyed successful careers, will now build their homes, start families, and one day tell their children of their grandfather, who stood all his life for what he believed was right.

INDEX